Jedediah Smith

THE OKLAHOMA WESTERN BIOGRAPHIES
RICHARD W. ETULAIN, GENERAL EDITOR

This rather poor image, the only known "portrait" of Jedediah S. Smith, is said to have been made shortly after Smith's death by a contemporary who knew him. Courtesy of Research Center, Utah State Historical Society, Salt Lake City.

Jedediah Smith

No Ordinary Mountain Man

Barton H. Barbour

UNIVERSITY OF OKLAHOMA PRESS : NORMAN

Also by Barton H. Barbour
(comp. and ed.) *Tales of the Mountain Men* (Santa Fe, 1984)
Fort Union and the Upper Missouri Fur Trade (Norman, Okla., 2001)
(ed.) *Reluctant Frontiersman: James Ross Larkin on the Sante Fe Trail, 1856–57* (Albuquerque, 1990)
(ed.) *Edward Warren/William Drummond Stewart* (Missoula, Mont., 1986)

Library of Congress Cataloging-in-Publication Data
Barbour, Barton H., 1951–
   Includes bibliographical references and index.
   ISBN 978-0-8061-4011-7 (hardcover : alk. paper)
   ISBN 978-0-8061-4196-1 (paper)
   1. Smith, Jedediah Strong, 1799–1831.   2. Pioneers—West (U.S.)—Biography.   3. Explorers—West (U.S.)—Biography.   4. Trappers—West (U.S.)—Biography.   5. Frontier and pioneer life—West (U.S.)   6. West (U.S.)—Discovery and exploration.   7. West (U.S.)—History—To 1848.
8. West (U.S.)—Biography.   I. Title.
   F592.S649B37   2009
   978'.02092—dc22
   [B]

                                                      20089038490

Jedediah Smith: No Ordinary Mountain Man is Volume 23 in The Oklahoma Western Biographies.

The paper in this book meets the guidelines for permanence and durability of the Committee on Production Guidelines for Book Longevity of the Council on Library Resources, Inc. ∞

2 3 4 5 6 7 8 9 10

For Penny and Vachel

The difficulties and dangers to be encountered,
the perilous adventures, and hair-breadth escapes of which
we have read and heard, have thrown over that whole land,
a fearful kind of romance.

Anonymous eulogy for Jedediah Strong Smith,
Illinois Monthly Magazine, June 1832

Contents

Illustrations

Series Editor's Preface

STORIES of heroes and heroines have intrigued many generations of listeners and readers. Americans, like people everywhere, have been captivated by the lives of military, political, and religious figures and intrepid explorers, pioneers, and rebels. The Oklahoma Western Biographies endeavor to build on this fascination with biography and to link it with two abiding interests of Americans: the frontier and the American West. Although volumes in the series carry no notes, they are prepared by leading scholars, are soundly researched, and include a discussion of sources used. Each volume is a lively synthesis based on thorough examination of pertinent primary and secondary sources.

Above all, The Oklahoma Western Biographies aim at two goals: to provide readable life stories of significant westerners and to show how their lives illuminate a notable topic, an influential movement, or a series of important events in the history and cultures of the American West.

In this book, Barton H. Barbour furnishes the new biography of Jedediah Strong Smith we have needed for a long time. For more than half a century, scholars and general readers have relied on Dale Morgan's earlier work, *Jedediah Smith and the Opening of the West* (1953). This fresh life story replaces Morgan's pioneering book. Barbour makes particularly good use of new findings in Mexican archives concerning Smith's controversial months in Spanish-Mexican California. He also tells an engrossing story that moves—following Smith in his journeys crisscrossing the plains, the Rockies, California, the Pacific Northwest, and the Southwest. No one will come away from

Barbour's *Jedediah Smith: No Ordinary Mountain Man* without being impressed with his protagonist's courage, ambition, and diligence.

Barbour also furnishes a complex, valuable portrait of Smith's extensive contacts with dozens of Indian peoples in the American West. As the author's evenhanded account reveals, Native groups repeatedly aided Smith with needed food, directions, and even horses. He got along well with most of the Indians he encountered. But on some occasions, these contacts turned violent, leading to conflicts brought on as much by the misdeeds of Smith and his men as by their Native competitors. To his credit, Barbour presents these varied cultural contacts thoroughly and does not shy away from outlining their manifold causes and tragic consequences.

The author's adept handling of human-environmental interactions is also of a high order. Readers will be drawn to Barbour's appealing, sometimes poetic, descriptions of the terrain through which Smith and his men pass. As Smith marches, wanders, and sometimes drags himself across these landscapes, Barbour shows repeatedly how these natural settings sustained or nearly defeated Smith's valiant efforts. This book is alive with the allure and dangers of the mountains, rivers, plains, and deserts of the American West.

Finally, Barbour also understands the tendency of many historians and biographers to transform Jedediah Smith into an entirely heroic, larger-than-life western figure. Throughout his biography the author demythologizes Smith, depicting him as a courageous and ambitious but also flawed human being. The result is an appealing, balanced new treatment of a major western figure and thus a valuable addition to The Oklahoma Western Biographies Series.

Richard W. Etulain

Acknowledgments

IT has been a privilege and a pleasure to work on this new biography of Jedediah S. Smith. Sometimes daunting, often frustrating, my investigation of Smith's life is the product of several years' work. Even in the final months of my work on the manuscript, I reconsidered some well-known evidence and reexamined more recently uncovered materials that called for yet another of many revisions. The final product, I hope, will tell Smith's story in an engaging narrative with sufficient detail and analysis. Because of the requirements for inclusion in The Oklahoma Western Biographies series, this book is not annotated, but a footnoted version of the manuscript will be placed on file at the University of Oklahoma Press for reference purposes.

A number of individuals and institutions have provided me crucial assistance on this project. The research phase of my work began in 1998, when I was employed with the National Park Service at the Southwest Regional Office in Santa Fe, New Mexico. My work there included research and writing on fur trade history, and I was fortunate to be able to combine a research trip to gather information on early Fort Laramie with my initial collection of Jedediah Smith materials during a visit to the Missouri Historical Society at Saint Louis late in 1998. The Missouri Historical Society's fur trade history collection is a fantastically rich resource, and I gathered much useful material on Smith and his associates there. The State Historical Society of Missouri at Columbia, and the Kansas State Historical Society, Topeka, also aided me in this effort.

Presentations that I gave on my Smith research for the Friends of the Idaho State Historical Museum in January 2003, at the ninth North American Fur Trade Conference in Saint Louis in May 2006, at the Oregon State Historic Preservation Office seminar on Smith at Reedsport, Oregon, in September 2006, at the Longmont History Museum and Cultural Center in Longmont, Colorado, in October 2007, and at Rapid City, South Dakota, in May 2008 helped me rethink and refine my interpretation of Smith's adventures and his personality.

I offer heartfelt thanks for long-enduring patience to my good friends Richard W. Etulain, the editor of the Oklahoma Western Biographies series, and Charles E. Rankin at the University of Oklahoma Press. I also wish to thank my friend and fellow Jedediah Smith researcher James Auld of Seattle for many enlightening conversations as we pondered Smith's story and its importance. As well, Smith researcher James Hardee aided me in understanding some of the geographical fine points of Smith's travels. Final revisions of the manuscript greatly benefited from the assistance of an exceptionally able undergraduate student at Boise State University, Dane Vanhoozer, whose enthusiastic and patient help proved invaluable. Thanks also to Patricia Heinicke, Jr., for her fine copyediting, and to Vitrude DeSpain for preparing the index.

I am indebted to the Utah State Historical Society, Salt Lake City, the Bancroft Library, University of California, Berkeley, and to the Missouri Historical Society, Saint Louis, for permission to use some of the illustrations in this book. Thanks also to William Nelson for his fine maps.

Finally, to all of my family and friends who endured uncounted hours of my ranting about Smith, and without whose support and tolerance the book would never have been completed, I owe a lasting debt of gratitude.

Jedediah Smith

Introduction

IT is late spring in 1831. Six hundred miles west of Saint Louis on the trail to Santa Fe, a solitary mounted white man cautiously rides two or three miles in advance of the traders' wagon caravan in which he is a leading investor. The landscape presents a dusty expanse of treeless plains, the air is hot enough to make the man feel as if he were standing before an open oven door, and water is nowhere to be found. Squinting in the harsh sunshine, he scans the arid land for signs of verdure that would proclaim the Cimarron River and offer relief from the dehydration that threatens men and livestock alike. At length, the buckskin-clad rider spots a dip in the prairie—it must be the river, or at least a waterhole.

He rides closer and is startled when he comes upon several mixed-blood New Mexican traders. Perhaps he has heard tales of these men, called *comancheros*. Ever since about 1720, small parties of daring New Mexicans had carried on a precarious, risky trade with the Comanche nation. Having just concluded another trade session with their unpredictable Indian partners, they too are alarmed when they see the stranger on his jaded horse. Unwilling to risk their own lives on behalf of someone they do not know, the comancheros offer no assistance, but they signal that Comanches are nearby and that the man has no hope of evading the Indians. The white man rides forward. Reaching the edge of the prairie depression, he spots a party of warriors on horseback a half mile off, and they have seen him, too. The man braces for action, for he has participated in many ugly confrontations with Indians over the past decade. Checking the priming on his flintlock rifle, he glances at the pair of pistols holstered across the pommel of his saddle and steels his nerve. His right hand slips closer to the trigger of his gun even as he makes signs for peace to the approaching Indians.

Perhaps, as a terrific sense of peril gathers about him, the man's racing mind brings time to a stop for an instant, as happens to some people during moments of extraordinary crisis. Perhaps the man's imagination even involuntarily reviewed the strange and exhilarating years that had passed since he left family and friends to wander the uttermost reaches of North America's little-known "Far West."

All too quickly, he approaches the Comanches and about twenty of them boldly encircle him. A few minutes drag by while the hot, still air fairly crackles with tension. The Indians mutter phrases in Spanish that the man does not understand, but he must sense that he is going to die. Several Comanches attempt to spook the stranger's horse. Then one warrior darts out a hand to snatch at the white man's gun. Instantly the rifle belches forth a lead ball, spilling the Indian from his saddle. As other Comanches quickly close in, the white man drops his rifle and reaches for one of the heavy holstered pistols, but it is too late. A second shot rings out, this time from a Comanche's flintlock gun. The white man's upper body jerks, and he starts to slump from his horse. Long Comanche lances are thrust into him, and he is dead. The Indians methodically sift through the man's belongings. Taking such gear as might be useful, they mount their ponies and move on, leaving the corpse where it lies, never to be found.

In brazen silence, the afternoon sun crawls toward the horizon, its raking beams illuminating the lifeless body of Jedediah Strong Smith, aged thirty-two years. The principal eyewitnesses to Smith's murder were the Comanches who killed him, and they never offered an account of the event. Still, the comancheros almost certainly observed Smith's murder from a distance. Smith's companions searched in vain for two days to recover his body, and if the comancheros had been discovered, they probably could have led Smith's companions to the site of the murder. Smith's fellow travelers learned nothing of his fate until after they arrived at Santa Fe a few weeks later.

This re-creation of an explosive instant of violence that ended the brief life of one of North America's greatest explorers is speculative, but it is not merely imaginary. It is based on a few skimpy reports provided by Smith's companions shortly after his death. Scanty though it may be, the documentation of the circumstances of Jedediah Smith's death offers more detail than has been discovered in the records concerning his first ten years of life. Indeed, the final third of Smith's life is relatively well documented, but so slim is the record of his first twenty years that any summary of it necessitates a good deal of conjecture and inference.

Jedediah Strong Smith roamed through more of the American West than practically any man of his era. Until the 1840s his name and exploits were well enough known, but as the people who knew him passed away, his remembered fame flickered, and by 1900 it had almost been snuffed out altogether. Rescued from historical obscurity by the middle twentieth century, his life and achievements are now certain to be remembered. And his achievements were many.

In 1824 Jedediah Smith was among the second wave of Euro-Americans to traverse the South Pass; more importantly, he almost instantly recognized the relative ease with which future thousands might travel through it to the Far West. In 1826–27 Smith led a party of mountain men on a perilous trek across the Mexican northwest by way of what is now Utah and Nevada to the so-called Spanish missions in Mexican California, becoming the first Americans to reach California by traveling overland. He was the first white man known to make an eastward crossing of the Sierra Nevada, the first to lead men across the Great Basin, and the first to lead men on a northward trek along the seacoast from California to Oregon. Fewer than a dozen years after Smith's death—by the early 1840s—the Platte River–South Pass route that he and other mountain men pioneered had become the preferred overland migration route for the yearly increasing throngs of Euro-Americans who believed themselves divinely ordained to wrest the Far West from the inept and feeble grip of Indians and Mexicans, and to drive Her Majesty Queen Victoria's interlopers from Oregon.

Jedediah Smith was no ordinary mountain man. A natural-born cartographer of rare talent, he alone transposed his mental map of the entire West onto paper. It is now known that Smith made numerous indirect but significant contributions to the most accurate maps of the American West published in the 1820s and 1830s. Snippets of documentary evidence indicate that Smith drafted several maps of the West. No one realized that he had transferred his vast geographical knowledge to a manuscript master-map—yet to be discovered—until the mid-1950s, when historical cartographer Carl I. Wheat and historian Dale L. Morgan identified a unique map of the American West covered with dozens of notations transcribed from one of Smith's maps. Called the Frémont-Gibbs-Smith map, it offers stunning corroboration of information recorded in Smith's own journals and letters and comments by his contemporaries.

Jedediah Smith was a supernova in the galaxy of mountain men who roamed the Rockies and helped make Saint Louis the queen city of the West by 1830. Modern-day Americans who familiarize themselves with Smith's life will better appreciate the convergence of powerful social, economic, and political currents that persuaded U.S. citizens to believe, for better or worse, that their nation's future power depended upon territorial expansion to the Pacific coast. Smith's life brilliantly reflects the ethos of "young America" during the ripest years of its celebrated frontier epoch.

Jedediah Smith's personality, attitudes, and behavior exemplify some of the bright and promising aspects of our national character, but they also reveal less appealing features such as Americans' habitually negative opinions about "Spaniards" and Indians. By the mid-nineteenth century, U.S. prejudicial attitudes about Mexicans and Indians had hardened, yielding the essential, if unpleasant, rationales that supported foreign policy in the Mexican-American War and a domestic Indian policy throughout the West. Rocky Mountain trappers' experiences with Indians and Mexicans often seemed to corroborate Americans' already negative characterizations and thus contributed to the ideology that produced such policies. Smith's encounters with British and Canadian fur traders likewise reflected and shaped U.S.-British relationships in the decades after the War of 1812. Stories of Smith's western experiences boosted Americans' interest in "the Oregon Country" and stoked Americans' fears that Great Britain might achieve supremacy in the region.

Jedediah Smith's western adventures became the stuff of legend, but mere legendry is not enough to make him a significant historical character worthy of attention. In a Rocky Mountain career that spanned the decade from 1822 to 1831, Smith began as a "greenhorn" with the famed Ashley-Henry trapping brigades, eventually became Ashley's partner, and later founded the successful firm of Smith, Jackson & Sublette. Several key events in Smith's career positively strain credulity. In 1823 he survived a terrible mauling by the fur traders' most feared antagonist, the grizzly bear. In 1823, 1827, and 1828 he walked away unscathed from the three deadliest encounters on record between western beaver trappers and Indians, while in each fight many of his fellow trappers perished. Smith was no braggart, and he never exaggerated his adventures. In a few instances, however, Smith did embroider the truth, most notably after two detentions in Mexican California when he wanted to appear beyond reproach as he complained of his treatment to U.S. authorities.

Although Smith was himself habitually self-deprecating and seems not to have courted publicity, his life seems tailor-made for mythologizing. Indeed, the mythic "Jed Smith" grew to heroic proportions in the twentieth century after a handful of less-than-scholarly writers rediscovered, and then bent to their own purposes, the story of his life. Jedediah Smith is reckoned by some to have been the first white man to preach the gospel to Indians beyond the "Shining Mountains." He is reputed to have been a devout, peace-loving, Christian teetotaler who rarely imbibed alcohol, never smoked tobacco, and never cursed. Some Christians have enlisted Smith as one of the "twelve apostles of California," eulogizing him as a "missionary" who preached not only to Indians but to the mountain men as well. According to some biographers he carried a Bible with him at all times over thousands of difficult miles.

Smith was no missionary. But he definitely stood out from his peers. Unlike most of his trapper brethren, Smith apparently never consorted with Indian women, and it is certain that he never married. Contemporaries universally considered him a superior leader of men, and his fellow mountain men willingly deferred to his wisdom in a multitude of emergencies. Though lauded as the finest cartographer among the Rocky Mountain men, Smith received no formal training in mapmaking, nor did he spend a single day in regular military service.

As of the year 2008 at least sixty-five monuments commemorate Smith's travels and achievements. A Jedediah Smith Society at the University of the Pacific in Stockton, California, hosts annual meetings and supports publication of Smith-related materials. He has been the subject of several biographies—including some marketed to young boys—as well as an epic poem and even a few verses of song. Thanks to Sidney Pollack's 1972 film, *Jeremiah Johnson*, the public often confuses Jedediah Smith's story with that of another legendary historical character, John Johnson. Even so, California boasts more roadside Smith memorials than any other state. A state park in the redwood country east of Crescent City is named for him, as are three rivers in Oregon and California, a public school, several hiking trails, and a northern California town. The Ashley National Forest, a wilderness area in Utah, memorializes the exploits of Smith and his patron and employer, William H. Ashley. At one time, Jedediah Smith's name even graced a sourdough theme restaurant located in Wyoming.

This enthusiasm for Smith's story is, however, a relatively recent phenomenon. Indeed, he was all but forgotten by about 1900, and the record of his achievements slumbered mainly in garbled tales of old-timers' folklore. Fortunately, legitimate twentieth-century historians such as Hiram M. Chittenden, Harrison Dale, Maurice S. Sullivan, and Dale L. Morgan rediscovered Jedediah S. Smith. Diligently combing through mounds of dusty business records, personal and official letters, journals, wills, and inventories in archives at the Missouri Historical Society and elsewhere, they recovered many documents that illuminated Smith's life and times. Morgan's bulky biography of Smith, published in 1953, which may be fairly described as "magisterial," remains in print today.

The past half-century of continued interest in Smith has churned up a welter of new information. Researchers such as George R. Brooks and David J. Weber brought to light a number of significant discoveries, including previously unknown portions of Smith's journals and letters, letters penned by some American associates, and documents generated by Mexican officials who dealt with Smith in California. Indeed, as recently as 2000 a hitherto unknown and wonderfully revealing 1831 letter from Smith to Secretary of War John Eaton surfaced in the National Archives in Washington, D.C. These archival bonanzas are among the principal reasons why a fresh biography of Smith is warranted. They open new windows on critically important but shadowy episodes of Smith's life.

Three dominant themes in Jedediah Smith's life were a razor-sharp ambition to succeed economically, an irresistible impulse to be and to be seen as an explorer, and a habitual predilection to wrestle with himself over his perceived spiritual failings. These often contrary impulses sometimes seem to have been locked in contention within Smith's agile mind. Still, the daily press of business affairs, the desperate, dangerous months on the trail, and his lengthy detentions in California comprise the bulk of his journal entries. It was only in rare moments of repose, or while confronting a grave situation, that Smith yielded to an urge to record his thoughts and feelings about things. Precious few as they are, those comments offer the best available insights into Smith's personality.

Aware that the historical Jedediah Smith differed from the mythic character that some writers made into a role model, Dale Morgan remarked, "Jedediah's years in the West are a sustained, almost unrelieved chronicle of physical endurance, unflagging courage and granitic purpose, with occasional climaxes in which his spirit burns clear and bright. Explorer, fur trader, fighting man—he was all of these; and as a symbol of the nation which launched him in the track of the sun, a great deal more. But

Jedediah the man tends to be lost in Jedediah Smith the hero, the trail breaker, the public personality."

Writing in the 1930s, Maurice Sullivan conceived of Smith as a "pious, but … vigorous, fighting Knight in Buckskin … [who] opened the gate through which passed the American builders of the West." No mere hagiographer, Sullivan was the first scholar to discover that Jedediah Smith planned to publish his journals, accompanied by "a map which changed the geographic conception of North America west of the Rocky Mountains." He also identified reasons that helped to explain why Smith's story had never been fully told. Two tragedies, according to Sullivan, "contributed to the amazing neglect of this extraordinary person." Smith's premature death, like that of Meriwether Lewis fifteen years earlier, eliminated the primary source of information and left a multitude of unanswerable questions. No contemporary writer fully documented Smith's experiences or promoted his achievements. At least, as Morgan and others pointed out, Lewis had William Clark to perpetuate his fame and celebrate his life's great work.

The second tragedy resulted from a series of fires. One fire destroyed most of Tracy & Wahrendorff's Saint Louis warehouse, where Smith or his patron, William H. Ashley, may have deposited Smith's papers. Some of Smith's journals, maps, and papers may have also been lost when fire demolished a house that Washington Irving occupied. Irving was supposedly preparing a manuscript on Smith that would have resembled the document-based books he eventually published about the Astorian enterprise (1836) and the travels of Capt. Benjamin L. E. Bonneville (1837). County courthouse fires in Ohio and Pennsylvania and the demolition of another courthouse in Ohio resulted in the loss of records dealing with Smith's early years. There is even a rumor that an unidentified family member burned some of Smith's records.

Sullivan feared it was "virtually certain" that Smith's original journals were destroyed some years after his death, cryptically noting that it happened "under circumstances which need not be recorded." After years of research and letter writing, Sullivan did recover portions of the transcript made by Samuel Parkman in Saint Louis, the version that Smith "intended to publish." Much of that manuscript had survived the ravages of time and fire, and in 1934 Sullivan published it along with a number of relevant documents. Though Parkman edited Smith's writing for spelling flaws, he did not impair what Sullivan denoted "a natural dignity of expression which a misspelled word could not mar."

Along with these incomplete copies of Smith's journal and a fragmentary journal in Smith's own hand, the journals of his clerk and friend Harrison Rogers, covering the two California expeditions, surfaced in Saint Louis early in the twentieth century. One of the most dramatic discoveries after 1950 was the recovery of Samuel Parkman's transcript of Smith's 1826–27 Southwest Expedition journal. It came to light at Saint Louis in 1967 as a gift to the Missouri Historical Society. George Brooks brought both Smith's and Rogers's California journals into print in 1977.

It is certain that Jedediah Smith drafted several maps. His greatest cartographic work, a large map covering several sheets, detailed his travels and was probably a composite of other maps. No original maps have been recovered, but much important information derived from Smith and his maps enhanced four of the most accurate and influential contemporary printed maps. Notations obviously lifted from a Smith manuscript map adorn an 1836 map of the West by Albert Gallatin, an 1839 map of the United States by David H. Burr, "Geographer to the House of Representatives of the U.S.," and two 1841 maps of the Oregon Country drafted by U.S. Navy Lt. Charles Wilkes.

The most thrilling authentic evidence of Smith's geographic discoveries and cartographic talent, however, is the spectacular Frémont-Gibbs-Smith map identified by Wheat and Morgan in 1954. It is a printed copy of Lt. John C. Frémont's 1845 map of the West published by the U.S. Congress, once the possession of George Gibbs, a mapmaker and ethnologist who worked in Oregon around 1850. Gibbs penciled many tiny notations onto the map, detailing routes and landmarks in descriptive language that could only have come from Jedediah Smith's master map. The emendations and additions conclusively demonstrate that Smith drafted a substantially improved map of the West, and that Gibbs had ample opportunity to examine it, possibly in the form of a copy he found at Fort Vancouver.

In his nine-year career as a trapper, Jedediah Smith endured unimaginable suffering, bitter defeats at the hands of Indian adversaries, and hazardous confrontations with wild animals. He also reveled in the soul-stirring novelty of probing the unknown reaches of western North America, and he remained ever cognizant that he was among the first Euro-Americans to see so much of the Great West. Smith keenly felt an obligation to record his western experiences, and he evidently aimed to publish his account one day. His journals and letters amply illustrate his compulsive urge to explore and to write things down, and they present a mind-boggling sequence of escapades. Unlike nearly contemporary nineteenth-century professional writers such as Washington Irving and Francis Parkman who published travelogues of their western adventures, Jedediah Smith went west primarily in search of wealth. Smith made a small fortune in a trade that was considered one of the most dangerous and exciting vocations to be found anywhere. By the time he was killed, Smith had gained wealth and reputation enough to pursue any number of new careers.

To be sure, not all the people with whom Jedediah Smith interacted thought highly of him. Contemporary Mexicans had reason to consider Smith a spy, or at least a snooping intruder in California. To British-Canadian competitors he presented an economic threat, and they generally characterized him as a "cunning Yankey." Many Indians, particularly Arikaras, Mohaves, and the northern California and Oregon tribes, likewise viewed Smith and his men with grave misgivings. But if any American of his time deserves the accolade of having lived larger than life, Jedediah Smith certainly is a prime contender. And yet, as is the case with many other "great" American personalities, it is no easy task to offer a "complete" depiction of the man. Indeed, it seems as if there were two Jedediah Smiths.

One is the result of a prescriptive myth conjured out of fanciful and heroic imagery, to some degree deliberately constructed in defiance of known facts to serve as an American civics lesson and to inculcate desirable moral or behavioral principles. The other is a historical character whose life can take shape only as the result of thoughtful reconstruction, founded upon a careful examination of documentary information reposing in widely scattered archives. This book attempts to depict Jedediah Smith as a not-so-simple man with human aspirations and failings who played a key historical role in the American West, in "Indian Country," and in the Mexican northwest.

Like hundreds of other young men from Virginia, Missouri, New York, and elsewhere in early nineteenth-century America, Jedediah Smith chose a career as a beaver trapper. But no more than a handful of his fellow "mountaineers" reached so high, suffered as greatly, or achieved as much. This book is based substantially on Smith's own writings, which have been extensively quoted in order to present his authentic voice to readers. (Some misspellings from the original sources have been left unaltered, but these should present no serious impediment to readers.) Its purpose is to tell Jedediah Smith's story, to frame his life and adventures within the contexts of Jacksonian America and the developing Rocky Mountain fur trade, and to highlight his contributions to the exploration and history of the American West.

CHAPTER 1

Jedediah Smith's Background

JEDEDIAH Smith's ancestors first reached American shores in 1634, when Samuel Smith's Puritan family departed Hadleigh, England, for the Massachusetts Bay Colony. Noted among other things for an emphasis on introspective self-criticism and an abiding revulsion from all things Catholic, the New Englanders' Puritan faith underwent change as time passed, commercial enterprises expanded, and new generations fanned out over the land. In the late 1730s an Anglican preacher named George Whitefield ignited a religious revival throughout British North America called the Great Awakening. Whitefield and the New Englander Jonathan Edwards became towering figures among supporters of the revival, called the New Lights. By 1750 the revivalism had crested and was in decline, but not before it laid the foundations for the American Methodist faith that Jedediah Smith's father, Jedediah Smith, Sr., embraced around 1790, and that Jedediah inherited as a youngster.

The Puritans' faith affected all aspects of life in early New England, but so did the harsh realities of eking out a living on a raw frontier and, from 1680 until 1760, the ever-present threat of French and Indian attacks. Decades of intermittent bloody conflict between the English and French—and their respective Indian allies—hardened New Englanders' attitudes about Indians and caused a goodly number of them to wonder if the violence was the Lord's way of testing their faith, or smiting them for their unrighteousness. As the Puritan ambition to erect a "Bible commonwealth" in the new American Eden faded, it was replaced by a modernizing, secularizing, and increasingly materialistic society that seemed more eager to gain wealth in this world than salvation in the next one. Thus was born the sharp-trading New England "Yankee" merchant whose economic enterprises attained a global reach. Jedediah Smith was in some respects the product of these historical experiences. The American Revolutionary War divided the Smith family. Some members remained loyal, while others took up arms against King George III. After independence, Jedediah Smith's grandfather and several of his sons lived in Vermont for a few years, having been granted lands there by the State of New York. Such grants were made because states had no money to pay soldiers who served in the Revolutionary War. But New Hampshire also granted Vermont lands to veterans, and the overlapping and uncertain grants nearly brought the two states to blows. In a lengthy lawsuit over the conflicting land claims, New Hampshire won the case. With the New York grants deemed invalid, the "Vermont Sufferers," as the New York grantees were called, received substitute parcels of land far to the west, in New York. So it was that members of the Smith family left New England, joining other outcast Vermonters in a westward migration.

Around 1795 Jedediah Smith, Sr., moved his father's family to New York. During a brief interlude at Spencertown, a hamlet east of the Hudson River, Jedediah, Sr., married Sally Strong, another descendant of an old-guard Puritan lineage whose family hailed from Northampton, Massachusetts. Her father, like her new husband, had received lands in western New York as a Vermont Sufferer. Perhaps both men had served in the same regiment associated with the State of New York during the Revolutionary War. In any case, the two families moved westward in tandem, taking up land in the Susquehanna River valley in western New York State. Helping to establish a town in Chenango County called Jericho, the Smiths remained there for about ten years, during which time five of their twelve children came into the world. By 1814 the town had been renamed Bainbridge.

Jedediah Strong Smith, the family's fourth child and second son, was born at Jericho on January 6, 1799. Two sisters and two brothers died in their infancy, but sisters Sally, Betsy, and Eunice survived to adulthood. Seven brothers—Ralph, Jedediah, Austin, Peter, Ira, Nelson, and Benjamin—also lived to adulthood. The last three sons were born after the Smiths departed Jericho for Pennsylvania shortly before the outbreak of the War of 1812.

Jedediah Smith, Sr., ran a general store at Jericho with his brother-in-law Cyrus Strong. The Smiths remained in the town until 1810–11, when the elder Smith became enmeshed in a legal problem, possibly for having inadvertently passed counterfeit coins. Shortly thereafter the family departed New York for North East Township, Erie County, Pennsylvania, where the elder Smith took up a farm. About this time young Jedediah Smith experienced his only exposure to military life. Family tradition holds that when brother Ralph enlisted in the New York militia to participate in Commodore Oliver Hazard Perry's successful Great Lakes campaign during the War of 1812, fourteen-year-old Jedediah tagged along. He briefly held a job as a "supercargo"—contemporary parlance for a clerk—on a Great Lakes vessel, so he may have possessed skills deemed useful in a naval operation.

By 1817 Jedediah's father augmented his meager farm income with odd tailoring jobs and had purchased a hilly, timbered parcel of land bordering a creek in the township. As a lad in Erie County, Jedediah Smith first made regular contacts with American Indians, for a mixed band of Delawares, Mohicans, Mohawks, and Wyandots lived nearby. Like most farming families in the region, the Smiths were relatively poor. On several occasions young Jedediah was obliged to rent oxen from a neighbor to plow his family's land. A few years later Jedediah, Sr., again led his family west, this time to Green Township near Ashtabula, Ohio. In February 1821, only a few months before he left his home, Jedediah Smith cast a ballot in a township election for justice of the peace—the only time he is known for certain to have voted in any political election.

Among the important influences on Smith's life during his formative years in the Susquehanna Valley and in eastern Ohio are his associations with three notable local men: Dr. Titus Gordon Vespasian Simons, Patrick Gass, and John Chapman. For many years Jedediah's family was closely associated with the Simons family. The doctor stood out as an educated man in a locale where few could boast similar attainments. Smith biographers Maurice Sullivan and Dale Morgan both speculated that Doctor Simons gave Jedediah a copy of Nicolas Biddle's 1814 edition of Lewis and Clark's journals.

It may be, however, that it was Jedediah's neighbor Patrick Gass who first introduced him to the expedition's narratives. One of four sergeants in the Corps of Discovery, Gass published his journal in 1807. Reprinted several times before 1812, it was the first authentic record of the expedition to appear. Several Gass family members resided in Richland County, in Green Township, Ohio, not far from the forks of the Mohican River and the town of Perrysville, Ohio, where the Smiths and the Simonses dwelled. Given the scarcity of literate persons in the area, it would be surprising if the three families were not acquainted. Patrick Gass's brother William was a locally prominent man who held several elective offices in Richland County, which he had helped organize in 1813.

Young Jedediah unquestionably read a number of contemporary expeditionary narratives. While coursing along the Missouri River during 1822, he wrote in his own journal, "The country has been well described by Lewis & Clark, therefore any observation from me would be superfluous." While in California in 1827, he forbore writing a detailed description of San Francisco Bay in his journal, since he knew it had been "well described by [Captain George] Vancouver."

Even if Dr. Simons was not the primary source for Jedediah's introduction to exploration literature, he played a substantial role in shaping Smith's outlook. Simons's medical practice kept him busy in western Pennsylvania and eastern Ohio, but he also made time to educate many rural youngsters over the years. He had known the Smiths well since they lived in New York and probably began teaching Ralph and Jedediah Smith after they migrated to Pennsylvania. By the time Jedediah reached the age of seventeen, his "formal" education was completed, and the doctor had done a good job. Jedediah Smith never forgot the intellectual debt he owed Dr. Simons and evermore held his first mentor in the highest esteem. He fondly referred to Simons in several letters he sent home from the Far West, and he occasionally forwarded money to the doctor as well.

Jedediah also became acquainted with the unusual man named John Chapman, destined for folkloric fame in the American Midwest as the celebrated "Johnny Appleseed." Born in Massachusetts, Chapman moved to the Ohio frontier in 1800 and was later one of the Smiths' neighbors. Besides planting fruit trees, Chapman also scattered seeds of the Swedenborgian variant of Christianity, which professed pacifism, humility, and personal conversations with spirits and angels. Chapman and the Smiths lived or owned land in Green Township and in neighboring Wayne Township, Ohio. Jedediah's brother Ralph and Dr. Simons each purchased land parcels adjacent to land Chapman owned, making it a virtual certainty that all three families were acquainted.

The foregoing spare account summarizes what is known about Jedediah Smith's background and youth. Most of the details of his upbringing remain in shadow despite the emergence of much new Smith-related information in the last half-century. Smith's associations with Dr. Simons, John Chapman, and probably Patrick Gass in western New York and Ohio likely had a lasting affect on the young man's intellectual development. Whatever the case may have been, it is clear that Jedediah Smith possessed a high degree of intelligence and abundant curiosity. His deep-rooted religious convictions found expression in Methodism, though as an adult he almost never attended a Methodist church, or any other for that matter.

It is also obvious—according to a number of surviving letters and several journal entries—that Smith was a devoted son and brother. And yet, in the course of his wanderings he sometimes berated himself for being so prodigal a son. Several of his letters refer poignantly to painful feelings of guilt and inadequacy for not living beside his aged parents and for failing to meet his filial obligation to provide for them. More than once he expressed grave doubts about his spiritual rectitude and fretted over being so bound up in the ultimately meaningless, materialistic "things of time." But as he wrote on Christmas Eve 1829, "[I]t is, that I may be able to help those who stand in need, that I face every danger." Jedediah Smith's motives for going west did include a nascent lust for fame and an insatiable curiosity, but also a burning desire to acquire wealth that he might share with his family and friends.

Virtually nothing is known of Jedediah Smith's early vocational training, though he no doubt acquired the hunting and woodcraft skills common among boys who grew up on the frontier. Thanks to Dr. Simons, Smith also mastered basic mathematical skills, as well as reading and writing, which to some degree set him apart from the average backwoods boy. His stint as a Great Lakes ship's clerk demonstrates that he could handle a job requiring literacy and familiarity with ledger-book accounting.

Jedediah Smith never married, but a vague family tradition suggests that he may have flirted with romance in Green Township. If true, this would constitute an event of singular importance in this solitary man's life. The most likely possibility would have been a connection with one of Dr. Simons's daughters. Jedediah's older brother Ralph married one Simons daughter, and one of the doctor's sons wedded Jedediah's sister Eunice. On the other hand, asserted a Smith descendant in 1933, "I have never heard that the 'fair sex' ever entered into the calculations of Uncle Jedediah. I suppose there was no room for anything 'weak' in his nature," though, she added, "the women of his family were too good to him to have a dislike for the sex." Perhaps Smith decided to defer any ideas about getting married until such time as he had achieved financial security.

Jedediah Smith might simply have grown up, gotten married, and lived and died in peaceful obscurity close by the hamlets where he spent his youth, but his life took a dramatic turn in 1822. When he was twenty-three years old he decided to go to Saint Louis, Missouri, the boomtown of the West. Like thousands of other young American men, Jedediah Smith set out in hopes of improving his own and his family's economic condition. Unfortunately, he came of age during a period of prolonged economic distress. Smith wrote nothing to explain his reasons for leaving Ohio to seek work at Saint Louis, but a brief summary of the nation's economic situation offers a context for his decision.

The United States' financial health was anything but good in 1822. Indeed, the economic outlook for many Americans had been bleak for several years. Recovery from the depression that followed the War of 1812 was sluggish, and in 1820 national commerce remained weak. Banking practices and financial affairs were in even worse condition. Early nineteenth-century banking, always poorly organized and volatile, collapsed after a parsimonious Congress dismantled the first Bank of the United States in 1816. As the nation slipped into fiscal chaos, government proved powerless to control rickety wildcat banks, whose operations were irresponsible at best, criminal at worst. When a financial panic ignited frenzied activity among bankers and speculators in 1819, nothing could stave off the impending disaster. Banks folded by the dozen and farm mortgage foreclosures skyrocketed, ruining thousands of rural debtors. Jedediah Smith's father, like many other local residents, became the victim of a busted Ohio bank in 1817 and he never recovered his vanished assets.

Few places offered a remedy for the widespread economic turmoil. One promising locale, however, was the bustling inland port town of Saint Louis. By 1764, when the French founded it as a trading post a few miles below the confluence of the Mississippi and Missouri rivers, France had already lost her North American colony. Indeed, in 1762 France ceded the whole of "Louisiana" to Spain rather than allowing it to fall to Great Britain, her archenemy and the victor in the Seven Year's War. Saint Louisans were eager to develop the fur and Indian trades, but during forty years of the Spanish regime these enterprises expanded very slowly. Napoleon Bonaparte forced the retrocession of Louisiana to France in 1800, but for the next two years nothing changed. Bonaparte's fantasy of reestablishing a French colony in North America quickly eroded under the financial and military exigencies of European war, and he sold Louisiana to the United States in 1803. Within a few months President Thomas Jefferson dispatched Lewis and Clark's Corps of Discovery on a two-year expedition to inventory the little-known assets in the enormous territory that the nation had acquired for a pittance.

The only readily exploitable sources of wealth, it turned out, were the legions of fur-bearing animals inhabiting the vast interior of the Louisiana Purchase. None were more valuable than the beaver, North America's largest rodent. Some beaver fur skins were used to trim clothing, but the principal buyers of beaver fur were hat-makers, who transformed the finely barbed fur into the world's best hat felt. Since the early colonial era the flourishing beaver trade had been among North America's leading frontier economic enterprises, and it remained important well into the early national periods in both the United States and Canada. The fur trade fostered exploration by Euro-Americans, provided economic foundations for English and French colonies, and underlay England and France's four wars for empire that ended with the ouster of France from North America in 1763.

For nearly two decades after the United States acquired Louisiana, the western fur trade remained relatively stagnant. Capital was in short supply everywhere, and the fur trade entailed far higher risks than most branches of commerce. Traders also lacked the necessary organizational framework, and perhaps the nerve, to push very far up the Missouri River. The Missouri had been touted as a rich source for fur-bearing mammals well before the Corps of Discovery returned to Saint Louis in September 1806, but few men dared to try their luck against the dangers of the upper river region and its sometimes hostile inhabitants.

In addition, British traders, under the banners of the Hudson's Bay Company (HBC) and the Montréal-based North West Company, already had fingers of influence at work among Indian tribes of the middle and upper Missouri, such as the

Arikara, Mandan, Hidatsa, and Blackfeet. Americans feared, with some factual basis, that British traders encouraged Indians to kill American traders or pillage their goods in order to eliminate competition. But the Indians were not mere stooges of British traders. They made decisions and took actions to advance their own commercial and diplomatic agendas and to prevent alien hunters from depleting their territorial resources. British and American interlopers alike might be the unlucky targets of tribal policies. For thirty years after 1790, the HBC men and "Nor'Westers" were so often at each other's throats that they paid little heed to their rivals from the south. But in 1821, with the HBC and the North West Company reeling and bloodied from their protracted struggle, parliamentarians and fur traders forged a formidable unification of the two great British-Canadian outfits.

Turning its attention to the troublesome Americans, the newly invigorated HBC threatened to hamstring their nascent plans to develop the Upper Missouri and Rocky Mountain Indian and fur trades, even though much of the region obviously lay within U.S. territory. At the same time, American frontier capitalists yearned to reclaim profits from the valuable fur resources, and some of their employees would delight in displaying a belligerent nationalism when confronting John Bull's minions in the Far West. It was this aspect of the fur trade that cloaked it with international diplomatic significance and informally vested the traders with the task of expanding and affirming U.S. sovereignty over the Far West in the 1820s and 1830s.

Jedediah Smith was a bright and ambitious young man, perhaps mature beyond his years. He analyzed options carefully, and his austere temperament would not permit superficial folly to run wild. Sometime in the winter of 1821–22, doubtless after sober reflection, Jedediah concluded that he would try his luck finding work in the western fur trade that was just beginning to blossom under the aegis of a handful of Saint Louis merchants. He had, by his own account, "passed the summer and fall of 1821 in the northern part of Illinois, and the winter of 21 & 22 at or near the

Rock River rapids of the Mississippi." He may have worked his way west from Ashtabula, Ohio, to Galena, Illinois, on one of the vessels that regularly plied the Great Lakes, before spending the winter hunting and trapping in the upper Illinois forests. When spring loosened winter's icy grip on the land, Jedediah headed downriver for Saint Louis. Probably in late March or early April young Jedediah Smith arrived at Saint Louis and set about looking for a job. Almost immediately, he encountered an intriguing advertisement that was published in several Missouri newspapers.

The notice first appeared in a mid-February issue of the *Missouri Gazette and Public Advertiser*, but identical advertisements soon followed in the *Missouri Republican* and the *Missouri Intelligencer*. Taverns, hotels, and mercantile houses in Saint Louis must have been abuzz with the exciting news. The now-famous solicitation—the first labor recruitment campaign launched in the United States by fur traders—informed readers that William H. Ashley and Andrew Henry aimed to hire one hundred "Enterprising Young Men." They were to "ascend the Missouri River to its sources, there to be employed" for "one, two, or three" years in the Rocky Mountains. Unstated in the vaguely worded invitation was the "enterprise" that Ashley and Henry had in mind for those young men: they would be betting their lives that they could earn money for themselves and their bosses by setting traps in cold mountain streams to catch beavers and other fur-bearing animals.

Jedediah began keeping a journal before he got to Saint Louis, but he had so far penned only a few brief lines. The record of his western career began when he laconically noted that Ashley and Henry were "fiting out for the prosecution of the fur trade on the head of the Missouri." He soon "called on Gen. Ashley to make an engagement to go with him as a hunter." A brief interview convinced Ashley of Smith's suitability as a contract hunter, and Jedediah noted simply that he "found no difficulty in making a bargain on as good terms as I had reason to expect." On May 8, 1822, after dozens of bales, kegs, and crates of merchandise were stowed aboard a keelboat and a full complement of boatmen and trappers was hired, Jedediah departed Saint Louis on the second of Ashley and Henry's keelboats bound for the Upper Missouri and the Rockies. Jedediah Smith had aspirations of financial success and fantasized about becoming an explorer, but he could not have known that he was about to embark upon a most remarkable western American odyssey.

Smith's employer, William Ashley, hailed from Virginia but migrated to Missouri in 1805 to develop a multifaceted career. Well connected socially, he secured a commission as a brigadier general in the territorial militia. In 1821, the year his first wife died, Ashley was elected as the state's first lieutenant governor. He would later serve Missouri in the U.S. House of Representatives from 1831 to 1835, and he died in 1836 shortly after a failed gubernatorial campaign.

By 1822, Ashley had already tried his hand at several commercial enterprises—lead mines, a gunpowder factory, surveying, and real estate speculation—with mixed results. For a few years following the War of 1812, he and a partner operated a saltpeter mine and gunpowder manufactory in Washington County, Missouri, not far from Saint Louis. But after several employees died in a spectacular explosion when the powder works blew up for a third time, they called it quits.

By 1821 Ashley and his new partner, Andrew Henry, a fellow mine operator and former militia officer, developed plans to break into the beaver trade on the Upper Missouri River, the Rocky Mountains, and even in the ill-defined Oregon Country. Ashley brought political connections and at least the appearance of money to the enterprise, but it was Henry who possessed the field skills required for success in the fur trade. A former partner in Manuel Lisa's Missouri Fur Company, founded in 1807, Henry was a seasoned Upper Missouri veteran. As one of Lisa's field commanders, Henry established a small log fort west of the Continental Divide in 1808 on Henry's Fork of Lewis' River, today called the Snake, but by 1811 Blackfeet enmity and supply shortages forced a retreat.

A decade later Manuel Lisa was dead, and without his guiding spirit his company barely managed to stay afloat. Ashley and

Henry concluded the time was ripe for a renewed campaign in the *pays d'en haut*, or "upriver" or "backcountry." Doubtless their decision was partly based on news of Lisa's death, but they also learned that a substantial impediment in their path was about to be eliminated. That barrier was the government-subsidized "factory system" of Indian trade houses.

The U.S. factory system resulted from the federal government's interest in fostering trade to promote friendly diplomatic relations with Indian nations living along the western frontier. The "factories" were small trading posts stocked with standard goods used in the Indian trade and operated by employees of the federal government called "factors." Initially implemented by Congress in 1796, the system was not intended to produce profits. Instead, it was meant to reduce the potential for abuses in the Indian trade by eliminating cutthroat competition in some areas, and by ensuring fair prices and outlawing the liquor trade with Indians at the government-run trading posts.

The triple purpose of the system, in theory, was to undermine British influence over Indians, improve relations between the U.S. government and Indian nations, and reduce the likelihood of frontier bloodshed. But in practice, the factory system failed to achieve its objectives. Scattered mainly along the Mississippi River and a few tributary streams, the factories did no business with Indians who dwelled in the distant plains and mountains, and thus did not enhance the standing of the government among tribes most likely to be courted by British rivals. The factories frequently stocked substandard, American-made goods that sold poorly to discerning Indian customers who preferred British-made goods, and the government traders rarely collected furs in sufficient numbers to offset annual operating expenses. The system failed primarily because the men who administered the program knew too little about the Indian and fur trades to make it work. Even so, the factory system generated unremitting hostility among American businessmen, especially the influential fur baron John J. Astor, who denounced the government-sponsored "monopoly" system for unfairly hampering entrepreneurs.

Years of vigorous and well-funded political lobbying produced victory for the system's opponents. When Congress dismantled it in 1822, Ashley and Henry put their ambitious scheme into motion. They were scarcely alone. The downfall of the factories stimulated an upwelling of capital seeking outlets, and in 1822 Saint Louis fur trade capitalists found plenty of men willing to risk their necks in the mountains. The result was a "fur rush" to the plains and mountains. Old and new firms jostled each other in a frenzied dash to assemble men and outfits and then reap the profits of a fur trade suddenly freed from government interference. Boosters claimed the newly opened trade would send one thousand Americans into the West to restore to their rightful claimants the fur harvests that hitherto fell into the HBC's lap.

Almost no one, it seems, lost sleep over the fact that federal law flatly prohibited non-Indian hunters from taking any game in Indian Country, an ill-defined but enormous region west of the Mississippi River. In fact, the business of trapping beavers—the enterprise so firmly associated with men such as Jedediah Smith—was entirely illegal in Indian Country. It was perfectly legal to trade with Indians, under federal laws that prescribed how licenses would be issued, bonds for good behavior negotiated, and so on, but trapping and hunting were explicitly forbidden in the trade and intercourse acts, a series of congressional laws passed between 1790 and 1832 designed to regulate the Indian trade. Enthusiasts blithely ignored this not-so-romantic legal reality when they celebrated the daring-do of the mountain men and applauded them for fulfilling the "manifest destiny" of the United States.

Not quite everyone was blind to this potential conflict. Upper Missouri Indian Agent Benjamin O'Fallon, a nephew of the explorer William Clark, wrote to Secretary of War John C. Calhoun in 1822 to suggest that whites should be permitted to trap on lands of Indian nations with whom the United States had no treaty agreements, but only until the fur traders drove out British competitors. Once that desirable end was achieved, O'Fallon thought, "hunting and trapping should be prohibited and our traders confined alone to a fair and equitable trade with [Indians]." But when Clark opined to Calhoun, "I am inclined to believe [that Ashley and Henry's license] will not produce any disturbance among the Indian tribes with whome we have much commerce," the matter was dropped. It resurfaced again in 1832, but neither Congress nor the executive branch of government ever seriously, or effectively, grappled with the issue.

Ashley and Henry intended that the men they recruited for their 1822 voyage would serve mainly as trappers, not as Indian traders. The trade license they received early in March permitted them "to carry on trade with the Indians up the Missouri," but it mentioned nothing about trapping or other activities. A local newspaper, the *Missouri Saturday News*, noted that Ashley's "young men … had experience as woodsmen, and a taste for the wild and rugged life of a hunter." Another paper, the *St. Louis Enquirer*, unequivocally stated that "the object of this company is to trap and hunt" and lauded Ashley and Henry's plans to project an armed and potentially aggressive American presence into a region beyond the Louisiana Purchase—the interior Pacific Northwest—where many feared that British influence operated to the prejudice of U.S. interests.

A few Americans already cast covetous glances toward the Oregon Country, though in 1818 American and British diplomats had signed a ten-year, renewable joint occupation treaty that left undecided the question of sovereignty over the region but permitted both nations to prosecute the fur trade. The treaty arrogantly ignored any preexisting claims of sovereignty by Indians who had long occupied the region and who had no hand in the agreement. Voicing the opinion of pro-Oregon expansionists, Representative John Floyd of Virginia placed several bills before the U.S. Congress in the early 1820s calling for immediate occupancy of the region. None of Floyd's bills ever became law, but they kept agitating the issue before a public increasingly eager to have Oregon.

Such was the general situation when Ashley and Henry's keelboats departed Saint Louis. The first to head out was under the command of Andrew Henry. Jedediah Smith was aboard a second boat named *Enterprize* and captained by Daniel S. D. Moore. Until 1831, when steamboat navigation began on the Missouri, keelboats served as the primary means of transporting men, goods, and furs on the streams that flowed through Indian Country. These ungainly wooden craft, about fifty feet in length, employed crews of ten to fifteen men to move several tons of cargo up the muddy river—slowly, and usually by muscle power alone.

There were three ways to get a keelboat upriver, and only one of them could be characterized as anything like pleasant. On most days, crewmen literally shoved the boats upstream, foot by painful foot, with fifteen-foot-long poles tipped with iron points. As a supervisor bellowed orders in French, crewmen lined up at the bow and faced the stern, poles in hand. At a word from the *bourgeois*, or "boss-man," the boatmen thrust their poles into the muddy river bed, braced their feet against wooden chocks fastened across the walkway, then marched to the keelboat's stern, each laborious step forcing the vessel a miniscule distance forward. Sisyphus-like, the men then hurried back toward the bow, reset their poles, and marched again, before the current dragged the boat downstream. Hour upon hour, day after day, this backbreaking work continued.

Rarely, when winds were cooperative, crewmen hoisted a square canvas sail up a simple mast amidships and the vessel beat sluggishly upriver while the boatmen enjoyed a welcome break. All too often, however, crews were obliged to unlimber the much-hated *cordelle,* a heavy hempen cable of perhaps two hundred feet in length. Whenever the river ran too deep or too rapid for poling, or when prairie winds blew contrarily, crewmen had no choice but to plunge into the muddy water near the riverbank and drag the boat upstream by brute force. Slippery steep banks, tangles of downed trees, and nearly impenetrable underbrush made cordelling an exhausting job.

Downstream travel was usually a far less taxing operation. Crews had only to keep the keelboat drifting along in the six- or seven-mile-per-hour current and prevent its arrest by sandbars,

snags, logjams, and "sawyers," a boatman's term for broken tree
trunks that oscillated invisibly in the muddy current and could
easily rip apart a keelboat's hull. Valued employees on the river—
though they could be an obstreperous lot—almost all boatmen
were French Canadian or Upper Louisianan *engagés* (hired
men). Some fur traders believed that Frenchmen were naturally
docile and hardworking, thus perfectly suited to a species of
labor that many Anglo-Americans refused to perform. Their
ubiquitous presence on keelboats and trading posts throughout
the West deeply influenced the fur traders' multiethnic frontier
society, and illustrates the importance of Franco-Americans in
U.S. history long after France's ejection from North America.

Having been hired as a hunter, Smith avoided most of the
drudgery that the boatmen endured; he also dodged what he
called the "dull monotony" of having to stay near the keelboat
as it crept upriver. Instead, he traveled along the shore ahead of
the vessel, taking in the vast prairies, killing game, and hanging
fresh quarters of meat at highly visible locations for the crewmen
to pick up. Then, only three weeks and about 260 miles from
Saint Louis, a costly mishap occurred near Fort Osage. Established by William Clark in 1808, the recently decommissioned
U.S. Indian factory in western Missouri still offered shelter and
rest to passing wayfarers. Captain Moore was cautiously negotiating a river bend twenty miles below the fort that was chock
full of sawyers. Somehow the *Enterprize*'s mast got entangled in
the branches of an overhanging tree. With its mast caught fast
and the vessel inexorably moving with wind and current, the
Enterprize instantly capsized, spilling cargo and crew into the
turbulent Missouri. Able swimmers leaped into the river to fish
out a few floating boxes, but most of Ashley and Henry's ten-
thousand-dollar cargo simply disappeared in the coffee-colored
water. Captain Moore immediately set off on foot for Saint
Louis, arriving around June 4 with bad news for Ashley. Meanwhile, Jedediah Smith and the others encamped at the site of the
wreck to await further developments.

Sorely disappointed but undaunted, Ashley soon replaced the
boat and its cargo and hired another forty-six crewmen and

hunters. Leaving nothing to chance, he decided to lead the expedition himself. A month of hard driving reunited him with his marooned men, and the keelboat proceeded up the Missouri. Ashley had brought along plenty of bacon and pilot bread to reduce his men's dependence on game alone for their food. Still, Jedediah Smith was among the few "good and active hunters" who procured bear, deer, elk, raccoons, and turkeys along the riverbanks and discovered plenty of honey in bee trees along the way.

Ashley, Smith, and the others soon passed the mouth of the Platte River, deemed the gateway to the Upper Missouri region. A few more days' travel brought them to the Council Bluffs, where the U.S. Army built Fort Atkinson in 1820 to replace the temporary Cantonment Missouri, established in 1819. Fort Atkinson's garrison mustered about five hundred soldiers under the command of Colonel Henry Leavenworth. Despite the loss of his keelboat and goods, Ashley was pleased to reach the fort safely and remained optimistic that success would crown his efforts.

CHAPTER 2

Bitter Lessons

UPON passing the Council Bluffs, Jedediah Smith and the other Ashley men entered the homelands of relatively unknown Indians. Almost two decades earlier, Lewis and Clark's Corps of Discovery had encountered the Ponca, Omaha, Lakota Sioux, Arikara, Mandan, and Hidatsa nations, but since then only a handful of North West Company traders had been among them. The land looked strange, too. Stretching to the limits of sight in all directions lay an extensive undulating prairie, bright with flowers in springtime, lush with nutritious forage for the game that abounded. Trees were exceedingly rare on the prairie, though dense groves of cottonwood and other species filled some of the rich bottomland along the river. This was ideal habitat for bison, and the trappers marveled at their numbers.

No animal was more important to Plains Indians than the bison, and many millions of them roamed the prairies. Bison provided Indians with high-protein meat; hides that could be stitched together with sinews to make lodge covers and furnishings; thick, bullneck rawhide for making war shields; and enough materials to craft a host of other utilitarian and decorative objects. Bison also constituted a major theme in Plains Indian religious practices and were considered sacred creatures. Within a few years after 1822 the bison robe trade became an important element in the Indian trade, accelerating the transformation of plains societies as Indians grew increasingly reliant on the white men's trade goods. As many as two hundred thousand robes went down the Missouri River bound for eastern markets each year from about 1835 to 1870. The robe trade generated robust profits for a few large companies until after the

Civil War, when the U.S. Army turned its attention to the Far
West, and the nation's wars against western Indians began in
earnest.

Jedediah had seen Indians before, but the Missouri River Indians were unlike those he had previously encountered. Smith was
especially impressed with the Lakotas, also called Sioux. He
likened their bison-skin lodges to "a stack of grain or perhaps a
Large Shock of tall hemp," noting that the distant lodges "cannot
fail of pleasing" an observer who was "not accustomed to such a
sight." The lodges were amply furnished with fur skins and buffalo
robes, willow-rod backrests mounted on tripods, and parfleche
containers to hold all sorts of things, and Smith judged them to
be "verry comfortable" and much warmer in winter than one
might suppose. Indeed, so seductive was the combination of
beautiful prairie setting and the Lakotas' picturesque skin lodges
that he thought it could "almost persuade a man to renounce the
world, take the lodge and live the careless, Lazy life of an indian."
Despite the tone of such statements, Jedediah Smith admired the
Sioux. Characterizing them as "generally above the common
stature and of a complexion somewhat lighter than most Indians,"
he added that their "intelligent countenances" placed them "in the
moral scale ... above the mass of indians."

Several Sioux nations had left ancestral homelands near the
western Great Lakes around 1700 to take up new lives on the
buffalo plains. Smith was unaware that when he first met the
Sioux they were engaged in an aggressive expansion deep into
the northern plains, powered by hundreds of mounted, highly
mobile warriors. In their successful bid for regional supremacy,
the Sioux disrupted older Indian power relationships, created
new ones, and made many enemies. They had only recently
ousted the Crow nation from its territory in the Black Hills area
of present-day South Dakota. Likewise, Sioux pressure was forcing the Assiniboines northward from the Missouri toward the
ancestral forests and parklands south of Hudson's Bay that they
had left sometime around 1800.

A very different nation, according to Smith and other American fur hunters, were the Arikaras, the northernmost Caddoan-

speaking Indians. They lived on the Missouri between the Heart River and Knife River but were related by blood, culture, and language to the Skidi Pawnees, southern cousins who dwelled along the Loup River north of the Platte in modern Kansas and Nebraska. Like their Upper Missouri neighbors the Mandan and Hidatsa, the Arikara were agricultural and trading people whose domed, earth-lodge villages overlooked the river.

For protection against the Sioux and other assailants, the Arikara, Mandan, and Hidatsa villages lay safely within defensible palisades. Indians in the region had built such enclosures since at least the fourteenth century. A short distance from the log palisades lay fields that yielded abundant corn, beans, squash, tobacco, and a few other crops. Missouri River village Indians also relied upon bison for meat and other products, including hides that women tanners painstakingly transformed into luxurious summer and winter robes.

These three nations had long enjoyed an enviable status as middlemen in the dispersion of Indian-produced goods over a large territory. Likewise, they were perfectly situated to move Euro-American trade goods up the Missouri and farther west. Food surpluses and Euro-American trade goods helped ensure safety for the exposed village dwellers, who employed diplomacy and trade to maintain a volatile peace with their more bellicose neighbors. Jealously protective of their position and angered by the rising number of white fur hunters roaming through their land, the Arikaras kept a close watch on the perceived usurpers of their role in the river trade.

For their part, the Americans, like the French and Spanish before them, paid little heed to the finer points of intertribal politics. Instead, they grew suspicious of the Indians, particularly the Arikaras, also called Rees, resenting what seemed to them dangerously unpredictable behavior. Arikaras and American trappers were on a collision course that would produce a clash in 1823. But in the autumn of 1822 relations remained peaceable.

On September 8 Ashley's keelboat anchored below the pair of Arikara villages located at the mouth of the Grand River, today the site of Mobridge, South Dakota. Having decided to split his

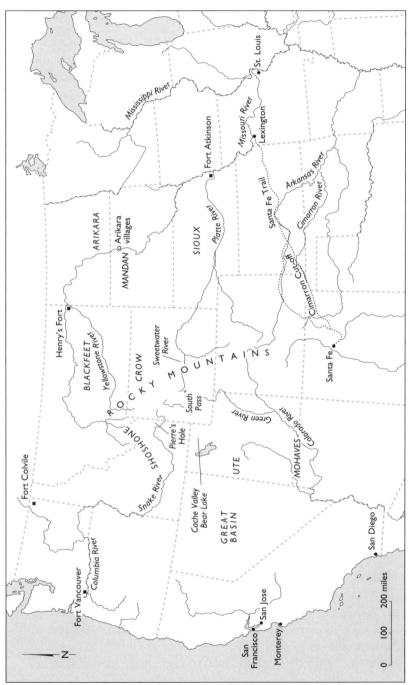

The Far West in the early nineteenth century

party, Ashley needed to purchase livestock. One contingent would continue up the Missouri with the keelboat, while the other hastened overland to the Yellowstone River, where Henry was building a new fort, to take part in the fall hunt. Jedediah Smith would accompany Ashley's overland party. Exercising due caution, Ashley traded goods for Arikara horses. Then he handed out a few presents and assured tribal leaders that he would trade no weapons to their enemies because his men would do their own fur hunting.

Moving a few more miles upriver, the trappers spent a day at the Mandan villages where Lewis and Clark wintered in 1804–1805. Ashley's horsemen headed northwest toward the Yellowstone, reaching Henry's new fort without incident on October 1. Two days after leaving the Arikara villages, the trappers found themselves in the heart of the buffalo country, and Jedediah first glimpsed a truly enormous herd. "It seemed to my unaccustomed eyes," he wrote, "that all the buffalo in the world were running in those plains.... [T]hey moved in deep dense and dark bodies resembling the idea I have formed of the heavy columns of a great army."

Ashley's keelboat soon arrived at the fort, where crewmen offloaded trade goods and stowed the past year's peltry harvest aboard the vessel. A few days later Ashley set out from Henry's Fort for Saint Louis. His mounted trappers made ready to winter closer to the mountains, so as to steal a march on their Missouri Fur Company rivals when the spring thaw came and beaver fur was in prime condition. Jedediah Smith and several other men traveled up the Yellowstone to trap, hunt, and collect skins to use during the coming winter.

In early November, Smith and the wintering party left Henry's Fort and rode up the Missouri to the mouth of the Musselshell River, where they constructed several rude huts. Finding no bison about, Smith and other hunters killed many antelope and deer and dried the meat. Neither Smith nor many of his companions knew that bison generally left the open plains to winter more comfortably among the cottonwood groves in the Missouri River bottoms. After the river froze hard, the trappers were "astonished to see the buffalo come pouring from all sides into the valley," and for the rest of the winter they had only to "select and kill the best for our use whenever we might choose." Rich, lean bison meat made first-rate fare for mountain men, who daily consumed several pounds of "hump ribs" and other choice cuts.

Livestock also needed survival insurance against the bitter cold that fast approached. A good camp required three things: fuel wood, water, and grass. The hunters' location offered plenty of firewood and drinking water, but what about grass, or its equivalent, for their horses and mules? From the more experienced trappers Jedediah learned that cottonwood was "an article indispensably necessary in wintering horses." Mules and horses alike thrived on the inner bark of cottonwood trees. Sometimes the trappers stripped large limbs of their outer bark to expose the nutritious inner bark, but horses and mules themselves eagerly pulled the bark from smaller branches to get at the inner bark, of which they "became verry fond." In his journal Smith wrote, "strange as it may appear to those unacquainted with such things, [livestock] become fat and will keep so during the winter if not used," though the weight gain would be "worn off in a few days of hard riding."

Jedediah Smith's first winter in the Far West passed pleasantly indeed. "In our little encampment," he wrote, "shut out from those enjoyments most valued by the world, we were as happy as we could be made by leisure and opportunity for unlimited gratification of the indulgence in the pleasure of the Buffalo hunt and the several kinds of sport which the severity of the winter could not debar us from." Life for the mountain men did not get much better than this.

While Smith and his companions prepared to winter near the Musselshell, Ashley hastened to reach Saint Louis before the river froze. Upon arriving in mid-November, he delivered his packs of fur to the firm of Tracy & Wahrendorff, agents for his Boston creditors, Stone & Bostwick. Proceeds from the fur sale were insufficient to balance his account, but if things went well the next year, he stood a good chance of retiring his debt and realizing a profit. If things did not go well, his reputation would be ruined and his future in Saint Louis doubtful at best. Staking everything on the bet that he would come out ahead, Ashley assembled another outfit. In a striking display of his talents for deal-making and jawboning, Ashley almost single-handedly drained local suppliers' warehouses of goods, outmaneuvering and irritating his Saint Louis competitors in the process. In the following weeks he procured a new trade license from William Clark, ran new advertisements for hired men, and purchased more keelboats for another foray up the Missouri.

Ashley let it be known that he would engage trappers at a fixed rate of two hundred dollars per year, payable in advance, rather than on the commission basis he introduced in 1822. By 1823, thanks in part to Ashley's own success, large cash advances had become necessary as half a dozen Saint Louis outfits competed for the labor of a limited number of men. Good hunters, trappers, and boatmen were hard to find in the spring of 1823, and Ashley's second recruitment campaign produced a curious mixture of men. Several of the new hands would enter the pantheon of renowned American explorers and frontiersmen, but most remained anonymous drudges plucked from the Saint Louis riverfront.

For his recruiting officer, Ashley hired a Virginian named James Clyman, who recorded his adventures in colorful backwoods prose. Seven years older than Jedediah Smith and cut from rather rougher cloth, Clyman became a close friend and brother in arms to Smith. Clyman had served as a militiaman during the War of 1812, then drifted around Indiana and Ohio for a few years doing odd jobs: farming, working in a salt factory, and chopping wood. In the summer of 1822 he spent a few months surveying public land in Illinois, and in early February 1823 he showed up at Saint Louis to be paid. A few days later Clyman heard that Ashley was "engageing men for a Trip to the mouth of the Yellow Stone river." Seeking more definite information, Clyman presented himself to the "General," who offered a glowing account of the abundant deer, elk, bison, and other game to be found in the pays d'en haut. The Virginian grew more acutely interested when Ashley regaled him with tales about the "immence Quantities of Beaver whose skins ware verry valuable selling from $5 to $8 per pound at the time in St. Louis."

James Clyman liked Ashley's sales pitch, but he was not quite ready to sign up. Saint Louis was "a fine place for Spending money," so Clyman "loitered about" and enjoyed himself. A few days later, he bumped into Ashley on the street. Ashley said he wanted to hire Clyman to assemble a crew for the mountain expedition. Still jobless and perhaps running low on cash, Clyman accepted the offer. Advising Clyman that he would likely find the right sort of men "in grog Shops and other sinks of degradation," Ashley sent him out to scour the waterfront district. Any man signed up was to be sequestered until the day of departure in a rented house that was well supplied with bread and pork, the better to keep them from running off with their cash advances. Clyman soon collected a suitable crowd of rowdies. As he put it in the reliable narrative he penned almost fifty years later, "[a] description of our crew I cannt give but Falstafs Battallion was genteel in comparison." Probably the new men differed little from the crew collected the year before, when Jedediah Smith signed on with Ashley.

On March 10 two new keelboats, the *Rocky Mountains* and the *Yellow Stone Packet*, pulled away from Saint Louis loaded with men and trade goods. Aboard were Clyman's seventy recruits, a mixed gang of raw greenhorns and veteran mountain men. Keelboat men formed a separate class of laborers, and Ashley had recruited most of them from among the local French populace, the "St. Louis gumboes," according to Clyman.

To make certain that local citizens remembered him come election time, "General Ashley" decided to embark his keelboats at sunset with sails unfurled and flags waving. In a gaudy flourish, Ashley hired some musicians—perhaps a string band or a small brass band—to accompany the keelboats a few miles up the Mississippi while performing a farewell serenade for the benefit of his crew and any spectators who happened to witness the launch of his daring venture.

Whatever excitement the musicians generated soon dissipated, for a series of problems bedeviled Ashley. One keelboat crashed into an obstruction and sprang a bad leak before it even got out of sight of the Saint Louis riverfront. The steersmen managed to beach it and crewmen quickly set about repairing it. A few days later one trapper somehow fell overboard and drowned in the Missouri.

In the meantime, Ashley rode overland sixteen miles to Saint Charles to settle some last-minute matters before joining his boats. He had initially planned to get his expedition under way by mid-February, but delays had prevented the arrival of Stone & Bostwick's shipment of trade goods at Saint Louis until early March. About a week later a delivery wagon loaded with rifles, pistols, and three hundred pounds of gunpowder left Saint Louis to meet Ashley's keelboats at Saint Charles. Due to some mishap the wagon blew up, killing three unfortunate men. Though shocked by news of the wagoneers' deaths, Ashley could spare no time for hand-wringing. After seeing his keelboats off, he quickly found another wagon, purchased new weapons and gunpowder on credit from the famed Saint Louis gunsmiths, Jacob and Samuel Hawken, and headed again for Saint Charles. When his boats arrived, Ashley clambered aboard, had his gear stowed, and hoped that things would at last go according to plan.

During the first weeks of ascending the river, several malingerers deserted and were replaced, wrote Clyman, by "new men of a much better appearance than those we lost." Perhaps so, but a few days later, Ashley's hungry men went out hunting and decided instead to steal some "Eggs Fowls Turkeys and what not" from nearby farms on the outskirts of civilization. After devouring some of their ill-gotten provender, they burned the incriminating remnants. The next morning a number of irate farmers barged into Ashley's camp to demand the return of their poultry, but they discovered no evidence of the theft. Later that day, a fair wind began to blow and the delighted engagés put away the cordelle. No sooner was the sail unfurled, wrote Clyman, than "out drop[p]ed pigs and poultry in abundance."

(Perhaps the animals had been butchered and temporarily stored in the folded sail.) The bourgeois ordered a crewman into a skiff to rescue the stolen animals from the Missouri and the men prepared another feast.

When the keelboats paused briefly at the Council Bluffs, officers from nearby Fort Atkinson presented Ashley's men with some fresh garden vegetables, the last they would see for a long time. Having decided that river life was not for them, about ten more recruits took a final opportunity to quit Ashley's employ, placing themselves beyond his reach by immediately enlisting in the U.S. Army. Ashley in turn hired a handful of recently mustered-out soldiers. Leaving Fort Atkinson and its comforts behind, the expedition that would determine Ashley's future ascended the Missouri and entered the Indian Country, bound for the Arikara villages.

The next month defied Ashley and Henry's fond expectations, sorely tested their mettle, and nearly dashed their hopes altogether. They would suffer calamitous losses in goods, equipment, and men that shoved their enterprise to the verge of ruin. It would be a year of almost unbelievable challenges for Jedediah Smith, too. Nothing he had ever experienced could have prepared him for the trouble that lay ahead.

Ashley and Henry's greatest problem would flow from events with which they had no connection. In 1822 several competing companies built trading posts in the Upper Missouri region. The Missouri Fur Company erected a small fort on an island in the Missouri near the mouth of White River. Fort Recovery, also called Cedar Fort, lay about two hundred miles downstream from the Arikara villages. In the winter of 1822–23 a skirmish took place between the Arikaras and some Missouri Fur Company men. Then, just two months before Ashley's keelboats reached the Arikara villages, Missouri Fur Company men again clashed with the "Rees". A Sioux woman captive escaped and sought refuge at Fort Recovery, closely pursued by Arikara warriors. The Missouri Fur Company men opened the gates to rescue the desperate woman, and in the ensuing scuffle they killed two warriors. Consequently, the Arikaras declared war on the

Missouri Fur Company, essentially making any white men legitimate targets for retributive raids.

Meanwhile, sometime in early May, Andrew Henry dispatched Jedediah Smith from Henry's Fort on an urgent errand. Smith was to descend the Missouri, intercept Ashley's keelboats, and deliver Henry's request for Ashley to purchase another fifty horses for his trappers. Encountering Ashley a few miles below the Arikara towns, Smith explained Henry's state of affairs. On May 30 the keelboats anchored offshore from the Arikara towns and Ashley prepared to trade for horses, as he had the previous year. The villages occupied a commanding position above the Missouri on the left bank of a narrow horseshoe bend. A single navigable channel flowed beneath the villages and a half-mile long sand bar jutted out from the opposite riverbank, leaving vessels no alternative but to pass right under the watchful eyes of the Arikaras.

Eager to purchase horses for a second overland trip from the Missouri to the Yellowstone, Ashley and his men recklessly put themselves at grave risk. Ashley knew of the previous winter's skirmish and was even informed that the Arikaras "considered war was fully declared between them and the whites," but he evidently believed he could convince them that he was not to blame for the incident. As it turned out, he could not have been more mistaken.

When the keelboats dropped anchor before the lower village, Ashley's men immediately noticed numerous Arikara women hurriedly filling water containers at the river's edge and carrying them into the village. Freshly constructed palisades and a breastwork on the sand bar likewise excited the trappers' suspicions, but Ashley's need to acquire horses overcame his misgivings.

Keeping his vessels safely moored in midriver, Ashley and two men landed a skiff on the beach by the village. Meeting with two chiefs, The Little Soldier and Grey Eyes, Ashley presented some gifts and negotiated terms for buying horses. Grey Eyes informed Ashley that one of his own sons had died in the skirmish with the Missouri Fur Company men, and that his people were much aggrieved at the white men. Speaking through an experienced mulatto interpreter named Edward Rose, Ashley attempted to ease the tension. He assured the chiefs that he had nothing to do with the previous clash, and the Arikaras agreed to sell him horses.

Though he remained somewhat apprehensive of trouble, Ashley spent two days trading goods, almost exclusively gunpowder and lead, for about two hundred buffalo robes and nineteen horses. As dawn broke on June 1, a fierce wind began to blow. By evening it had increased in fury to a perfect gale, making a departure impossible. Forewarned by The Little Soldier that an attack might well come that night, Ashley planned to keep a strict lookout and make a speedy getaway early the next morning. But the situation had already spun out of his control.

In the wee hours of June 2 a few of Ashley's men foolishly accompanied Edward Rose into the Arikara village, most likely to exchange some "foofarow" (trade goods) with Arikara women for sexual favors. About an hour later three warriors stealthily boarded Ashley's keelboat, apparently intending to murder him. Awakened by their movements, he leveled a pistol at them and they beat a hasty retreat. A few moments later guards spotted numerous armed warriors taking up positions outside the village. Sometime around 3:30 A.M. Rose dashed into camp, shouting that the Arikaras had murdered Aaron Stephens, a discharged soldier that Ashley had picked up at Fort Atkinson. Rose warned Ashley that the Arikaras would "in all probability . . . attack the boats in a few minutes."

When the fight began, about forty of Ashley's men lay encamped on a sandy beach where the horse-trading had taken place. Jedediah Smith had been placed in command of the dangerously exposed shore party and their livestock. At sunrise the wind died, and instantly a massive fusillade of musket fire erupted from the direction of the palisaded village about one hundred yards off. Simultaneously, strategically placed Arikara archers launched flights of arrows into Smith's encampment. Within a few minutes, most of the horses and several men on the beach were dead or severely wounded. James Clyman tersely recalled the chaotic scene: "[W]e had little else to do than to Stand on a bear sand barr and be shot at, at long range."

The killing range of the smoothbore flintlock trade guns favored by Indians was roughly eighty yards, but the Arikaras' gun positions overlooking the bar enabled them to unleash a hail of lead on the shore party. Moreover, some warriors doubtless crept close to the sandbar to shoot at exposed trappers. Ashley later admitted that the Arikara marksmen managed their "London Fusils" with "as much experience as any man I ever saw handle arms." White participants later calculated that the Arikaras possessed between five hundred and eight hundred flintlock guns. Perhaps they exaggerated, but Arikara guns were numerous enough to kill one of every six among Ashley's men.

In the midst of the commotion Jedediah Smith displayed stalwart and cool-headed leadership. Sorely beset but loathe to flee, Smith and the others hunkered down behind dead and dying horses and stubbornly returned fire, with but little effect. Dense smoke and whistling musket balls made it nearly impossible for the trappers to take aim at their concealed antagonists. From hiding places among the dead livestock, some trappers beseeched the keelboats to approach and render them assistance, but Ashley's crewmen were almost paralyzed by fear. Instead of aiding the beleaguered shore party, they milled about in confusion. After Ashley started bellowing orders, a skiff manned by a daring few rowed close enough to shore to evacuate some wounded men and anyone else able to clamber aboard.

Many bullets slapped into the dead horses and more men dropped around Smith on the sand bar. Some wounded men desperately lurched into the river, only to vanish beneath the muddy current. The air grew heavy with howls of dying men and beasts. Ashley again ordered his keelboat men to make landings with two skiffs—and some did—but with "the shot coming thicker and faster," one crew weighed anchor and someone severed the other keelboat's cable with an axe. Both vessels began drifting gawkily down the Missouri.

While Ashley gaped impotently, his shore party doggedly continued to load and fire, but their situation was obviously hopeless. A week later he noted that his boatmen were so "panic struck, that they would not expose themselves in the least," while the shore fighters bravely stood their ground. This emanated, Ashley thought, "from a predetermination on their part not to give way to the Indians as long as it was possible to do otherwise, [and] the most of them refused to make use of that opportunity of embarking." Jedediah Smith was among the most stalwart fighters, and he emerged without a scratch.

A dozen men were dead or mortally wounded by the time the keelboats' skiffs landed to extract survivors. After evacuating some men from the sandbar, the boatmen somehow lost control of one of the skiffs; perhaps they cowered in fear, or perhaps too many were wounded. Amid dying men and shrieking musket balls, James Clyman dashed into the Missouri and secured the skiff before it drifted beyond reach. He nearly drowned before he could shuck his rifle, belted pistols, shooting bag, and leather coat and start swimming toward the boat. A fellow Virginian named George Gibson was mortally shot through the bowels while he pulled Clyman aboard.

Clyman rowed the skiff to the opposite bank and leaped ashore, knowing that he had to outrun several Arikara warriors whom he saw crossing the river. At length he left his pursuers a good quarter mile behind him and stopped to catch his breath. He "made them a low bow with both my hand[s] and thanked God for my present Safety and diliveranc[e]." A lucky survivor named Jack Larisson showed up at Ashley's camp two days after the fight, "naked as when he was born and the skin peeling off of him from the effects of the sun." Shot through both thighs by a single Arikara ball, Larisson had lain in agony between two dead horses "untill the boats left." Knowing he was a dead man if he remained on the bar, Larisson pulled off his clothes and leaped into the Missouri with several warriors in hot pursuit, but he made good his escape.

The harrowing firefight probably consumed no more than a half hour and ended with the last survivors of the shore party scrambling aboard a skiff and Ashley's entire party in disorderly retreat down the Missouri. Fourteen men had been killed outright or were mortally wounded, and another dozen were less seriously injured. All nineteen of the dearly purchased horses lay dead. Especially galling to the trappers was the horrid certainty that the victorious Arikaras would scalp and mutilate the comrades they left dead on the beach. Indeed, they already knew that Aaron Stephens' eyes had been gouged out and his decapitated body was horribly mangled. The "Ree fight," one of the bloodiest in the Rocky Mountain fur trade era, had a distinctly sobering affect on Ashley's greenhorn "Mountain Boys." Before that deadly encounter, many had fancied themselves genuine "ringtailed roarers" in the best frontier tradition. Clyman wryly recalled, "few men had Stronger Ideas of their bravery and disregard of fear than I had but standing on a bear and open sand barr to be shot at from bihind a picketed Indian village was more than I had contracted for and some what cooled my courage."

After drifting twenty-five miles downstream, Ashley halted the keelboats and assessed his dismal state of affairs. Several men he had intended to send to Henry were dead, and so were all the horses. His French crewmen stood on the threshold of mutiny. Bristling, he exhorted them to make another attempt to run the Arikara gantlet, but few stepped forward. The despondent crew appeared ready to quit altogether and leave Ashley in the lurch. Sure enough, a number of men did soon desert.

Admitting the impossibility of advance upriver, Ashley decided to dispatch two expressmen with an urgent plea for Henry to rush reinforcements from the Yellowstone post. For this weighty responsibility he selected Jedediah Smith and an experienced French Canadian. Before the two men set out, however, Jedediah conducted a brief funeral service for a dead comrade named John S. Gardner. A trapper named Hugh Glass penned an obituary letter to Gardner's parents, noting that "Mr. Smith a young man of our company made a powerful pray[e]r wh[ich] moved us all greatly." Glass's brief comment is the only recorded evidence that Smith ever delivered a public, ceremonial expression of faith.

Ashley's keelboats retreated about one hundred miles below the Arikara villages to the mouth of the Cheyenne River, where he halted to await further developments. Within a month Smith and the anonymous Canadian reached Henry's Fort and then returned to Ashley's camp, likely in some form of watercraft, with reinforcements and the past winter's collection of furs. They had managed to slip unmolested past the Arikara villages. Ashley's crewmen transferred some cargo from the undermanned keelboat *Yellow Stone Packet* to the smaller *Rocky Mountains* and loaded his peltry onto the *Yellow Stone Packet*.

Ashley called upon a man named Samuel M. Smith to convey the peltry to Saint Louis. This was a weighty responsibility indeed. Ashley and Henry's success depended utterly on the men entrusted to undertake this final, critical leg of the journey. It may have been Samuel Smith who informed military authorities at Fort Atkinson of the Arikara attack and secured their assistance. On June 18, after an uneventful ten-day voyage, the *Yellow Stone Packet* docked at Fort Atkinson. In command was Col. Henry Leavenworth, a career soldier with a distinguished War of 1812 record. Leavenworth would prove incapable of resolving Ashley's conflict with the Arikaras. His name would forever be wedded to the humiliating Arikara Campaign, a pointed demonstration that the U.S. Army's systems of command, supply, and tactics needed to change if soldiers were to fight and win battles against Plains Indians.

After Smith briefed Leavenworth, the colonel put together a plan to punish the Arikaras. Mustering about 250 soldiers comprising six Sixth Infantry companies and a few artillery men, Leavenworth left Fort Atkinson on June 22. Bolstering his force were Joshua Pilcher, the Missouri Fur Company's leading partner, and sixty Missouri Fur Company men, along with a mixed band of Teton Sioux warriors, pleased to have white men help them rub out their enemies. In late July Leavenworth found Ashley's party encamped near the Teton River, also known as the Little Missouri. About eighty Ashley-Henry men joined the march, all of them eager to spill rivers of Arikara blood to avenge lost comrades and soothe injured pride. Jedediah Smith and Hiram Scott each commanded a forty-man squad of Ashley-Henry trappers. Unfortunately, Smith wrote nothing about his role in subsequent events, though a few other participants left summaries of what followed.

Leavenworth's colorful corps, which Pilcher dubbed the "Missouri Legion," halted just below the Arikara villages on August 9, two months after the bloody affray. Pilcher had urged Leavenworth in the strongest terms to "strike a decisive blow … for the safety of every white man on the river above the Council Bluffs." Soon after the soldiers arrived, the fearful Arikaras began shooting at them from their palisades, and Leavenworth's little army returned a desultory fire. Clyman described a hellish scene of "pandemonium": the "wa[il]ing of squaws and children the Screams and yelling of men the fireing of guns the awful howling of dogs the neighing and braying of hosses and mules … all intermingled with the stench of dead men and horses made the place the most disagreeable that immagination could fix Short of the bottomless pit." The trappers passed the night in anxious anticipation of the bigger battle to come—and the chance to even the score with the Arikaras—but they would soon taste bitter disappointment.

Ignoring Pilcher's advice, on August 10 Leavenworth launched a poorly coordinated, half-hearted infantry assault on the fortified village. Sporadic artillery fire killed the Arikara leader Grey Eyes and several men and women but did little other damage. The Teton Sioux quickly lost interest in the battle, contenting themselves with raiding Arikara cornfields and killing a few stragglers they caught outside the village. With Leavenworth's supplies dwindling and the Sioux no longer willing to fight, indecision in the absence of orders from a superior officer got the better of the colonel, and he abruptly terminated the assault. The Arikaras immediately called for peace talks. Advised by some of the fur traders, Leavenworth parleyed with The Little Soldier and other leaders and concluded a peace treaty on August 11.

Joshua Pilcher indignantly refused any part in the treaty negotiations and waxed apoplectic over Leavenworth's feeble efforts. In his opinion the campaign's sole outcome was to convince the powerful Sioux that the Americans were stupid weaklings. The miscreant Arikaras, meanwhile, got off with virtually no punishment for wholesale murder and theft. Pilcher later aired his views in an angry letter to Leavenworth that the *St. Louis Enquirer* published. Denouncing Leavenworth's "shameful conduct before the [Arikara] villages," Pilcher claimed that the colonel had only made the situation "ten times worse." "The imbecility of your conduct," he fumed, had done nothing but "impress the different Indian tribes with the greatest possible contempt for the American character."

True, Leavenworth's campaign resulted only in a temporary closure of the Upper Missouri to fur traders and did nothing to advance U.S. Indian policy. Ashley received, so far as is known, not one cent of indemnification for lost goods, horses, or men. On the other hand, partial responsibility for the disaster must be chalked up to Ashley's trappers. They helped precipitate the bloody affray by prowling through Indian Country and hunting game in blatant violation of common sense as well as federal Indian trade and intercourse laws. Their mere presence threatened the Arikaras' delicate position in Upper Missouri politics and commerce, and if the trappers were ignorant of this fact, the Arikaras were not. As well, their midnight dalliance with Arikara women was—to say the least—ill advised.

The federal government also bore some responsibility for Leavenworth's inconclusive campaign. With no effective Indian-fighting frontier army at its disposal, the trade and intercourse laws became unenforceable dead letters, and Indian policy drifted impotently. Not only were fur traders virtually free to do as they pleased, so were the western Indians, practically none of whom saw any reason to respect federal authority.

No doubt infuriated by Leavenworth's inconclusive bungling, Ashley and his men could do nothing but continue up the Missouri. The Arikara fights resulted in grave setbacks for Ashley and Henry, but they marked a turning point in Jedediah Smith's career. He had emerged from the rank and file of trappers as an unusually trustworthy, resourceful, and clear-headed man, respected for his leadership abilities. Clyman singled out Smith as one of the "honorable exceptions to the character of the men engaged at St. Louis" and joined his fellow trappers in dubbing Jedediah "our Captain." Just a few weeks later, though, while

Smith led a trapping party northwest along the White River, the young partisan's resourcefulness would again be tested. Persuaded that he would save time by taking a shortcut across a deep meander in the river, Smith set off overland. Under a blazing sun he led his men through a treeless desert strewn with prickly pear cactus. A water hole they located was empty, and his party found themselves facing heat prostration and dehydration. The line of march stretched ragged and thin, each man making his way as best he could. When two exhausted trappers dropped beside the trail, Smith halted to bury them in damp sand up to their necks, preserving their lives for a few more hours in case someone found water. Fortunately James Clyman happened upon a spring. Firing his gun to alert his parched companions, he plunged headlong into the life-giving water. By nightfall all but the two buried men had stumbled into camp. "Capt Smith Being the last who was able to walk," wrote Clyman, "he took Some water and rode about 2 miles back bringing up the exhausted men which he had buried in the sand." Smith's remarkable capacity to endure heat and thirst and his willingness to carry water to foundering comrades would save men's lives on several more occasions.

After resting for a few days, Smith and his men crossed the White River and continued northwest, headed for the South Fork of the Cheyenne, an affluent of the Missouri. Encountering some Oglala Sioux, they paused briefly to trade for horses and then moved on. At length Smith's brigade crested a ridge of what they called the Black Hills and began a descent westward toward the Powder River. By late September, Smith had dispatched his guide, Edward Rose, to discover the whereabouts of the Crow nation, with whom the Americans intended to trade. The stage was set for another famous mishap involving young Jedediah Smith.

One afternoon, while Rose was off searching for the Crows, Jedediah led his mounted trappers in a single file through a narrow, brush-choked river bottom. Suddenly they heard a heavy thrashing in the underbrush next to the trail. A split second later, a large sow grizzly bear burst from the thicket and crashed into the center of the slow-moving line of men and horses. As trappers and livestock leaped to safety, the bear quickly turned and began running parallel to the line. Clyman, the only eyewitness to record what happened next, wrote that "Capt Smith being in the advanc[e] he ran to the open ground and as he emerged from the thicket he and the bear met face to face[.] Grissly did not hesitate a moment but sprung on the capt[ain] taking him by the head first."

The enraged bear hurled Smith to the ground, seizing his upper body in a deadly hug while its fearsome jaws again enveloped Jedediah's head. The savage embrace alone could have been fatal, but the bear's killing power was blunted when its five-inch claws raked across Smith's hunting pouch and sheathed butcher knife. Still, the grizzly snapped several of Jedediah's ribs. Far worse, the grizzly's teeth transformed Smith's head into a gruesome tangle of lacerations, dangling flesh, and flowing blood. But Jedediah was still conscious. One of the trappers killed the bear when it momentarily turned away from Smith, but as Clyman wrote, the rest of the men milled about distractedly, "none of us having any su[r]gical Knowledge."

No one had the least notion of how to proceed, and not one man had nerve enough to lay his hands on Smith's mangled face. Clyman lamely "asked the Capt what was best." Somehow, Smith regained his composure and began to issue instructions. After sending a couple of men to fetch some water, he told Clyman, "[I]f you have a needle and thread git it out and sew up my wounds around my head." Clyman rummaged through the packs of goods, pulled out a pair of shears, and began snipping away hair from Smith's scalp, which hung in tatters beside his face. With only a sewing kit, no medicines, and nothing whatsoever to dull Smith's pain, Clyman performed his first—and last—surgical operation. Dutifully threading his needle, Clyman sewed up Jedediah's wounds in the "best way I was capabl[e] and according to the captains directions."

As Clyman struggled to gauge the extent of Jedediah's facial injuries, he realized that the grizzly had "taken nearly all of his head in his captious [capacious] mouth close to his left eye on one side and clos[e] to his right ear on the other and laid the skull bare to near the crown of his head leaving a white streak whare his teeth passed[.] [O]ne of his ears was torn from his head out to the outer rim." The bear had very nearly removed Smith's scalp. Marshalling every bit of his prodigious instinctual self-mastery, Jedediah suppressed his shock and pain, knowing that he must remain conscious in order to survive.

Jedediah's nearly severed ear proved more than a match for Clyman's limited suturing skills. After a few moments' contemplation, he told Smith he "could do nothing for his Eare." This Jedediah refused to accept, and he pathetically insisted, "O you must try to stitch up some way or other." Steadying his nerves, Clyman got back to work and finished the job of reassembling Smith's face: "I put in my needle[,] stitching it through and through and over and over[,] laying the lacerated parts togather as nice as I could with my hands."

A few minutes after Clyman completed the operation, Jedediah Smith forced himself to mount his horse and ride a mile to water and camp. There he was lodged in the party's only tent while his comrades made him "as comfortable as circumstances would admit." Clyman concluded his brief recital with a fine bit of gallows humor: "This gave us a lisson [*sic*] on the char[a]cter of the grissly Baare which we did not forget." Within two weeks of the attack Smith was well on his way to recovery, though whatever boyish good looks he possessed had vanished. For the rest of his life he wore his hair long on the right side to camouflage his disfigured ear and the ragged scars on his face.

It so happened that the "grissly" taught the trappers two lessons that September. Hugh Glass was the second Ashley man to fall victim to a grizzly in the fall of 1823, and his story became even better known than Smith's encounter. "Old Glass," as his fellow trappers called him, was wandering ahead of his party on a tributary of the Missouri, headed for the Yellowstone. This was routine behavior for Glass, a tough, solitary man who hated to take orders. Fed up with Glass's customary insubordination, one trapper complained to a companion, "I wish some Grizzly Bear would pounce upon him & teach him a lesson of obedience to orders, & to keep in his place." A few days later, when Glass was "dodging along in the forest alone," he startled a female "white bear" with two cubs. She instantly attacked Glass and "tor[e] the flesh from the lower part of the body, & from the lower limbs— He also had his neck shockingly torn … an aperture appeared to have been made into the windpipe, & his breath to exude at the side of his neck."

A few trappers ran up and killed all three bears, then hastily prepared a litter for Glass and carried him into camp. His wounds were so severe that everyone assumed he would be dead within hours, or at most a day or two. Fearful of being exposed to Indian attacks and duty-bound to continue their march, the trappers could not afford a prolonged deathwatch for the injured man. After a harangue from the bourgeois and an offer of a hefty cash bonus, two men volunteered to watch over Glass until he died. But the spark of life lingered, and despite his awful wounds "Old Glass" stubbornly refused to die. Unmanned by fear of hostile Indians the blackguards who were paid to bury Glass lost their nerve and abandoned him after just three days. When they slinked away they even took his gun and gear.

Several excruciating weeks passed as Glass recovered his strength. Subsisting on rotting carcasses, berries, rattlesnakes, and whatever else he found, Hugh Glass started crawling toward Fort Kiowa, two hundred miles away. Weeks later he showed up at the post looking like a walking skeleton, unrecognized by men who knew him. Glass's subsequent confrontation with the cowards who left him to die—one of whom reportedly was the youthful James Bridger—became a cautionary tale repeated beside many a Rocky Mountain campfire.

The chilly days of autumn found Smith and a dozen men moving westward in the high country. Still partially incapacitated, Jedediah sent Clyman ahead to reconnoiter the southern Black Hills and the Cheyenne River. Smith's party proceeded to the Powder River and camped with a band of Crow Indians, from whom they traded some horses. After crossing the Big Horn Mountains, Smith and his men turned south toward the Wind River in central Wyoming. There they encountered some of Ashley and Henry's trappers led by a Danish former sea captain named John H. Weber. He had accompanied Andrew Henry to the Yellowstone fort in 1822, and then led a brigade across the Continental Divide to begin a two-year trapping expedition. During that time he discovered Weber Canyon and the Weber River in Utah.

Smith and Weber and their men wintered among the Crows. The Absarokas, as they called themselves, were generally friendly hosts to white men. The Crows produced superior bison robes and their land was famed for its fine beaver fur. Mountain men kept a close watch on Crow warriors, however, for they were consummate horse-thieves. To the Absarokas' way of thinking, horse thievery was a fine and noble art. As some Crow warriors put it to a mountain man named William Gordon, who recounted the story to a congressional committee in 1831, "if they killed [us], we would not come back & they would lose the chance of stealing from us.... They ... talk over their past thefts ... with all possible frankness and indifference." Despite occasional friction, and rare violence, over differing views on what constituted stealing, the Crow nation remained at peace with American trappers and never made war on the U.S. Army.

Winter passed in relative comfort, and when signs of spring appeared in February 1824, Jedediah had fully recovered. It was time once again to find good beaver-hunting territory while the fur remained in its winter prime. He led his men toward Union Pass at the northern side of the Wind River Mountains, but a heavy snowpack blocked his way and forced a retreat. A second attempt in February likewise failed, but then helpful Indians offered the mountain men a much-needed geography lesson. Consultation with the knowledgeable Crows initially presented difficulties since no one in Smith and Weber's party spoke their language. But James Clyman "spread out a buffalo robe and covered it with sand, and made it in heaps to represent the different mountains ... and from our sand map with the help of the Crows, finally got the idea that we could go to Wind River, called by them Seeds-ka-day." In fact, *Seeds-kee-dee-Agie*, meaning "Prairie Hen River," was a Shoshone name for the Green

River. Even so, from his Indian informants Jedediah learned that following the Popo Agie River (the south fork of the Wind River) would take him to a pass that led to the southeastern margins of the Wind River Range.

In mid-March he sallied forth again, this time crossing the Wind River Range along a divide between the Popo Agie and the Sweetwater River in what is today Fremont County, Wyoming. The pass lay between the Sweetwater, which flows east to join with the North Platte, and the Big Sandy River, which flows southward into the Seeds-kee-dee, or Upper Green River. So it was that in March 1824 Smith and his men became the "effective discoverers" of the South Pass, a twenty-mile-wide swath of unimpressive highland dividing the waters that flowed from the Rockies toward the Pacific and Atlantic oceans.

They named it South Pass to distinguish it from the inhospitable "Northern Pass" over which Lewis and Clark struggled in 1805, a punishing trek from Lolo Pass to Lemhi Pass on what is now the Montana-Idaho border. South Pass is no dramatic passage through steep mountain ranges, but it was a discovery of major significance because it provided an easy traverse of the Continental Divide. Connecting the Platte River valley to the Sweetwater River, the pass formed the crucial link that later enabled thousands of ox- and horse-drawn wagons to cross the continent. Jedediah Smith and other fur traders would use what they called the "Platte River Road" to haul goods and furs across the plains for the next fifteen years. After 1840 the extended road divided at Fort Laramie and stretched all the way to the Pacific coast, gaining fame as the Oregon-California Trail. More than a quarter-million emigrants followed the trail across South Pass into the Far West until 1869, when the transcontinental railroad rendered it obsolete.

Jedediah Smith and his trappers were not the first white men known to cross South Pass. In 1812 Robert Stuart had led the "Returning Astorians" through South Pass on their way back to Saint Louis. Some of Andrew Henry's Missouri Fur Company trappers in 1811 and some HBC men in the early 1820s may likewise have used South Pass. More than his predecessors and contemporaries, however, Smith quickly grasped the pass's probable future import.

Smith's men suffered severely on their trek and were likely in no condition to celebrate their discovery of a new pass. Some men had gone without food for several days while trudging through a frozen landscape, where howling winds made it impossible even to light a fire, much less keep one burning. Relief came when James Clyman and another member of the party, William Sublette, killed a buffalo. Slicing hunks of raw flesh from the steaming carcass and wolfing them down as only starving men can do, the trappers hid under blankets and buffalo robes and waited for the bitterly cold and stormy weather to change.

After the blizzards abated, Smith and his men worked their way down to the Big Sandy River and moved on to the Green River, an American name that reflects a Spanish precursor, the Rio Verde. The Green offered excellent prospects for beaver trapping, so the hunters divided into two groups to maximize the spring fur harvest. Smith led six trappers, and another trapper, Thomas Fitzpatrick, led three others, among whom was the chronicler James Clyman. Smith's men made their way downstream to Black's Fork of the Green, while Fitzpatrick's trappers worked upriver. Fitzpatrick lost all his horses to a party of Snake (Shoshone) raiders but recovered most of them after threatening to kill the horse thieves when their trails again crossed. The event was commemorated in the naming of Horse Creek. From the Green, Fitzpatrick headed for the Sweetwater River, where he was to rendezvous with Smith's outfit.

Arriving at the Sweetwater in advance of Smith's party, Fitzpatrick opened a cache of goods, buried a few months earlier, to air out and repack the gunpowder supply. Jedediah and his trappers soon rode into camp bearing many furs. The two leaders decided that Fitzpatrick and two men named Stone and Branch would convey the packs of beaver skins down the Sweetwater to the Platte and then down the Missouri to Saint Louis. Fitzpatrick was to deliver Smith's information on South Pass to William Ashley, who would see to it that local newspapers trumpeted the news. Clyman had also been in on the discovery, but

Fitzpatrick had dispatched him on a scouting mission weeks earlier. When he failed to return to camp, his fellows assumed Indians had killed him. Clyman did eventually reach Saint Louis, but Smith would not learn what happened for another year.

Clyman suffered fearfully on his journey, beset by starvation and exposure and in constant danger of being cut off by hostile Indians. Several months of hard traveling brought him staggering into Fort Atkinson on the Missouri. Just ten days after Clyman's arrival, his trail-weary and half-starved cohorts Fitzpatrick, Stone, and Branch showed up from Smith's camp on the Sweetwater. They were, as Clyman put it, "in a more pitiable state if possible than myself."

After recovering somewhat, Fitzpatrick recited a tale of suffering and privation to rival Clyman's. Hoping to save time and effort, he and his men had constructed a "bull-boat" to transport the furs. This Indian-inspired craft featured a frame of bent willow branches lashed together with rawhide and covered with "green" (untanned) bison hides stitched in place, the seams being caulked with a mixture of resin or grease and ashes. (Indian bullboats were small and circular, but the traders built oblong bullboats, large enough to carry a ton or more of freight.) After loading the bull-boat, Fitzpatrick and the others set off down the Sweetwater, perhaps anticipating a pleasant river voyage. Within a short time, however, they nearly came to grief. Drifting into a turbulent rapid at the Devil's Gate, about six miles west of the landmark they called Independence Rock, their clumsy boat capsized, dumping the packs of furs into the stream. They managed to recover most of the furs but realized too late that no bull-boat could navigate the treacherous Sweetwater. Transporting the heavy packs of fur on their backs was impossible, so they cached the furs near the Sweetwater and made their way down the Platte to Fort Atkinson. Upon arriving there, Fitzpatrick penned a letter to William Ashley in which he described the discovery of South Pass. In early September Fitzpatrick arranged to borrow some horses from the fort, and the three men returned to the Sweetwater to raise their cache of furs.

Finding the furs in good condition, Fitzpatrick and his men loaded them on the borrowed horses and returned without incident to Fort Atkinson on October 26, 1824. William Ashley had arrived just a few days earlier. Despite his difficulties, Fitzpatrick's venture along the Platte River, like Jedediah's 1823 cross-country trek, proved that men, goods, and furs might travel overland instead of relying solely on the perilous Missouri River route. These realizations yielded the Platte River Road and soon transformed the American system of supplying and exploiting the Rocky Mountain fur trade.

Based on information that Ashley distributed after receiving Fitzpatrick's description of South Pass, several Missouri newspapers printed windy assertions that a highway across the continent already existed. The *Missouri Advocate and St. Louis Enquirer* in March 1826 boldly proclaimed: "[T]hose great barriers of nature, the Rocky Mountains, have been called up in judgement against the practicality of establishing a communication between this point and the Pacific Ocean. But the Great Author of nature in His wisdom has prepared, and individual enterprize discovered, that 'so broad and easy is the way' that thousands may travel it in safety, without meeting any obstruction deserving the name of a MOUNTAIN." Likewise, the *Missouri Herald and St. Louis Advertiser* in November 1826 enthused that "[t]he whole route lay through a level and open country, better for carriages than any turnpike road in the United States."

So it was that the fur traders—whether they knew it or not—served as advance agents of empire. Their explorations stoked aspirations that eventually found voice in a peculiar American concept of providentially ordained national expansionism. Culminating with the Mexican-American War of 1846–48, American territorial gains came at the expense of Mexicans and Indians. And Jedediah Smith, unlike many beaver trappers, well understood that exploration of the "unclaimed" Indian Country between the Rockies and the Pacific had profound implications for the national destinies of the United States and British Canada.

Smith's primary obligation as William Ashley's employee was to hunt beavers, but he yearned with a lover's passion to "discover" new country. Shortly after seeing Fitzpatrick off in July 1824, he found an opportunity to launch a daring scheme that merged his interest in exploration with his duty to Ashley. Jedediah set out to probe beyond South Pass. Perhaps, even, he could open a way for Ashley and Henry's trappers to the Columbia River and the Oregon Country, where HBC domination of the fur trade seemed unassailable. As it turned out, Smith and the Ashley men would directly challenge Britain's primacy in Oregon.

Few Americans had ever seen the Oregon Country, and to the vast majority it would have seemed a mysterious, half-fabulous place. But even before Lewis and Clark's Corps of Discovery returned in 1806 to tout its riches, some men believed that Oregon offered enormous potential benefits for the future development of the United States. American interest in the region dated from Capt. Robert Gray's voyages to the Pacific Northwest in 1792 and 1793. For the next decade, French, Russian, British, and U.S. vessels regularly plied northwest waters in search of sea otter skins, the most valuable of all furs. The sea otter trade inaugurated commercial relations with Indian nations such as the Chinooks and Clatsops, who traded skins and other products to the newcomers for manufactured goods, liquor, and guns.

Commerce with the sailors also introduced syphilis, smallpox, and other diseases that ravaged Indian populations, and over-hunting of sea otters pushed the animals almost to extinction. By 1824 several hundred commercial ships had visited the Pacific Northwest and the sea otter trade was in decline. Coastal Indians had long been capable traders and sharp bargainers, but interior nations also learned much about the newcomers. By the late 1820s tribal people had become only too familiar with white men and their goods.

Spain, Russia, Great Britain, and the United States all staked sovereign claims to the Pacific Northwest region by the "right of discovery," arrogantly disregarding centuries of Indian occupancy of the land. As of 1824 only Great Britain and the United States remained in contention for the Oregon Country in its entirety. Spain relinquished its Pacific coastal claim above Alta California in the 1819 Transcontinental Treaty (also called the Adams-Onís Treaty), while Russia consented in 1824 to keep its

Russian American Fur Company traders north of 54° 40'. American proponents of sovereignty claimed that possession of Oregon would foster continental nationhood, provide access to the China trade, and erect a bulwark against further British meddling in U.S. affairs. The British thought of Oregon primarily in terms of its economic value in the fur trade and showed almost no interest in colonizing it.

North West Company trading posts began to appear in the Pacific Northwest a few years after Alexander Mackenzie's epic 1793 journey to the ocean. Establishing a half-dozen posts along the upper Columbia River and its tributaries, North West Company traders encountered no serious competition until 1811, when John J. Astor's Pacific Fur Company built Fort Astoria near the mouth of the Columbia.

More than a year after the War of 1812 broke out, some Nor'Westers and a British naval vessel appeared almost simultaneously at Fort Astoria and forced its surrender. Astor's field partners, some of whom were Canadians, sold out to the North West Company at a bargain price in late 1813, dooming his plan to establish a beachhead of American global commerce on the Oregon coast. North West Company traders simply renamed the post Fort George and resumed operations. The 1814 Treaty of Ghent stipulated restoration of Astoria to Astor, but by then his economic interests lay elsewhere and he no longer wanted it. Some Americans continued to call for a U.S. takeover of the Pacific Northwest, but no action took place in the decade before Jedediah Smith and the Ashley men appeared.

After its 1821 merger with the North West Company, the HBC set about tightening John Bull's grip on greater Oregon. Fort Nez Percés, a North West Company post near the confluence of the Snake and Columbia rivers, became the HBC's depot and jumping-off place for the famed Snake Country Expeditions of the 1820s. First set in motion by the Nor'Wester Donald Mackenzie in 1818, the Snake Country brigades gathered respectable fur harvests. Mackenzie's brigades trapped in territory the United States claimed as part of the Louisiana Purchase and in colonial territory feebly held by once-mighty Spain.

Within two years New Spain rebelled, achieving independence in 1821 as the Republic of Mexico, but the infant nation developed no significant presence in the Oregon Country.

Mackenzie's brigades introduced innovations in the far western fur trade that predated by several years Ashley and Henry's adoption of similar practices in the Rocky Mountains. Rather than relying upon Indians to exchange beaver furs for trade goods, Mackenzie's men acquired beaver skins by trapping the animals themselves. Mackenzie's system reduced the necessity to build, stock, and maintain expensive trading posts, and it used horses instead of boats to carry peltry from the field to transshipment depots. Furthermore, even as it maximized trappers' productivity, it also tended to increase their dependence upon the company (and its goods), since they might remain in the field for years at a stretch. Most importantly, Mackenzie's North West Company brigades began returning profits from a region that formerly produced lackluster fur harvests.

The 1821 merger brought a powerful new player to the scene, the cynical and cantankerous HBC governor, Sir George Simpson. The HBC's chief executive in North America, George Simpson was an exceptionally able administrator, brutally frank in his assessments of men and conditions in the company's westernmost fur trade district. Simpson aimed to achieve two major objectives in the Oregon Country: reduce excessive operating expenses and keep American fur hunters like Jedediah Smith out of the Columbia-Snake drainages. Simpson and the HBC leadership believed that if American trappers could be excluded from the Oregon Country and prevented from establishing connections with the many U.S. vessels that visited the region, then not only would fur trade profits fall into British hands, but Great Britain might also secure much of today's Idaho, Washington, and Oregon. Indeed, fur traders and governments often operated in a symbiotic harmony of interests. Fur trade dividends enriched HBC stockholders and simultaneously bolstered British imperial ambitions. In the United States, too, fur trade advocates usually found sympathetic ears in the halls of Congress and even in the White House.

Taking a cue from Donald Mackenzie, Sir George Simpson determined to send strong trapping parties into the Snake Country to eliminate beaver populations and create a "fur desert," thus preventing American competition. Year after year the Snake Country brigades cleaned out streams, sometimes bringing in as many as seven thousand beaver skins in a single season. In the 1820s Alexander Ross and Peter Skene Ogden led the HBC's Snake Country Expeditions. Jedediah Smith would deal with both of them, but it was Ogden, who led brigades from 1825 to 1830, who would became Smith's "opposite number" in the northwestern fur trade.

Mutual distrust and little else defined Jedediah Smith's relationship with Peter Skene Ogden. They shared a passion for geography and exploration, but their personal and economic competitiveness and the fact that they represented contending national interests poisoned their interactions. Smith rarely wore his patriotism on his sleeve, but he certainly understood that American trappers were in a position to strengthen U.S. territorial claims, and he knew that Ogden's company was likewise determined to advance Britain's imperial designs on the West.

Simpson's policy failed to dissuade ambitious Americans from trapping in the Snake Country. Spurred by partisans like Jedediah Smith, Ashley's men soon attempted to dismantle the HBC's façade of regional hegemony. But Jedediah Smith and the Ashley men were not the only Americans who roamed through the British fur traders' interior northwest domain. Others came from as far away as the Mexican territory of New Mexico.

Initially established in 1598 as a Spanish missionary outpost among the Pueblo Indians, by 1700 New Mexico and the other northern frontier provinces served primarily as buffer zones to deter invasion by French, English, and later American interlopers. After several false starts, American trade with Mexico began to flourish in 1821, when Mexico became independent and the Santa Fe Trail opened. Trade with foreigners had long been forbidden under Spain's imperial policy, but the Republic of Mexico almost immediately legalized trade with American *gringos*.

Down the Santa Fe Trail came men eager to sell inexpensive textiles, hardware, and other goods to equally eager New Mexican consumers. Many beaver trappers came too, and they soon set traps along the Colorado, Gila, San Juan, and other rivers. The northern village of Taos, safely distant from the provincial capital at Santa Fe, was the main base of operations for mountain men seeking to dodge inquisitive Mexican authorities, licensing laws, and export duties on furs. Many illegal trapping expeditions departed from Taos in the 1820s and 1830s. A few other small towns also became desirable wintering spots, offering comfortable adobe houses, liaisons with Hispanic women, and plenty of the raw New Mexican corn liquor called *aguadiente*.

From Taos the trappers rode north into the Rocky Mountains and west across the Continental Divide. James Ohio Pattie, Ewing Young, Kit Carson, Old Bill Williams, and Étienne Provost were among the first trappers who wandered from northern Mexico to the Columbia River in quest of prime beaver fur. Some American and Canadian trappers became Mexican citizens and acquired licenses to trap, hunt, or trade. Many, however, did not, and considerable friction marked the complex relationships between mountain men and the Mexicans among whom they dwelled.

In 1824 Jedediah Smith first came into Oregon and Alexander Ross led his last brigade into the Snake Country. Before dispatching Ross's expedition, Simpson had specifically ordered him to avoid "opening a road for the Americans," but that is exactly what happened and it was not entirely Ross's fault. On June 12, while Ross's brigade was trapping the Snake River near today's Blackfoot, Idaho, several of the "Iroquois" in his party departed for a hunt. (Some of these men actually were Iroquois, but the HBC men applied the term as a catchall description for mixed-blood hirelings of various tribal affiliations.)

In the course of their travels, the Iroquois clashed with some Snake raiders, losing most of their gear and horses. Jedediah Smith and his trappers happened to be working nearby, and when he ran into the "pillaged and destitute" Iroquois they begged him to accompany them back to Ross's camp. Undoubtedly motivated by more than mere humanitarian concern, Jedediah seized an opportunity to take the measure of his British competitors. When the Iroquois returned to camp with Smith and his men, Ross was much put out. Not only had they brought in few beaver skins, they also thoroughly violated Simpson's directive. Irritated, Ross noted that, "With these vagabonds arrived seven American trappers from the Big Horn River; but whom I rather take as spies than trappers."

Rising to the occasion, Smith spun a tale about his fear of exposing his small party to grave danger and requested that Ross permit them to accompany his brigade to Flathead Post, near today's Thompson's Falls, Montana. Unaccountably, Ross acquiesced, enabling Jedediah Smith, whom one HBC clerk characterized as a "sly cunning Yankey," to acquire important firsthand information about Ashley's chief rivals. When Ross's brigade arrived at Flathead Post with the unwelcome strangers in November 1824, they met an icy reception from Peter Skene Ogden, just arrived at the fort a few days earlier.

Ogden was the son of well-to-do loyalists who fled to England and then returned to Canada after the War for Independence. His father and brother became prominent Montréal lawyers, and Peter received at least some legal education. Instead, he chose the dangerous career of a fur trader. As a North West Company employee from 1810 to 1821, Ogden's reputation for a hair-trigger temper and coarse sense of humor earned him many enemies. He delighted in bullying and cursing his competitors. In 1818 the HBC had him indicted for murdering an Indian, but the case went nowhere. No one disputed Ogden's ability to command the rowdy underlings in the trade, but when the two companies amalgamated, he was summarily dismissed. Even so, Ogden's special abilities soon caught Simpson's attention.

Not without reservations, Simpson hired him in 1822 for service at Spokane House, an HBC post in the Oregon Country. Within two years Simpson decided to demote Alexander Ross, whom he thought "empty-headed" and "full of bombast," to the role of post factor and place Ogden in charge of the demanding Snake Country Expeditions. Simpson needed a hard-driving bourgeois to tame the Snake River trappers he considered "the very scum of the country and generally the outcasts from the [HBC] service." Ogden seemed the sort to brook no nonsense from "the most unruly and troublesome gang to deal with in this or perhaps any other part of the world." Still, Simpson suspected Ogden was himself an unprincipled man who might "soon get into the habits of dissipation if he were not restrained by the fear of those operating against his interests."

Ogden came to Flathead Post just in time to encounter Jedediah Smith, and Alexander Ross's demotion took effect the day after Ogden and the Americans arrived. Over the next three weeks Ogden assembled trade goods, gear, men, and livestock. In the meantime he implemented one of Simpson's harsher cost-cutting measures. Abruptly dismissing more than twenty engagés from the HBC's service, Ogden immediately reenlisted them as "freemen." As HBC "servants," engagés customarily received lodging, board, and the occasional petty luxury at company expense, but freemen were contract hunters who sold their furs to the company and received no benefits. Simpson's economy-minded parsimony would cause much grief for Ogden and the HBC.

On December 20, 1824, Ogden departed Flathead Post for the Snake River country. His brigade mustered seventy-five well-armed men and boys, many accompanied by their wives and children, along with 352 beaver traps and 268 horses. Before leaving the post, Smith and his men traded forty-nine beaver skins to Alexander Ross, at freemen prices, the lowest HBC rates for beaver, undoubtedly to procure necessities such as powder and lead. The seven Americans set out before Ogden, and he was not pleased when they showed up at his camp a few days later.

Shadowed by the Americans, Ogden's brigade steered a southerly course along the Bitterroot River past the Camas Prairie, then cruised the valleys dividing the Bitterroot and Lemhi ranges. Crossing the mountains over Gibbon Pass and Lemhi Pass, they reached the Snake River Plains near today's

Blackfoot, in southeastern Idaho. Pushing southward, they trapped around Bear Lake astride the Utah-Idaho border, then headed toward the Great Salt Lake. Several weeks later Ogden reversed course, leading his brigade north back across the Snake before traversing southern Idaho. Moving west through the area around present-day Boise, they regained the Snake River at Burnt River, near what is today Baker City, Oregon. Late in October they rode northwest across the Blue Mountains to their final destination, Fort Nez Percés, where the Snake joins the Columbia. It was during this trek that Ogden and his men became "discoverers" of the Great Salt Lake, though in reality credit must be distributed among Ogden, Jedediah Smith's party, and Étienne Provost, for they all saw it between the fall of 1824 and the spring of 1825. On November 21, 1825, after only eighteen days recuperating and resupplying at the fort, Ogden would set out on his second extended Snake Country Expedition.

The Americans had traveled with Ogden's brigade for three months, though they were rarely mentioned in the HBC party's surviving documents. In March 1825, hoping they were safely beyond the reach of Blackfeet warriors who assaulted British and American trappers without much distinction, Smith's men departed from Ogden's brigade after again purchasing some goods. William Kittson, Ogden's clerk, noted, "The Americans traded some ammunition and Tobacco from us for Beaver at the same price as our freemen." The next day he wrote, "About noon they left us, well satisfied I hope with the care and Attention we paid them. For since we had them with us no one in our party ever took any advantage of or ill treated them."

For several more weeks the two parties trapped in close proximity, often experiencing actual or threatened harassment from Blackfeet raiders. By the time Ogden reached the Portneuf River in southeastern Idaho in mid-April, his limited patience with Smith's Americans was badly frayed. He detailed some of his trappers to "keep in Company with them so as to annoy them & with the hopes they will Steer another course."

Late April found the rival outfits on the Bear River. There they separated, the HBC men heading south in search of the Bear's source while the Americans trapped upstream on a nearby fork. Ogden was disappointed to find the lower Bear River thoroughly trapped over, but worse, he discovered evidence that even more Americans were in the area. At that moment, the stage was set for an alarming encounter between Ogden's brigade and the Americans. It precipitated an international incident that reverberated all the way from the Snake River wilderness to the halls of government in London and Washington, D.C.

American trappers certainly irritated Ogden, but his own undisciplined freemen had also grown troublesome of late. Resentful over the HBC's low prices for their beaver skins and high prices for goods, Ogden's trappers refused to guard their horses at night, losing many to Indian thieves. Fearful of more Blackfeet depredations, they bickered with Ogden over what route ought to be taken, and they even "expressed their determination of abandoning the Country," complaining that "at the commencement of the season . . . already one Man has been killed, and one half of our horses have been stolen."

The freemen may also have "loaded" beaver skins with sand to boost their weight. The chief factor at Fort Vancouver, John McLoughlin, complained in June 1825 that the "Snake Beaver was full of sand and evidently had not been beaten since the Freemen gave them in." Yet without freemen, the Snake brigades would be far less productive, so Ogden had no recourse but to yield—at least sometimes—to the pressure tactics of his disgruntled hirelings.

Another of Ogden's problems was his frustrating quest to discover the elusive Rio Buenaventura, which was depicted on numerous maps and widely believed to lie somewhere south and west of the Great Salt Lake. This mythical river was supposed to flow from the Salt Lake region to the Pacific Ocean near San Francisco. Well-informed fur traders, including Ogden's HBC superiors, suspected it was real. In truth, no such river existed, but in 1825 British fur traders were as eager as the Americans to find the mysterious "river of the west."

In mid-May, Ogden's freemen were setting traps along the Weber River, near present-day Mountain Green, Utah. A pair of men who deserted from Flathead Post in 1822 showed up on May 22, bearing disturbing news. They told Ogden they had lately been trapping in company with Étienne Provost and thirty Americans from Taos who claimed New Mexico lay only fifteen days' march to the south. Indeed, the freemen reported, "the whole Country is over-run with Americans." Not only was Jedediah Smith's party still in the neighborhood, but so was John Weber's large contingent of Ashley men, as well as Provost's independent trappers. Ogden had plenty to worry about, including the distinct possibility that more freemen might desert or sell their furs to the Americans. Events soon took a surprising and unpleasant turn, one that amply justified the British-Canadian's fears.

Among Weber's mountain men were a handful of "free trappers," analogous to the HBC's freemen. One of them was a belligerent strutter named Johnson Gardner. Gardner probably entered the trade in 1822 as an Ashley man, but within two years he became an independent operator. On May 24 Gardner blustered into Ogden's camp leading a "Strong party," waving an American flag and talking tough. According to Ogden, Gardner "lost no time in informing all hands in the Camp that they were in the United States Territories & were all free [whether] indebted or engaged." Urging Ogden's men to desert and renege on their debts, Gardner brusquely informed the Snake Country men that British law and contracts had no force in "US territory." The truth is that none of these trappers were in the United States; they were not even in the British-American joint occupancy region as established in 1818. Instead, they were, to a man, trespassers on Mexican soil, though knowledge of that fact would probably have mattered not at all.

The other key actors in this drama were Ogden's Iroquois. Most likely, Old Pierre Tevanitagon or his fellow mixed-blood Ignace Hatchiorauquasha, known as John Gray, persuaded the Iroquois to desert Ogden's brigade. A veteran trapper, "Old Pierre" is said to have discovered Pierre's Hole in Idaho. It was also Old Pierre who had led the party that Jedediah Smith accompanied to Fort Nez Percés the preceding autumn after the

Snakes robbed them. Ogden saw both as troublemakers, and Alexander Ross characterized John Gray as "a turbulent blackguard, a damned rascal."

Irrespective of who spoke for the HBC freemen, Gardner's assurance of $3.50 per pound for their beaver, much more than the HBC paid, and "goods cheap in proportion" was inducement enough to convince about twenty-four of Ogden's men—almost half—to leave with Gardner. Following a brief, noisy debate over international lines and legal points, the deserters simply rode out of camp. As a result Ogden's brigade was weakened and the HBC forfeited several hundred beaver skins. In an ironic turnabout, the freemen, to whom the HBC owed no patronage, displayed an independence not seen since the amalgamation. Before the Americans came, such wholesale desertion would have been impossible. Jedediah Smith played no role in this incident, but Gardner's high-handedness seemed to substantiate Ogden's already deep mistrust of Smith or any other Americans.

Reports of Gardner and Ogden's altercation infuriated HBC officials far and wide. From his newly established headquarters at Fort Vancouver in August 1825, chief factor John McLoughlin circulated a letter to HBC traders bemoaning "the mortifying intelligence of the desertion of our Freemen in the Snake and the threats made by a Mr. Gardner that the Americans ... would drive us from their Territory." The deserters, McLoughlin asserted, "evinced the most disgraceful I might say criminal neglect, of their bounden duty in not supporting Mr. Ogden." Early the next year the HBC's London governing committee informed Simpson that in view of diminishing beaver returns, good policy required "keeping all the frontier country hunted close, and ... [sending] trapping expeditions in those territories likely to fall within the Boundary of the United States."

The HBC elected to jettison customary conservation practices in Oregon in hopes that a "fur desert" would clip the wings of U.S. interest in the interior northwest. But Gardner and a handful of beaver hunters unofficially warned Britain that U.S. citizens had grown restive under joint occupancy and would no longer stand idly by while the HBC alone profited in Oregon. Johnson Gardner was a hard-talking thug with a chip on his shoulder, but inducing a few dozen HBC men to sell furs to Americans would not bring about permanent changes in fur trade supply and transport systems, nor would it tilt the balance of imperial power in favor of the United States. A scheme that William Ashley hatched far from the Snake River country in the spring of 1825, however, might just do the trick.

Like the Nor'Westers before him, Ashley came to realize that his profits could improve if he maximized his trappers' time in the mountains. He decided to send a caravan with an ample supply of goods to the trappers in their mountain haunts, and then send it back to Saint Louis with the winter fur harvest. Ashley's successful "rendezvous system" operated for the next fifteen years (1825–40) and left an enduring legacy, but he did not originate the idea. The French word *rendezvous* itself indicates that Ashley borrowed the concept. Decades earlier the North West Company began sending annual canoe fleets into the pays d'en haut. Loaded with goods and supplies on the outbound voyage, they returned to Montréal with hundreds of bales of furs. Ashley's innovation consisted in his substitution of horses and wagons for canoes, keelboats, and the like to transport men, goods, and furs; and instead of a water route he used the alternate Platte River Road that Jedediah Smith and others followed to the mountains. Among other benefits, the Platte River Road promised to eliminate further conflicts with the Arikaras or other Missouri River tribes.

When Thomas Fitzpatrick met with Ashley late in 1824, possibly at Fort Atkinson, he offered news of Jedediah Smith and the discovery of the South Pass. Ashley and Henry's economic prospects still looked grim. A small army of creditors nipped at their heels, and Henry seemed ready to call it quits. Ashley faced the distinct possibility of a complete financial collapse and the premature termination of his nascent political ambitions. With much at risk and desperate to do anything he could to ensure success, Ashley had already decided to lead the supply expedition himself.

On September 24, 1824, he secured a license from Superintendent of Indian Affairs William Clark to trade for three years "West of the Rocky Mountains, at the junction of two large rivers, supposed to be branches of the Buonaventure and the Colorado of the West." After assembling and dispatching an outfit mustering twenty-five men, fifty packhorses loaded with trade goods, and the first horse-drawn wagon to cross the prairie, Ashley left Saint Louis. Traveling up the Missouri, he reached Fort Atkinson on October 21. Diarist James Kennerly, who happened to be at the fort, heard that Ashley's party of "Trapers and hunters" was bound for "the Spanish country," obviously beyond the limits of Clark's licensing authority. At the fort Ashley wrote to Governor William Carr Lane of Missouri on October 29 that he meant to "accompany my party of Mountaineers to their place of destination."

Departing Fort Atkinson on November 3, he caught up with his brigade two days later. Between November 1824 and August 1825, forty-six-year-old Ashley logged about three thousand miles over punishing landscape, much of the journey taking place during a harsh winter. As Ashley followed the Platte River to the Pawnee land, he was repeatedly beset by shrieking winter storms that broke down men and livestock. Food was scarce, and he found no Indians from whom he could buy more horses. One of Ashley's trappers, a mulatto named James Beckwourth, recalled that "no jokes, no fire-side stories, no fun" enlivened their frozen and desolate encampment. For two weeks the mountain men ate nothing but a half-pint of flour gruel each day. In early December, Ashley caught up with the Grand Pawnees near Plumb Point, in modern-day western Nebraska, while they were en route to spend the winter encamped on the Arkansas River. They advised him to remain with them for the winter, warning him that forage and firewood were scarce on the trail ahead. Ashley declined their invitation.

Proceeding to the "Forks of the Platt," Ashley located the Loup Pawnees, with whom he traded goods for "twenty three horses and some other necessary things." On December 24 he set out for the south fork of the Platte, which the Pawnees told him furnished better wood and forage. The party soon encountered bison, and circumstances appeared to improve, but then another storm overtook them and more broken-down horses were abandoned. Despite the brutally cold weather, Ashley's men performed their duty "with alacrity and cheerfulness," and their "privations in the end became sources of amusement to them."

From late January 1825 until the end of February, Ashley's party crept ever closer to the Rockies, camping for days at a stretch while scouts searched for a route through the snow-locked mountains. In late March a difficult three-day crossing of the Medicine Bow Range brought the party to the Laramie Plains, close to the Continental Divide, where forage was relatively abundant. The party had lost many horses to weather and Indian thievery, but Ashley's leadership—a combination of threats, cajolery, and camaraderie—kept the party together.

By mid-April, thanks to Indians' advice and some cautious reasoning, Ashley figured he was near the Sweetwater, south of the Wind River Range in southwest Wyoming. Continuing westward, his men commenced trapping the Seeds-kee-dee Agie, or Green River. Downed trees along the banks and other signs persuaded Ashley that it formerly "contained a great number of Beaver," and he surmised that the river had been "trapped by men in the service of the North West Company some four or five years ago." Beaver were still about, so his men set traps while Ashley laid plans for the first Rocky Mountain rendezvous.

Ashley dispatched four trapping brigades, one of which was to determine the whereabouts of Jedediah Smith's and John Weber's men. In letters to each brigade leader, he directed them to assemble in mid-July. He would locate a "place of deposite" somewhere near the Green River that would serve as "the place of rendavose for all our parties on or before the 10th of July next." Tall trees stripped of their bark would mark the spot. If no timber grew near his cache (the "deposite"), Ashley would "raise a mound of earth five feet high or set up rocks the top of which will be made red with vermillon[.] [T]hirty feet distant from the same—and one foot below the surface of the earth [in] a north-west direction will be deposited a letter communicating to the party any thing that I may deem necessary."

Thinking the Green River a likely candidate for the Rio Buenaventura, Ashley resolved to explore it, becoming one of the first Americans to document a voyage on the Green. His trappers constructed a large bull-boat "about the size and shape of a common mackinaw boat," some sixteen feet long by eight feet wide. Ashley and a six-man crew embarked on April 22, 1825. The initial stage of the river trip was deceptively pleasant. Ashley paused for a few days while his crew built a second bull-boat, and the party made other stops to hunt game and to cache goods for later use. On May 3 he identified a creek that seemed to answer his needs for the July assembly, and he named it "Randavouse Creek." Today called Henry's Fork of the Green River, it flows eastward just north of the Uinta Mountains, entering the Green near what is now called the Flaming Gorge.

Ashley did not know when he re-embarked on May 5 that his salad days on the river were over. Two days earlier, even as he rejoiced to see "much beaver sign" along the river, he had also noted ominously that the mountains thereabouts presented an "alltogether exceedingly gloomy" prospect, what with their beetling cliffs and icy slopes lashed by frigid winds, snow, and rain. Sure enough, the next three weeks brought a ceaseless round of suffering—terrible weather, dangerous rapids, and continual drenchings, an aggravating food shortage, and many arduous portages around impassable falls. The Green offered no shortcut to success or anywhere else. Ashley's skin boat repeatedly dodged calamity, but on one occasion it nearly came to grief.

On May 14 Ashley heard the roar of white water several hundred yards ahead. The current was rushing along so fast that he could not beach his bull-boat, leaving him no choice but to "run" the heavy rapids. Beset by standing waves and flying foam, the boat filled with water and threatened to capsize. With fatal catastrophe looming, wrote Ashley, "two of the most active men then leaped in the water[,] took the cables and towed her to land. Just as from all appearance she was about making her exit and me with her for I cannot swim."

A few days later, in a long-odds encounter, Ashley's haggard party happened to meet some "Frenchmen" from Taos, New Mexico. First entering the Great Basin from New Mexico in 1824, Étienne Provost and his partner, a man named LeClerc, had returned with thirty men to trap the Weber and Green rivers in the spring of 1825. Among them were several Iroquois and other freemen who had deserted an HBC expedition in 1822.

Provost's trappers informed Ashley that the country thereabouts was "Entirely destitute of game" and that hostile Indians had recently killed or robbed about twenty men. Bad news indeed, but with no ready alternative Ashley proceeded on. By this time, leaky bull-boats and generally wretched circumstances had forced Ashley to cache most of his remaining goods where Ashley's Fork enters the Green, not far from today's Dinosaur National Monument. He carried a surprising variety of materials, including bolts of blue and scarlet cloth, bags of coffee and sugar, axes, hoes, and horseshoes, sixty-pound bars of lead, and several "bags" of gunpowder weighing seventy-five pounds each. Little wonder, then, that his overloaded bull-boats were so often in danger of capsizing.

The weary men paddled into the spectacularly carved canyons and badlands of northeast Utah. A few days' drifting brought them to the Duchesne River and the Wonsits Valley on the southern edge of the Uinta Mountains. There, Ashley jettisoned his played-out bull-boats, and his men adzed out a pirogue from a giant cottonwood trunk. After dispatching some men to hunt for badly needed game, Ashley and three crewmen continued downstream, hoping to find Indians willing to trade some horses. Starvation hovered over them until about May 25, when they met a Snake Indian who told Ashley that other Snakes were close by and would likely be willing to sell some horses. Having experienced more than enough river exploration, Ashley wanted only to reunite with his trappers at their "place of deposite," the rendezvous. During the last few days in May he traded two horses from the Snakes, who owned "a great number of good

horses" but refused to part with any others. Then Ashley found
Provost's "Frenchmen" encamped about fifteen miles up the
Uinta River and secured three more horses.

At last mounted and freed from the river's caprices, Ashley's
small party set out overland on June 3. Trapping as they went,
the party generally retraced portions of routes through the
desert that had been pioneered in 1775–76 by the Franciscan
fathers Francisco Garcés, from Arizona, and Francisco Silvestre
Vélez de Escalante and Francisco Atanasio Domínguez, from
New Mexico, who first called the Green River the Rio Buenaventura. This route, potentially connecting New Mexico to
California, saw very little use until the mountain men came into
the West, and by 1830 they called it the Old Spanish Trail. Along
the way Ashley again encountered Étienne Provost's trappers,
who informed him that Johnson Gardner's party was nearby. It
was late June when Ashley's and Provost's men hastened toward
the Great Salt Lake to rejoin Ashley's trappers at the rendezvous.

Finally, on July 1 Ashley wrote, "all the men in my employ or
with whom I had any concern in the Country, together with
twenty nine who had recently withdrawn from the Hudson bay
Company, making in all 120 men, were assembled in two camps
near each other about 20 miles distant from the place appointed
by me as the general rendezvous." The first of fifteen annual
Rocky Mountain fur traders' grand frolics, the "rendezvous,"
was about to begin.

CHAPTER 3

Ashley & Smith

UPON arriving at the rendezvous, Ashley was no doubt delighted to greet Jedediah Smith. His "very intelligent and confidential" young partisan recounted his adventures of the past year and informed Ashley that HBC traders and trappers were scattered "on both sides of the Rocky Mountains ... 60 of whom were generally employed as trappers" in the Snake Country. Jedediah estimated that in the past four years the HBC had harvested about eighty thousand beaver pelts, amounting to at least one hundred thousand pounds of fur. So thickly populated with beavers was the Snake Country, Smith told Ashley, that some of his own trappers had caught "upwards of one hundred in the last spring hunt out of streams which had been trapped ... for the last four years." He described the Great Salt Lake and its extensive salt deposits and presented Ashley some samples "equal in appearance and quality [to] the best Liverpool salt." Jedediah Smith also told his patron that a vast number of bison roamed the country "in almost any direction."

Shooting matches, displays of horsemanship, and general raucousness enlivened the rendezvous scene as the trappers welcomed veteran comrades, lamented the fate of men who had disappeared or died, and enumerated their many exploits. A few days of brisk trading substantiated Ashley's hopes that financial success might be within his grasp. He took in about 675 pounds of beaver skins from free trappers and 8,829 pounds from his hired men, including 668 pounds from Smith's detachment. He also received orders from Johnson Gardner and another free trapper for goods amounting to several hundred dollars. No liquor was sold at the first two rendezvous, though in subsequent years whiskey would be vended in large quantities, generating large profits and contributing to the enduring "hell-roaring" mythology of the Rocky Mountain rendezvous era.

Annual rendezvous continued until 1840, when a sharp decline in beaver fur prices ended the era of the Rocky Mountain men, though low-intensity beaver trapping never ceased. During the same years an ever-increasing consumer demand for luxurious bison robes caused a major shift in the Indian trade. Unlike the beaver hunts, the robe trade required reliance on Indian men, who hunted bison, and Indian women, who processed and tanned the robes exchanged for manufactured goods at fixed trading posts scattered throughout the West. Jedediah Smith would not live to see these changes, but he helped identify the potential for an expanding bison robe trade.

For each of the finest beaver skins Ashley exchanged trade goods nominally worth about five dollars, but his goods fetched highly inflated "mountain prices." Markup on most goods used in the fur and Indian trades hovered around 100 percent. Some items yielded greater profits, such as the Sheffield butcher knives that cost Ashley about ten cents each but sold in the mountains for $2.50 apiece.

Those hefty mountain prices may strike modern readers as extortionate, but in addition to Ashley's profit margins, they reflected transportation expenses, labor costs, and the multiple risks involved in the worldwide fur trade. Many goods had to be imported from Britain, especially high-quality woolen "point blankets" and other textiles, guns, knives, and hardware. All glass beads came from Venice, which had monopolized the glassblowing industry for centuries. Brilliant vermilion powder, a face paint and all-purpose pigment, was found only in China. Customs duties boosted operating expenses, as did insurance premiums and transportation charges to move goods from New York, Philadelphia, or New Orleans to Saint Louis and into the West. Other costs included wages for hired men and money to purchase keelboats, livestock, and gear. At any rate, for two years the mountain men either paid Ashley's prices or went without necessities and luxury goods. On the other hand, Ashley paid his trappers more than the HBC offered for equivalent skins, which helps explain why many freemen temporarily deserted the HBC.

As the rendezvous came to an end, Ashley prepared to convey his rich harvest of beaver fur to market at Saint Louis. Using crude timber-built devices, his men pressed the furs into fifty-pound packs containing about thirty skins apiece. To carry the furs Ashley borrowed packhorses from "our Salt Lake friends," Provost's trappers. A few of them guided Ashley's men to "Wind River, one of the branches of the Yellowstone." Detailing twenty men to escort the furs down river with him, Ashley assigned thirty others to return Provost's horses. When Ashley's contingent left the rendezvous on July 2, Jedediah Smith probably led a trapping party through South Pass and continued on to the Yellowstone, where he would rejoin Ashley.

Ashley's crew first headed for the Sweetwater to retrieve forty-five packs of fur that Smith cached in 1824 and 1825. Soon after raising the cache, however, Ashley met more setbacks. A Blackfeet raiding party ran off all of his livestock save two horses, forcing a halt while he procured additional mounts. Two days later, Crow raiders attacked his camp. One Crow was killed and one wounded, but Ashley's brigade suffered no casualties. On August 7 he reached the Bighorn River and followed it to the Yellowstone. About ten days later he came to the confluence of the Yellowstone and the Missouri. There, fortune smiled broadly upon William Ashley and he sensed that the worst was over.

On August 19 "General Ashley" and twenty-four men with one hundred packs of beaver fur happened upon Camp Barbour, a temporary military cantonment on the Yellowstone near the site of the recently abandoned Henry's Fort. As luck would have it, he had encountered the Yellow Stone Expedition, several hundred soldiers commanded by Gen. Henry Atkinson on a summer tour of the Upper Missouri River. Indian Agent Benjamin O'Fallon accompanied the soldiers in order to secure treaties with several Indian nations, the first such negotiations with the Upper Missouri tribes. Atkinson's expedition was meant to awe Indians with the military strength of their "Great

Father" and to repair some of the damage resulting from Leavenworth's bungled 1823 campaign.

General Atkinson offered space in the expedition's keelboats to transport Ashley, his men, and his furs down to Council Bluffs. With financial security now virtually assured, he could dare to hope that his creditors would soon be silenced, and that his postponed political career might yet flourish. While his trappers rested and swapped stories with the blue-coated soldiers at Camp Barbour, Ashley learned that General Atkinson planned to explore the Missouri River and he decided to join the entourage.

Ashley and Atkinson, with 330 soldiers and a small cannon, boarded five army keelboats rigged with experimental, manually operated paddle wheels. The vessels bore distinctly unmilitary names, such as *Mink*, *Beaver*, and *Muskrat*, symbolic testimony that in 1825 the fur trade overshadowed military adventurism on the Upper Missouri. Atkinson's six-day excursion more resembled a sporting event than any species of serious exploration. During the characteristic "hot sultry" days of a northern plains summer punctuated by a few "thunder gusts," Ashley and the soldiers shot bison, elk, deer, antelope, and a grizzly bear, but they saw not a single Indian. On Friday, August 26, Atkinson's party returned to their base camp, and the next morning the keelboats set off down the Missouri, often drifting more than sixty miles a day.

The generally tedious trip offered a few memorable highlights. One night a crazed buffalo bull charged through the camp and nearly knocked down Maj. Stephen Watts Kearny's tent before it leaped into the river, only to be shot dead. A few days later, in genuine mountaineer style, Ashley treated the soldiers to three cooked beaver tails that he purchased from a "French" trapper thirty miles above the Arikara villages. The next day the soldiers stopped to trade the Arikaras some goods—including guns and ammunition—for corn. Whatever thoughts Ashley, Smith, or the other mountain men entertained at passing the site of their 1823 defeat went unrecorded. A trapper in Ashley's party, James Beckwourth, remembered the river cruise as a "jovial time," noting that the trappers amused themselves by "telling stories, cracking jokes, and frequently making free with Uncle Sam's 'O be joyful' [i.e., liquor], of which there was great plenty for the supply of rations for the troops."

A more serious incident occurred on September 13 when the *Muskrat* got impaled on a "snag," boatmen's parlance for a sunken tree buried in muck under the Missouri's opaque current, and sank in three feet of water. After pounding blankets into the multiple punctures, crewmen bailed out and repaired the keelboat. No cargo was lost, but the next day Ashley requested a halt at a sandbar to unpack, dry out, and repack twenty-five bales of drenched beaver fur. Six more days brought the little fleet safely to Council Bluffs. The Missouri had exacted a heavy toll from the experimental riverboats, most of which were in a sorry condition. On October 3 advance reports of Ashley's impending arrival stirred Saint Louis, and the "General" himself showed up four days later.

"Our enterprising fellow-citizen," the *Missouri Intelligencer* crowed, returned with a "rich cargo of beaver" to "confirm the accounts we have had of the wealth of the fur regions beyond the Mountains." Ashley's furs were "supposed to be worth $50,000," something of an overestimate. Other newspapers trumpeted similar accounts of Ashley's "heroic enterprize." One report noted ominously that the HBC were "believed to have 1,000 men in their employment west of the Rocky Mountains," claiming that a single HBC brigade had taken "beaver to the amount of $200,000" within the "territory of the United States." Such exaggerated commentary agitated the growing tensions surrounding the unpopular 1818 treaty that permitted British and United States traders to operate freely in the Oregon Country but did nothing to resolve questions about overlapping jurisdiction.

For instance, William Clark, superintendent of Indian Affairs at Saint Louis, informed Secretary of War James Barbour on October 25, 1825, that he had issued Ashley a license to trade "West of the ridge of Rocky mountains." But Clark wondered if the joint occupation treaty nullified "the operation of the Laws

& regulations, that govern our Indian intercourse East of those mountains." He also wondered, in a telling query, "is a citizen of the United States licensed to trade with the Indians, & who does hunt or trap in those regions, liable [to] the penalties inflicted by the Intercourse law of 1802, and to the forfeiture of their bond given on the receipt of their license [according to provisions of] the act of 6th May 1822?" This was no mere idle speculation. Clark's question raised doubts about the applicability of the trade and intercourse laws that regulated the Indian trade from 1796 to 1834, and that coincidentally laid the foundation for nineteenth-century U.S. Indian policy. According to those federal laws, as Clark knew, it was illegal for men licensed as Indian traders to set traps or to hunt game in Indian Country.

Clark's uncertainty highlighted important issues having to do with both the history of the western fur trade and the story of Jedediah Smith. "Indian traders" like Ashley and Smith were practically always involved in trapping operations, but the intercourse laws' prohibition of hunting was never enforced. This was because the smoldering contest over sovereignty in the Pacific Northwest in the 1820s and 1830s generated enough acrimony to trump such fine legal points, and the U.S. government chose to wink at American trappers' continual violation of its own trade and intercourse laws. Fur hunters such as Ashley, Smith, and their cohorts thus served as unofficial agents of U.S. expansionism, and their role in that capacity was evidently deemed too important to curtail. Consequently, Indian nations' legitimate complaints against illegal hunting and trapping would never receive serious or effective attention from the government that solemnly—and often— pledged itself a genial and protective "Great Father" to the "untutored children of the forests."

If Jedediah Smith pondered such ethical conundrums he did not record his thoughts. After three years as a mountain man, however, Smith had mastered the trapping craft and proved himself a capable, dependable partisan. He had learned much about Indians, western geography, British competitors, and how to manage the roisterers in his brigades. He likewise benefited from his association with Ashley, who was at first simply his employer but quickly became Jedediah's mentor and friend. The two men shared an enthusiasm for exploration, and Jedediah Smith willingly placed his geographical knowledge at Ashley's disposal. Smith's intelligence, reliability, youthful verve, and keen observational senses surely impressed the older man.

These were valuable assets, and Ashley soon put them to good use. Sometime before the close of 1824 Andrew Henry terminated his partnership with Ashley and retired from the fur trade, as indicated by the absence of his name on the September license that William Clark issued to Ashley alone. Of necessity, Ashley assumed the responsibility for transporting goods to the mountains and returning furs to market in 1825, but this he saw as a temporary expedient, not something he wished to continue indefinitely. Ashley needed a new partner to haul goods to the mountains and oversee his interests there, and he decided to offer Smith a partnership. The two men came to an understanding at the 1825 rendezvous, and when Smith returned with Ashley to Saint Louis he was no longer a mere hunter or partisan. He would henceforth codirect the company and receive a larger share of whatever profits accrued. Greater responsibility offered the promise of enlarged economic opportunities, and this change marked a new phase in Smith's career. He was now a bourgeois and had risen to that lofty position in just three years.

When Ashley arrived at Saint Louis he delivered his furs to Tracy & Wahrendorff, who were no doubt relieved to see his debt retired. With his catch sold and hard money in hand, Ashley assembled his men and paid them off in silver coin. He then bankrolled a boisterous two-day drunken frolic at Le Barras's Hotel. James Beckwourth claimed that Ashley even pledged to cover the expenses of carriage rides around the city, and that the mountain men "did not fail to take into our party a good share of lasses."

Ashley had good reasons to celebrate, despite the frenzied pace of his life. Tracy & Wahrendorff had successfully peddled the preceding year's fur harvest in New York, receiving an astounding $6.25 a pound for the excellent Rocky Mountain fur, which for several years thereafter fur-buyers would dub "Ashley beaver." Plans for a second marriage demanded Ashley's attention as well, and he set a date in late October to wed Eliza Christy, the daughter of a prosperous tavern keeper, landowner, and well-connected politician. He and Jedediah Smith also assembled a twenty-thousand-dollar outfit of men, livestock, trade goods, guns, saddles, and tack, and a multitude of other necessities to be sent into the mountains under Smith's command.

Smith spent four harried weeks helping Ashley. Some mountain men became notorious for reveling in the liquor-drenched atmosphere of Saint Louis's bawdy, bustling riverfront neighborhood, but Smith was cut from different cloth. Rarely critical of behavior that ran contrary to his own prescriptive framework, he still saw much in Saint Louis and the mountains that offended his pious sensitivities. Ignoring as best he could the bordellos, barrooms, hustlers, and general clamor, Smith methodically visited the merchants and tradesmen who catered to the Indian and fur trades and who conducted their business in shops, warehouses, and offices along the colorful streets flanking the river that was the lifeblood of the city.

On November 1, 1825, Jedediah Smith's caravan, mustering about seventy men and 160 horses and mules left Saint Louis. In an 1826 letter, Smith noted with a hint of pride that he rode out of the city as "a partner of *Gen Wm* Ashley's in the Fur Trade and Trapping Business." Traveling along the Kansas River, the brigade passed by Fort Riley around January 1, 1826. They wintered with the Pawnees of the "Republican Fork" near Grand Island, Nebraska, where Smith and Campbell lodged with a hospitable chief named Ish-Ka-ta-pa. Trappers could survive on Pawnee corn, but the fierce weather killed so many mules that a few men returned to Saint Louis to order new livestock. In March the trappers prepared to head up the Platte River and on April 1, Ashley arrived with men, mules, trade goods, and supplies. Jedediah and "Black" Harris hurried ahead to convene the mountain trappers' rendezvous at Willow Valley, twenty miles north of Salt Lake.

Jedediah's brigade practiced rigorous diligence during the trip and suffered no incidents of theft or other trouble. Hard-won experience yielded organizational principles that helped guarantee safety on the trail. Selecting certain "confidential and experienced" men as assistant leaders, Smith assigned the remaining men to "messes" of eight or ten trappers. Each mess was supervised by a man filling the role of sergeant who was directed to "make known the wants of his mess, receive supplies for them, make distributions, watch over their conduct, enforce order, &c. &c." The contents of every numbered pack of goods, as well as a tally of horses and mules entrusted to each man, were entered into a ledger book in a rudimentary form of "inventory control" tactics.

At the end of every day's travel, the trappers set up camp with strict attention to security. Members of each mess piled their packs and saddles to form a defensive breastwork in case of Indian horse raids or attacks. Horses and mules were turned out to graze under the watchful eyes of guards, then carefully picketed inside the camp perimeter at sundown. Livestock were secured to thirty-foot ropes fastened to iron picket-pins driven into the ground. The pins were placed far enough apart to ensure that every animal would find sufficient grazing for the night and not become entangled. Sentries kept watch while the rest of the men slept under the open sky, wrapped in buffalo robes or blankets. When dawn lightened the eastern horizon, mounted scouts rode out to reconnoiter the neighborhood, hoping to flush out any daring Indians who might be plotting an early morning raid.

After the scouts returned to camp, "camp keepers"—the least experienced men—kindled fires and prepared breakfast. Horses and mules were again put out to graze and then rounded up as the brigade got into motion, mess by mess. While en route, "spies" or flankers rode at a distance on all sides of the line of march, constantly scanning the landscape for signs of trouble. Only by assiduously adhering to these practices would safety be ensured; otherwise, as the trappers knew, disaster might smite the unwary with devastating fury. Few mountain men were so callous as to murder Indians for no reason, but all knew that their survival depended on conscientious attention to precautions and a willingness to defend their lives and property at all costs. Trapping in Indian Country was not a vocation for the lackadaisical or fainthearted.

Smith and Ashley's wintering trappers managed to survive the inclement season. A good many of them wound up encamped in the temperate Salt Lake Valley, where snow was scanty and buffalo were plentiful. In time their tales of the isolated and beautiful valley attracted the attention of Brigham Young and the other Mormon leaders who led the Saints' exodus to "Deseret" in 1846. Ashley's man John Weber established a camp on the Weber River, and when spring came and the weather moderated, he divided his brigade into smaller parties, each comprising of perhaps twenty-five trappers. One contingent encountered Peter Skene Odgen and the HBC's Snake County brigade. Another Ashley & Smith party, under the direction of Thomas Fitzpatrick, trapped along Bear River and some branches of the Snake River. In what the trappers called Willow Valley, Fitzpatrick's men dug a cache for some seventy-five packs of beaver fur. Their excavation caved in and buried a man named Marshall, yielding a new name for the place, Cache Valley, which is still used today.

While Ashley & Smith's trappers worked streams to the north and east, Jedediah led his own detachment northwestward from Great Salt Lake into a little-known region that some men believed would reveal the source of the fabled River of the West, sometimes called the Rio Buenaventura. Several contemporary maps of western North America, based on speculative Spanish predecessors, depicted an anonymous river flowing west from a lake that sometimes appeared on early maps as Lake Timpanogos. Ashley and others supposed it to be the Great Salt Lake and suspected the river was the Rio Buenaventura, but in actuality the garbled, vague Spanish information doubtless referred to what was later named the Humboldt River. The only significant stream within the Great Basin, the Humboldt flows westward from mountains west of Salt Lake, only to dwindle to nothing amid the desiccated wastes of the Humboldt Sink in central Nevada.

As summer approached, Smith's men probably crested the rugged Promontory Mountains, not far from where the first transcontinental railroad's celebrated "golden spike" would be driven in 1869. Dropping down into the Salt Lake Valley, Jedediah again confronted one of the West's genuine oddities: a huge expanse of water saltier than the ocean, unfit for men or horses to drink, and bordered by salt-encrusted swamplands. Smith evidently dispatched four men in a bull-boat to coast the lake, seeking an outlet that he might follow. The crew probably consisted of James Clyman, James Bridger, Moses "Black" Harris, and a German immigrant named Henry Fraeb. Four weeks of fatiguing exploration produced nothing but disappointment, for the Great Salt Lake has no navigable outlet. But the bull-boaters did glean some geographical truth about the region.

The fruitless cruise around Salt Lake only whetted Jedediah's appetite, and he decided to examine the practically unknown terrain west of the lake. Smith's brief foray in the spring of 1826 amounted to a dress rehearsal for his famed Southwest Expedition, which came later that year. His first effort yielded considerable frustration and some useful lessons. Plunging into what is now Nevada, Smith encountered a harsh desert environment that even today challenges travelers in high-speed, air-conditioned automobiles. Springs and watercourses were dangerously scarce, and game was almost nonexistent. It became painfully obvious that this was no land for beaver hunters. Within a short time Smith decided to strike northward toward the Snake River, where beaver were still relatively plentiful despite several years of high-intensity trapping campaigns.

In late May and early June, Peter Skene Ogden received disturbing reports that Smith's men were once again in his bailiwick. Snake Indians informed him that "a party of Americans about 30 in number" had arrived at Salmon Falls Creek "on their return from Salt Lake without beaver." Ogden also learned that the Americans' attempt to locate good hunting ground south of the Snake had come to naught, and that "Starvation had driven them back.... [W]hen last seen they were destitute ... and were Killing their Horses." Entering present-day Idaho, Smith's

This image shows a southeastern Idaho landscape adjacent to the Snake River Plains through which Smith journeyed several times. "Big Blackfoot Valley," chromolithograph from Pacific Rail Road Surveys, vol. 12, book 1. Author's collection.

mountain men trapped along the Snake, Boise, and Payette rivers, taking a respectable haul of beaver fur. Then they headed southeast across the tortuous lava flows dotting the Snake River Plains in southern Idaho toward the rendezvous site at Cache Valley, near today's Hyrum, Utah.

Ashley had departed Saint Louis in early March with a large assortment of trade goods and twenty-five men. Before leaving he penned a curious note to Missouri Senator Thomas Hart Benton that reveals the cross-grained, symbiotic relationship linking the interests of fur traders and the U.S. government. The greatest western "booster" of his time, Benton was a keen observer of the fur trade, ever mindful of its role in advancing the cause of national expansionism. Saint Louis merchants reckoned him an important political ally and a powerful advocate for their interests. In what Ashley suggested would be a "*mutually*" advantageous" arrangement, he urged Senator Benton to persuade the government to hire him as an Indian agent. Ashley pledged that if he were permitted to serve as the government's representative, he would inform the western Indians about their "relative political condition, with us and the British." In exchange he requested that he be issued "a commission or letter of instructions" and "a contingent fund [to] cover his compensation." The senator obligingly forwarded Ashley's proposal to Secretary of War James Barbour.

Secretary Barbour responded that, while he had "no doubt of the friendly dispositions" of Ashley, he was obliged to point out (with no hint of irony) that the proposal "might be esteemed as conflicting with decisions which have been had upon this subject." Adding that it might conflict as well with "the interests of others who are or who may be engaged in the same trade in that quarter," Barbour politely declined Ashley's offer. Such were the antics of clever men who scrambled for political preference and economic advantage in the age before conflicts of interest supposedly became subject to legal or governmental oversight.

Denied a government subsidy, Ashley reunited with Smith and their men at the rendezvous in early July. There he vended goods to his own trappers, as well as to a mixed assemblage of Indians, free trappers, and some HBC deserters. He took in about 125 packs of beaver fur, enough to pay off his debts and leave him with a small fortune in hand if all went well. Four years of high risks and hard work had paid off, and Ashley decided the time had come for him to quit the mountains. Jedediah Smith, his ambitious and capable partner, was willing to buy him out, and Smith already had two experienced men in mind to join him in the new venture.

One of them, David Jackson, was credited with the discovery of Jackson's Hole in Wyoming and may have become an "Ashley man" in 1823. Jackson probably was among Smith's party that explored the terrain northwest of the Great Salt Lake in the spring of 1826. Better known is William L. Sublette, the eldest of five brothers from Kentucky who were all engaged in the western fur trade during its heyday. An "Ashley man" since 1823, Sublette had amply proved his mettle.

Energetic, daring, and highly motivated, William Sublette first went to the mountains as a tubercular seeking the "prairie cure" in an era before doctors knew how to treat the deadly ailment. Sublette would outlive Smith by a dozen years and become wealthy, though in 1845 he succumbed to the lung disease. From 1832 until he died, Sublette operated a partnership with a Scotsman named Robert Campbell, another Ashley veteran whom Jedediah Smith esteemed enough to name as executor of his estate in an 1826 will. Closely associated with Smith, Jackson, and Sublette, Campbell never became a partner in their company. He engaged in a variety of his own mercantile pursuits and died in 1871 as one of Saint Louis's richest men.

Nine months' partnership with Ashley had placed Jedediah Smith in a position to be the new firm's undisputed leader. Thanks to his own and Ashley's associations, Smith was well known to the Saint Louis mercantile community, and Ashley's reputation would help secure the critically important credit that fueled the fur trade. Fur trade entrepreneurs almost never laid out cash to purchase a year's outfit of goods, gear, keelboats, or livestock. Instead, they relied upon long-term loans at annual interest rates of between 2 and 4 percent. Typically, two to three years passed before money invested in the fur trade returned a profit. Trapping expeditions spent at least one year in the mountains, and the better part of another year went by before peltry was marketed and transformed into cash, or into credit lines in ledger books that eliminated debts. Such practices necessitated a good deal of trust among fur producers, venture capitalists, and providers of goods, transportation, and the like. Fortunately for Jedediah Smith, in 1826 Ashley's golden reputation opened the right doors.

On July 18, while still at the rendezvous, Smith and his new partners signed an agreement with Ashley. Smith received a five-thousand-dollar credit for his share of Ashley-Smith profits, which may in part reflect dividends on his prior investment in the firm. Ashley sold all his remaining goods, valued at about sixteen thousand dollars, to the new firm, called Smith, Jackson & Sublette. Smith anted up more of his own money, perhaps augmented by several thousand dollars from Jackson and Sublette. When the debits and credits were calculated, Smith, Jackson & Sublette owed Ashley roughly eight thousand dollars, a debt they hoped to repay quickly. The new outfit also bought the contracts for about forty of Ashley's trappers. Ashley pledged to furnish them goods, transport their furs to Saint Louis, and see that they were advantageously marketed. For his services Ashley would receive $1.12 for every pound of beaver fur that he sold.

Soon after signing the agreement, Ashley bid his farewell to the mountains and to the mountaineers who had made him wealthy. During the remaining decade of his life Ashley engaged in state and national politics, with but moderate success. Serving from 1831 to 1837 as a U.S. congressional representative from Missouri, he sponsored no significant legislation. Many contemporaries doubted his proclaimed allegiance to the nationally dominant Jacksonian Democrats, and he often voted as an independent Whig. His fame rests mainly on his achievements as a fur trader and explorer rather than on his uninspired political career.

Ashley departed the rendezvous with a list of goods that Smith, Jackson & Sublette desired for the coming year. Enumerating many standard trade items, the order also indicates the mountain prices at which they would be sold. Examples include "Three point blankets at nine dollars each," "North West Fuzils at twenty four dollars each," "Squaw axes at two dollars fifty each," and "Beaver traps at nine dollars each." Smith, Jackson & Sublette also requested such items as "washing and shaving soap," allspice, raisins, dried fruit, and—correcting a deficiency of the first two rendezvous—"fourth proof rum" for the mountain men.

The articles of agreement further stipulated that Ashley would haul the supplies to "the west end of the little lake of Bear river a watter [*sic*] of the pacific ocean on or before the first day of July 1827 without some unavoidable occurrence should prevent." Ashley required Smith, Jackson & Sublette to confirm their order by sending a messenger to Saint Louis by March 1, 1827. He promised to do business with no one else "other than those who may be in his immediate service," and to deliver to the next rendezvous goods valued at "not less than Seven thousand dollars nor more than fifteen thousand."

When Ashley returned to Saint Louis in late September, local newspapers proclaimed that he brought in furs valued at sixty thousand dollars, a princely sum. One report gushed that the country Ashley had traversed was full of game, offered plentiful water sources, and presented an easy route to the Far West. The same report indicated that the mountaineers who had already spent four or five years in the West were "too happy in the freedom of those wild regions to think of returning to the comparative thraldom of civilized life." By 1826 the mythology of the hyperindividualist mountain men had already taken root in the American imagination, and it contained more than a kernel of truth.

Ashley's successes lured new and powerful competitors to the mountain trade. In early 1827 John J. Astor, America's richest fur trader and eventually its first millionaire, was trying to hammer out a deal with a Saint Louis outfit, Bernard Pratte & Company, to establish a western department of his American Fur Company. Astor avidly strove to engineer a fur trade monopoly and came closer to attaining that goal than any of his contemporaries. Ashley's well-advertised success in the Rocky Mountains and the burgeoning Upper Missouri trading post system pioneered by the Columbia Fur Company under Kenneth McKenzie's dynamic leadership persuaded Astor that the far western fur trade was about to start paying large dividends. After months of negotiation, in July 1827 Astor reached an accord with McKenzie's outfit and Bernard Pratte & Company, also called the "French Company." The result was the creation of the AFC's Western Department and its most profitable component, the Upper Missouri Outfit. The Upper Missouri Outfit achieved formidable power by the mid-1830s and would dominate the Missouri River fur and Indian trades until the late 1860s.

A year before Astor's agents courted the Columbia Fur Company and the French Saint Louisans, William Ashley made a deal of his own with Bernard Pratte & Company whereby it would supply him goods for Smith, Jackson & Sublette's mountain trade. A major player among Saint Louis's many fur traders, Bernard Pratte & Company purchased goods in such quantities that it often received discounts available to no one else. Ashley also contemplated bankrolling another group of trappers for the mountains, a move that would have irritated Smith, Jackson & Sublette and violated the spirit of their agreement. Perhaps Ashley was simply hedging his bet in the event that Smith, Jackson & Sublette folded prematurely, but when expressmen William Sublette and "Black" Harris arrived early in March 1827 to confirm the order made seven months earlier, Ashley cancelled his plans to compete against Jedediah and his partners.

Sublette and Harris had left their winter quarters at Salt Lake Valley on New Year's Day, 1827. Horses could not subsist on the scanty vegetation left on the frozen plains, so Sublette and Harris made the trek on foot and barely survived a harrowing midwinter ordeal. They carried snowshoes to use on stretches of the trail where snow lay deep or had drifted into heaps. Their only companion, "an Indian broken dog," somehow managed to get along under a fifty-pound pack stuffed with camp gear and dried buffalo meat. On January 15 they spent a frigid night at Independence Rock, where they carved their names and the date into the "register of the plains." Starvation soon overtook them, and they wound up killing and eating their dog. On some nights the exhausted pair had no choice but to keep marching in order to avoid freezing to death. Fortunately, they occasionally encountered Indians who sheltered them and provided them food.

Upon their arrival at Saint Louis, the order they had carried almost thirteen hundred miles was quickly filled. Ashley's men had already put up dozens of bales of goods and equipment in anticipation of a rapid turnaround. On March 6, 1827, Ashley posted a final recruitment advertisement in the *Missouri Republican* soliciting "FIFTY competent men" to accompany his caravan to the Rocky Mountains. By April 15, after purchasing about two hundred horses and mules along with saddles, tack, and so forth, he dispatched a heavily loaded party mustering about sixty men. Ashley sent his financial agent, James B. Bruffee, to keep track of the goods and gear and manage sales at the rendezvous, and he hired the veteran mountain man Hiram Scott to "pilot" the expedition to Bear Lake. Citing poor health, Ashley remained in Saint Louis. He never saw the Far West again. Before returning to the mountains, William Sublette secured a trade license from William Clark. Along with this caravan rolled the first wheeled vehicle to cross the South Pass: Two mules pulled a small iron cannon on a gun carriage all the way to the 1827 rendezvous.

Some time before Ashley's caravan reached the Bear Lake rendezvous, Scott had fallen gravely ill. It was obvious that he was in no condition to ride back to Saint Louis immediately. When James Bruffee departed the rendezvous he promised that he would wait for Scott on the homeward route at a prominent rock outcropping that overlooked the Platte. With two men who volunteered to care for him, Scott floated down the North Platte in a bull-boat to the place that Bruffee designated. By this time Scott was probably near death. After several anxious days passed and no one showed up, Scott's companions apparently decided to leave him to his fate. It happened that Bruffee had already come and gone, and his failure to redeem a solemn vow to await Scott condemned him to a lonely death near the landmark thereafter called Scotts Bluff, Nebraska, one of many names on the land that commemorate the exploits of the "Ashley men."

Bruffee's caravan continued down the Platte River Road without further incident, and around October 1 Ashley greeted it near Lexington, Missouri. David Jackson and William Sublette had accompanied the expedition and now set about balancing their account with Ashley. The two partners transferred $7,821 to Ashley, which retired much of their previous, original debt, and took possession of about $22,500 worth of goods they had ordered from him for the coming year. Offsetting a substantial portion of their new bill for goods, they delivered Ashley about 7,500 pounds of beaver skins, 102 otter skins, and 95 pounds of "Castor," or castoreum, a secretion from beavers' musk glands used as bait for traps and as an ingredient in medicines and perfumes. In the 1820s, Castor sold for about as much as beaver skins, making it a valuable commodity. Sublette and Jackson also promised to pay Ashley roughly four thousand dollars for the livestock that had carried their furs to Saint Louis, comprising eighty-seven mules and a dozen horses. To avoid the needless expense of sending the goods to the mountains with a separate caravan in the spring of 1828, they reloaded their horses and mules with packs of new goods. Within five days they were once again bound for the Rockies.

When Ashley's one-year deal with Bernard Pratte & Company profitably expired, the AFC and the French Company were still negotiating their deal. But by July 1827 Astor's representative Ramsay Crooks and Bernard Pratte & Company agreed to cooperate in an effort to seize control of the western beaver trade. Within months, Astor's Western Department initiated a major expansion program. In 1829 it constructed Fort Union at the confluence of the Missouri and the Yellowstone, and the trading post would soon send competition into the mountains. The 1830s would see the most intense competition ever to appear in the mountain fur trade. Numerous outfits vied for the remaining beaver fur supplies, and each year several hundred American and British-Canadian trappers scoured the Rockies for furs.

Jedediah Smith is notably absent from some of the events recounted above, yet they provide a necessary backdrop for developments in which he was directly involved. Even as Smith and his new partners organized their company, he was formulating plans for his most daring enterprise yet. In late September, when Ashley sold Smith, Jackson & Sublette's rich haul of beaver fur, Smith and a small party were more than one thousand miles away, encamped in the desert near the Mohave River. By the time Sublette and Harris left winter quarters in January 1827, Smith's party had been in California for two months and was making plans to depart the province. At midsummer, while Ashley and Sublette worked out their accounts and the AFC finalized its agreement with the Saint Louisans, Jedediah Smith and two companions were on the final leg of a desperate race to reach the 1827 rendezvous. Had he made no other exploration, his 1826 venture to California would have assured him a noteworthy place in the history of North American exploration.

CHAPTER 4

The Southwest Expedition

AS of July 1826, Smith, Jackson & Sublette was a going concern. While David Jackson and William Sublette busied themselves with matters crucial to the new firm's economic success, Jedediah Smith for the first time yielded completely to his compulsion to explore. His preparations for what he called the Southwest Expedition incorporated the important lessons he had learned about desert travel earlier in 1826 during his preliminary venture into the region west of the Great Salt Lake. When the rendezvous ended, he eagerly set out to make a closer examination of that strange and desolate country. Jedediah Smith evidently understood that he was about to take giant steps into American history.

Smith's 1826 expedition would bring the first Euro-Americans, so far as is known, into California from across the harsh Great Basin. And when Jedediah arrived at the 1827 rendezvous, he would become the first man to complete a journey from California eastward over the Sierra Nevada into the Great Basin and the Great Salt Lake Valley. Equivalent in some respects to Lewis and Clark's epic traverse of the northern portions of the Louisiana Purchase twenty years earlier, Smith's mountain crossing marked a major turning point in western American history. It would have a profound impact on the future of California and the Pacific Northwest. The Southwest Expedition must also be reckoned as one of the most daunting treks yet undertaken in the American West, and the fact that Smith and his companions survived it indicates just how tough and resilient they were.

Two remarkable documents from the expedition have also survived, both of them diaries chronicling the brigade's daily operations. One is a copy of Smith's own lost journal, which first came to light in 1967, and the other is an original daybook kept by his clerk, Harrison Rogers. Like other travel narratives, these journals present a running commentary on camp life on the trail and the many hardships Smith and his men faced, but they also offer a great deal more.

Smith's journal, covering the time from July 1826 to July 1827, with some lapses, forms the core of the next two chapters. Smith or his editor recast portions of his original diary sometime after 1827 in more "literary" prose, and the original diary's whereabouts remains a mystery, but the surviving document still exhibits much of the raw tone of an authentic trail journal. Unlike many nineteenth-century expeditionary diaries and overland trail journals, it contains far more than a terse catalog of mileage, landmarks, and weather conditions. Numerous entries indicate that Indians provided Smith with material assistance at critical moments and often shared vital geographical information. Some of Jedediah Smith's interactions with Indians were peaceable and friendly, but others were extremely violent. Together, Smith's and Rogers's journals provide a unique opportunity to examine the complexities of Smith's relationships with Indians. Smith's journal also exhibits a handful of thoughtful, deeply personal passages. No other documentary sources, including those that Smith himself wrote, offer better clues about how Jedediah dealt with his fellow mountain men, how he grappled with the meaning of his own life, and how he framed his relationships with Indians, Mexican Californians, and the landscape itself.

The morning of August 7, 1826, found Jedediah penning his first journal entry "at our rendezvous at a place known as the bend of Bear River." He and his partners had agreed that "in order to Prosecute our Business advantageously it was necessary that our company Should be divided." Sublette and Jackson were to head "north on to the waters of Lewises River [i.e., the Snake] and the Missouri" with some of the approximately forty trappers whose contracts the new firm had taken over from Ashley a few weeks earlier. Smith would "take the remainder of the men and go to the South." Though he admitted that his disappointing foray west of Salt Lake earlier in the year produced "comparatively little" information about the country to the southwest, he wishfully speculated that the "great and unexplored country" to the southwest might yet prove "as well stocked with Beaver as some of the waters of the Missouri." Then, in an introspective passage written sometime later (probably in 1829–30), he exposed some significant features of his temperament:

> In taking the charge of our S western Expedition I followed the bent of my strong inclination to visit this unexplored country and unfold those hidden resources of wealth and bring to light those wonders which I readily imagined a country so extensive might contain. I must confess that I had at the time a full share of that ambition (and perhaps foolish ambition) which is common … to all the active world. I wanted to be the first to view a country on which the eyes of a white man had never gazed and to follow the course of rivers that ran through a new land.

Seventeen men left the rendezvous under Smith's command. The expeditionary roster offers a revealing glimpse of the ethnic diversity that characterized the trapping fraternity, though of some members nothing is known beyond their names. Robert Evans hailed from "ould Ireland." Arthur Black came from Scotland, as did John Wilson, a thirty-year-old weaver. (The naming of Black's Fork of the Green River dated to the same time that "Smith's Fork" was first applied to a stream in the area, suggesting that Black likely traveled with Jedediah in 1824. A family tradition holds that Arthur Black killed the grizzly bear that attacked Jedediah in 1823 and perhaps saved Smith's life.)

James Reed, like Jedediah, was a New Yorker. Two members, Martin McCoy and John Gaither, grew up in Kentucky. Smith's clerk was a Virginian named Harrison Rogers. Like Jedediah, Rogers was a highly intelligent, literate young man whose personality traits reflected a firm religious upbringing, and the two became close friends. John Hanna was a Missourian, and Silas Gobel came from Ohio. Emmenuel Lazarus was born in Germany, and Peter Ranney (sometimes spelled "Ranne") was listed as an "E Frenchman," possibly indicating that he was a European rather than a French-Canadian. A man named Abraham Laplant, obviously of French descent, was from "Indiana," and Daniel Ferguson came from places "Unknown."

Manuel Eustavan (probably a corruption of "Estevan") was a "native Mexican," and a man named only "John" was listed as a "slave," without further comment. (Just possibly, this man, whom Harrison Rogers in 1828 referred to as a "coloured man" and who was sometimes identified as "John Ransa," was the property of Jedediah himself. One has to wonder what, apart from the instance of a stern owner, could motivate a slave to accompany such a high-risk expedition with no guarantee of remuneration. A few slaves are known to have been hired out to fur traders, but usually for a fixed annual fee at a trading post. Smith's ownership of slaves is treated in the final chapter.) Two original members were of Indian or mixed-blood ethnicity: "Robeseau" was called a "half breed" from Upper Canada; "Nipisang" was a Nipissing tribal member, resident in what Smith denoted "British America." Both brought wives and children with them, but nothing else is known about these men's families. A third Indian named Marion was listed in the 1826 roster as an Umpqua Indian "slave" but did not travel with Smith until the final week of his 1828 expedition into Oregon. (Smith or his editor evidently later incorrectly reconstructed the roster.)

Before Smith's party took the trail in earnest, they set their course for Soda Springs, in southeastern Idaho, then followed the Portneuf River to a suitable camping spot. There they halted "for the purpose of drying meat as the Buffalo were quite plenty and in fine order." Recalling the privations he had endured on his first venture, Smith recognized the "necessity of providing a supply of provision for traveling in a gameless country." Over the next three days, hunters killed several bison and the men dried "three horse loads of most excellent meat," amounting to about seven hundred pounds of "jerky."

The party proceeded to Cache Valley to retrieve some buried goods and a set of blacksmithing tools to make necessary repairs on their guns. A few men prepared charcoal and set up a temporary forge. Their blacksmith, possibly James Reed, had all the firearms in good order by about August 18. Before departing, Smith's men loaded their livestock with a variety of merchandise from the cache. Among the items the clerk Rogers dutifully entered into his daybook were four dozen butcher knives, two pounds of glass beads, a few two-and-a-half- and three-point blankets, eighteen looking-glasses, fifty-five pounds each of gunpowder and tobacco, and seventy pounds of bar lead.

Rogers debited several of the men in his ledger book for small purchases of personal goods for the journey. Some bought "wiping sticks" for their flintlock guns that could serve in a pinch as backup ramrods. Laplant and Robeseau bought soap. Jedediah bought three cakes of shaving soap, and Ferguson bought two. Almost all of the men, including Rogers but not the abstemious Smith, also procured tobacco and "rum" in anticipation of the traditional regale that usually marked the departure of trapping expeditions. On August 15 each of the drinking men consumed about a pint and a quarter of rum.

The day after their moderate celebration, the brigade moved out, heading across rugged mountains and down small river valleys southwest to Salt Lake, then south toward Utah Lake to cross the Weber River. The party encountered some Utes living along the Provo River, the first of many Indians with whom they would interact on their trek. Jedediah decided to stop and council with them to collect information about the "Country to the South." During their palaver he also negotiated one informal "treaty" intended to prevent recurring hostility between the Utes and Snakes and another one "by which the americans are allowed to hunt & trap and pass through their country unmolested." Such unsanctioned treaties possessed no legal standing but may have had a temporary salutary effect on local Indian-trapper relations.

Smith promised the Ute chieftain Conmarrowap that he would convene a second meeting between the two tribes when he returned from his fall hunt. As it turned out, Smith was unable to keep his promise. Jedediah found the Utes a pleasant people, "cleanly quiet, and active." He considered them "more honest than any I had ever been with in the country," adding his general opinion that "stealing and Begging are the most degrading features in the Indian character." He noted with interest that the Utes had "some communication with the Spanish villages of Taos and Santa fee," a commerce that provided them with more guns than their Shoshone (Snake) enemies.

To solemnize the negotiations, Jedediah distributed gifts such as a tin kettle, some powder and ball, and several knives, combs, rings, awls, needles, and hawk bells. He wrote that he had "been directed to do so by Genl Ashley who acted in the capacity of a sub-agent." As noted above, Ashley received no commission from the government, so Smith was mistaken in this assertion, though his error may have been an honest one. While at the Ute camp Manuel Eustavan purchased two recently captured Snake women, running up an additional twenty-seven dollars of personal debt for goods in Rogers's book.

Accompanied by some Utes for a few days, Smith's party followed part of the eastern segment of the Old Spanish Trail. Smith and his men would fall upon sections of the old trail again and again during their trek because they and the Spaniards, for the most part, simply followed well-marked Indian trails. Smith's party probably passed from the eastern shore of Utah Lake in the vicinity of present-day Provo, Utah, to the east where they crossed Soldier Summit, near what is today the Ashley National Forest. Descending from the mountain ridges that divide the Great Basin from the Colorado River drainage, Smith's men likely fell upon the Price River, where they stopped a few days to hunt beavers. After investigating a "verry barren and Rocky" country to the east that offered disappointing prospects for trapping, Smith decided to take his men southwest through Castle Valley, following a part of the Old Spanish Trail that today closely parallels State Highway 10 in Utah.

Jedediah Smith was about to enter the spectacular, eerie landscape of the red sandstone canyon country. Sunbathed under late September's azure sky and with the "harvest moon" beginning to show, the jagged cliffs and dazzling perpendicular spires presented strange vistas. Smith's well-traveled mountain men had seen nothing to compare with this otherworldly landscape. Only a handful of American trappers had passed this way by 1827, and they had come from the south, from the adobe-built towns of New Mexico.

Smith must have pondered that tortured landscape with awe and perhaps a hint of trepidation. But his keen eye and instinct for comprehending geography and the urgent need to make progress would have arrested whatever tangential ruminations crossed his mind, and he soon turned his attention to pragmatic speculations about the best route to follow.

A few days later Smith encountered an "old squaw," too slow to flee with the rest of her people of the "Sampatch" tribe (San Pete or San Pitch Utes) when they detected the approaching white men. Coaxing the woman into camp, Jedediah offered her a badger his men had killed. To his surprise she immediately tossed the creature on a fire and when it was "about half cooked" she "commenced eating[,] making no nice distinction between hair pelt entrails and meet." After she finished her meal, Smith offered the woman some presents, requesting that she bring others of her tribe to see him. Later that night a few curious San Pete Utes tentatively appeared at the camp. Using sign language, the lingua franca of the western Indians, Smith quizzed the Indians for geographical information. Upon learning that a large river lay to the west, Jedediah managed to hire a man to guide his party.

Three more days' travel brought them to the banks of a broad stream, sixty yards wide and with a muddy current. Smith named it "Ashley's River," but today it is called the Sevier. Finding some encouraging evidence of beavers, his men commenced trapping, but with little success. As they moved down the river, Smith's men passed some of the San Pete Ute lodges that dotted the margins of the narrow river bottom. Soon they encountered members of an unfamiliar nation, the Paiutes. Ungenerously, Jedediah judged them to be "in the mental scale lower than any I have yet seen." Eking out a precarious living in the harsh land by subsisting largely on roots, these Indians were later disparagingly labeled "Diggers" by white soldiers and travelers, who sometimes callously murdered them. In the following weeks, Smith grew better acquainted with the Paiutes, and perhaps his opinion of them softened a bit.

Moving on the next day, Smith became aware that he was being observed by unseen Indians who employed "a peculiar method of conveying intelligence of the approach of danger." He had taken notice of the little piles of firewood that lay beside every lodge he passed, and now he realized they were not intended solely for cooking purposes. When Indians spotted strangers in their territory, they lit signal fires, a process repeated over miles of landscape "with the greatest rapidity." Upon perceiving the smoke from such fires, the Indians threw their few belongings into pack baskets and hastened to hiding places until the potentially dangerous visitors were gone.

With beaver too few to warrant further trapping, Smith followed the Sevier several more miles, then shifted westward through Marysvale Canyon and over a pass that brought his party to a small creek near the present site of Cove Fort, a Mormon outpost erected around 1855. During a brief excursion to examine some streams that flowed to the west, Smith was "not a little surprised to find they all sunk in the sand." Admitting that it was "useless for me to look for Beaver where there was no water," he camped for the night.

The next day Smith's party traveled about twenty miles to the southwest in hopes of discovering a river to follow. "To my great Surprise," Jedediah wrote, "instead of a River an immense sand plain was before me." Scanning the shimmering horizon with his spyglass, Smith discerned no evidence of water, only an "interminable waste of sand," which is today called the Escalante Desert. With this daunting prospect in view, Smith backtracked to his previous camp to think things over. By this time some of the horses had already "given out" and had to be left behind. After recovering a few stragglers the next morning, Smith mounted the strongest horse and rode out to reconnoiter the country. Fifteen miles of persistent searching took him to the summit of a high hill from which his telescope disclosed distant indications of trees and possibly water. During his absence, his hunters killed a pair of antelopes, and after the men butchered and packed the meat, the party set off again. By day's end they reached the trees that Smith had spotted and were relieved to find them bordering "a creek 20 yds wide running West with some little Beaver sign."

At this camp the trappers discovered evidence of recently departed Indians, and again spotted the now familiar smoke signals on distant hilltops. Smith's horsemen discovered and overtook two frightened Paiute men, who indicated "by a continued gabering and signs their desire that my men should go one way and they would go another." After presenting them with some small gifts as peace offerings, Smith made camp. His men began setting traps along the creek bed, only to find that it disappeared in the sand. So again the brigade moved on.

When Smith's party neared the Parowan Valley around September 13, Robeseau and Nipisang dropped out of the expedition, having decided to leave with their wives and children and go their own way. They were quickly followed by Manuel Eustavan, who, Smith wrote, "ran off" at night with the two Snake women he had bought, taking "a horse Rifle and ammunition belonging to the Comp[any]" and leaving behind his unpaid debt. Two other anonymous Indian women evidently joined the expedition at some unknown point, a fact disclosed only months later in California, when one of Smith's men, John Wilson, informed Mexican authorities of their presence.

By mid-September the party had almost exhausted their supply of dried meat. The barren and broken country supported practically no game, and the men and women trod mile upon mile with aching bellies. They came to a river that Jedediah named "Adams River," to honor President John Quincy Adams; today it is called the Virgin River, after Smith's companion, Thomas Virgin. Correctly guessing that it flowed into the Sevier, Jedediah followed it for a few miles. Searching without success for game, he was amazed to find remnants of Indian corn "hills," which had been planted several years earlier in "this lonely country." Two days later, while riding in search of a suitable campsite on the Santa Clara River (he named it "Corn Creek"), Jedediah spotted an Indian and hailed him. The man brandished his bow and arrows in an apparent gesture of defiance and Smith prudently retreated.

Later that day, while setting up camp, Smith's men detected more than a dozen Indians "skulking around among the rocks." Jedediah quickly got his men "prepared for the worst," then walked out alone to invite the Indians—they were Southern Paiutes—into camp. One trembling Indian ventured into the white men's encampment, holding in his outstretched hand a rabbit that betokened friendship. Accepting the gift, Jedediah spoke kindly to the Indian to signify his peaceful intentions. A few minutes later several other Paiutes cautiously approached, each bearing an ear of corn as "an emblem of peace."

Smith commenced swapping some goods for corn and pumpkins to feed his hungry men. He found the Indians most eager to trade for bits of iron that they used to fashion knives and arrow points. As the pile of Paiute farm produce grew larger, the starving mountain men's flagging spirits lifted. Recalling his own past experiences, Smith noted, "[I]ndifferent as this may seem to him who never made his pillow of the sand of the plain or him who would consider it a hardship to go without his dinner[,] yet to us weary and hungry in the solitary desert it was a feast." Indeed, the prospect of abundant food "made [his] party in their sudden hilarity and Glee present a lively contrast to the moody desponding silence of the night before." During the ensuing few days, while his party and their livestock recuperated, Smith traded for more food. He also dispatched two men to scout down the river and two more on the back trail to retrieve a pair of fagged-out horses that had been left behind. The Virgin River supported few beaver, so trapping operations were again suspended.

Smith's innate curiosity impelled him to spend some time visiting nearby Indian lodges. Paiute farmers planted corn and pumpkin hills along the narrow bands of arable bottomland that were refreshed every spring when the river flooded and deposited rich silt and organic matter. They cooked and stored their food in well-fired earthenware, and they also grew some tobacco. Unlike the mountain tribes with whom Smith was more familiar, the Paiutes refrained from passing pipes around when they smoked; instead, "each man smokes for himself." Jedediah exchanged a few items for a "fine clouded marble" Paiute pipe that he later gave to William Clark at Saint Louis. He remarked that some of the Paiute men sported "the scalp of an antelope or a Mt sheep with the ears on for a hat," and he described two plants unknown to him, manzanita and some type of cactus.

Smith was not the sort of man who simply moved through landscape with nothing in mind but arriving at his destination. He was constantly observing, ceaselessly taking the measure of everything around him. Smith's comments on the Paiutes were later corroborated by Lt. Amiel Weeks Whipple, an army surveyor who mapped a potential southern transcontinental railroad route in the mid-1850s.

On the next day the brigade moved down the river, which wended its tortuous way "among the rocks and ravines." Taking to higher ground to survey his surroundings, Smith found himself at the lip of a deep canyon. His party descended the precipitous slope to reach water. In fading daylight Smith made camp at a place where there was no grass for the horses. Luckily, Jedediah and another man each shot a mountain sheep, which "relished verry well with men who had been for several days deprived of their accustomed rations of meat." The mountain men ordinarily consumed several pounds of meat per day and considered doing without it a disagreeable hardship, even when other food was at hand.

After breaking camp the next morning, the men followed the stream another dozen miles through a narrow canyon whose towering walls were lost in the glare three or four hundred feet above them. Jedediah noted "a good many" hot springs along the Virgin and found what he believed was evidence of iron deposits, but he saw little sign of Indians. Emerging from the shadowy chasm into a land less broken but still "extremely barren," the party discovered a stream falling into the Virgin from the west, bordered by some large cottonwood trees. Known as

Beaver Dam Wash today, Smith called it "Pauch Creek." During his second crossing of the desert in 1827, Smith would choose it as an alternative to the arduous and time-consuming Virgin River canyon passage.

Four days' uninterrupted travel brought the party to another Paiute settlement, where they traded for more vegetables and established their camp. Smith again employed sign language to make inquiries about the country ahead and whether it contained beaver. The Indians indicated that many beavers lived beside a large river at some distance, but Jedediah grew suspicious, remarking, "[I]t is a general characteristic of indians to answer your question in the manner they think will please you but without any regard for the truth." The Paiutes certainly knew about beavers, for some of them sported beaver-skin moccasins. The Indians' responses to Smith's queries probably reflected a desire to be rid of potentially troublesome strangers whose motives for being among them were unclear. Still, the Paiutes remained guardedly friendly and offered Smith information about a nearby salt cave that he planned to visit.

Of more immediate interest was the presence of two men from the Mohave nation, the first Smith had met. The Mohaves confirmed the Paiutes' story that one more day's travel would bring Smith to a large river where beaver abounded and where the Indians possessed horses. Noticing that the two men adorned themselves with bits of blue yarn and possessed some iron utensils, Smith "judged they had some intercourse with the Spanish provinces." This inference came at a critical moment in Jedediah Smith's journey, for he had evidently been giving some thought to the notion of retreating to more familiar country. Instead, he wrote, "I engaged these Indians as guides for I might as well go on as undertake to return."

The belief that he might be nearing the "Spanish provinces" undoubtedly figured in Smith's calculations, though in fact he and his party had been in Mexican territory ever since they left Bear River. Several horses had already given out on the grueling journey, and others were in such poor condition that they could barely carry a load. If the Mohaves told the truth, Jedediah thought, it might be feasible to keep his men busy trapping all winter in "this moderate Climate" and thus provide him ample time to purchase new mounts. "These considerations," Smith wrote, "induced me to abandon the idea of returning to the mountains until I should have gone somewhat further in exploring the secrets of this thus far unpromising country." Perhaps, too, Smith was doggedly determined to reap some benefits from this grinding trip, and simply refused to concede the possibility that his efforts might not pan out.

After people and horses rested for two days, Smith's small brigade again took to the trail, accompanied by their new Mohave guides. During the day's march Smith called a temporary halt. While his companions rested, he clambered up a steep slope overlooking the west bank of the Virgin River to visit the salt cave that Paiutes and Mohaves frequented. With a small axe he chopped out some samples of the crystalline mineral. Along with the Paiute pipe he collected, Smith eventually gave the salt specimen to William Clark to put in his "museum" at Saint Louis. Continuing a few more miles beyond the salt cave, which Smith called "Adams Cave," the footsore party encamped. (In 1936 Adams Cave, like much of the path Smith followed that week, would be inundated when Hoover Dam arrested the flow of the Colorado River and flooded the Virgin River's Boulder Canyon, creating the gigantic Lake Mead.)

Around October 4, after a fifteen-mile march, Smith found the big river of which his guides had foretold. About two hundred yards wide with a "deep and strong current," this "could be no other but the Colorado of the west," as Jedediah put it. He correctly surmised that it was the same river whose northern branch the mountain men called by its Crow name, Seeds-kee-dee-Agie, also known as the Green. When the guides indicated that it was necessary to cross the river at this place, Jedediah and his men hastily constructed a driftwood raft. After loading packs of goods and gear on the raft, some of the men poled it across while others swam the horses to the far shore. Upon landing, Smith traded some pumpkins, squashes, and beans from a Paiute family that dwelled at the crossing site.

This circa-1855 image shows an idealized view of the southwestern rivers that Smith passed on his way to California in 1826 and 1827. The Bill Williams Fork enters the Colorado River about fifty miles south of present-day Needles, California. "Valley of Bill William's [*sic*] Fork," chromolithograph from Pacific Rail Road Surveys, vol. 3. Author's collection.

Smith's Indian guides told him of a better ford downstream, later called the Mohave Crossing. Beyond this, the river entered an impassibly rough and fractured country. Smith learned he must journey overland for better than a day before he encountered the next water source. Even this late in the autumn, the noontime desert temperatures could reach distressing heights, so the trappers spent the daylight hours resting in camp, then headed out as dusk deepened. Traveling at a brisk pace until about midnight, the men unpacked and hobbled their horses and the party caught a few hours of sleep.

Another hard, dry-throated day's journey brought them to water, but once again the campsite lacked grazing for the horses. When day broke, Smith discovered that his guides had vanished, but their footprints in the sand pointed toward a

narrow, rock-strewn ravine. Smith went ahead alone to reconnoiter, fearful that horses might be unable to negotiate the
stony descent. Finding that they had no choice but to forge
ahead, Smith returned to camp and ordered the march to continue until approaching darkness checked further movement
and the exhausted brigade made camp. By morning their situation seemed dangerously bleak. One trapper had become "so
lame that he could not walk," but with a yawning canyon
obstructing their path, the party was obliged once more to proceed overland in order to regain the river. When the fatigued
party at length reached the Colorado, they rested for two days,
trading for more Indian crops and catching fish with some
lines and hooks they had packed with their gear.

By this point many of the horses were too far gone to carry
anything. Fortunately, however, the travelers began to
encounter numerous Mohaves, and Smith hired some to help
lug his bundles of goods to their village. He called them "A-muc-
ha-bas," noting that they "appeared quite friendly" and proved
willing to trade food for "Beeds Rings vermillion &c." But they
refused to part with any of the few horses they possessed, so
Jedediah gave his brigade another two-day rest while he sorted
out their prospects. Some of the Mohaves spoke a smattering of
Spanish and so did one of Smith's men, probably Abraham
Laplant. As a result, Smith learned that much larger Mohave settlements lay about thirty miles down stream, and he decided to
make for them.

Every time that Jedediah met with Indians in the Mohave Valley, they treated him hospitably and offered him melons and
roasted pumpkins "in great abundance." Smith considered the
Mohaves a "tall and well formed" people, noting that they "did
not appear much inclined to steal but are quite fond of gambling." Their homeland consisted of many clusters of lodges scattered along a thirty-mile stretch of the Colorado, which was
thereabouts a wide and deep river edged with broad ribbons of
bottomland densely cloaked with cottonwood and mesquite
trees. Bounded by "a chain of Rocky hills" that ran parallel to the
river at a distance of about ten miles, the valley itself was lush and

This 1850s-era artist's rendering of Mohave Indians was made about thirty years after Smith encountered them. "Mohave Indians," chromolithograph from Pacific Rail Road Surveys, vol. 3. Author's collection.

green, but the land beyond the river bottom presented an inhospitable wasteland of prickly pears and desert shrubs.

Smith observed that Mohave men and women wore no hats, leggings, or moccasins, and that the women wore nothing but a "peticoat made of a material like flax." He was surprised to find men working alongside women in the fields, "which is quite an unusual sight among Indians." He noted that few of the men possessed bows and arrows, and he penned brief descriptions of the Mohaves' housing, hairstyles, food preparation, and cooking gear. Jedediah also noticed that some of the men sported brightly colored woolen serapes, indicating that perhaps the Mohave land lay relatively close to the "Spanish" settlements.

Finding beaver still too scarce to justify trapping, Smith rested his men and horses for a few more days while he gleaned further information from the Mohaves as to possible routes. They described a desolate and uninhabited land to the south but told

Mohave Indians are here seen on the shore of the Colorado River at
the Mohave Crossing. "Rio Colorado Near the Mohave Villages,
View No. 3," chromolithograph from Pacific Rail Road Surveys, vol.
3. Author's collection.

Smith that about ten days' travel westward would bring him to
the "spanish settlements in California." With this destination in
mind, Jedediah managed to trade his poorest horses for a few
healthier Mohave horses, but despite his offer of more trade
goods, the Indians refused to part with any others.

One morning in mid-October, Smith learned that some
Mohaves had killed one of his horses and were preparing to feast
on its flesh. Though he must have been irritated, Jedediah took
no action and no trouble ensued. Perhaps the Mohaves had simply exacted a sort of toll from Smith for crossing their land, or
maybe the horse killing portended worse things to come. In any
event, more than a week's sojourn among the Mohaves persuaded Smith that it was time to move on, so he "determined to
prepare myself as well as possible and push forward to California where I supposed I might procure such supplies as would
enable me to move on north."

Jedediah continued to hope that he would discover good stocks of beaver farther west, as well as "some considerable river heading up in the vicinity of the Great Salt Lake." Finding that river would be a great coup, and it might also enable him to return to the next summer's rendezvous on schedule. Smith's expectation of locating a river in California that he could follow upstream to the big lake reflects the persistence of the Rio Buenaventura in the geography of imagination. His journey would help unravel that conceit and replace it with more reliable information.

Smith attempted to hire a Mohave guide, but not one of them volunteered to take the job, so he settled for a general description of the path ahead. On the day of departure the trappers again lashed together a driftwood raft, loaded it, and crossed with their goods and horses. Steering a westward course through the heart of the Mohave Desert, they marched about fifteen miles before making camp. During the night, some Mohaves managed to steal the "most valuable" horse right from under the eyes of Jedediah's guards.

With two horses lost in short order, Smith must have been torn between conflicting urges to take vengeance for the thefts and to get away as fast as possible. Despite his mounting anger and suspicion, Smith chose not to confront the Mohaves. The next day found his brigade scrambling through a labyrinthine landscape, fissured by "high hills and deep ravines in every direction" and totally lacking water. In frustrated consternation Jedediah wrote, "the Idea came forcibly to my mind that it was the policy of the Indians to send me into the desert to perish."

Passing to the west of the Paiute Range the trappers became disoriented in the splintered and arid terrain of southeastern California, about twenty miles from the Nevada border. Galled by the apparent impossibility of forward movement, Smith resolved to retrace his path to the Colorado. While backtracking, he surprised two Indians picking their way along his trail. Fearing they were up to no good, Smith forcibly detained one of them and returned to the previous evening's campsite. Somehow the captive made off during the night and Jedediah grew even more concerned for his party's safety. Worry coalesced into genuine alarm when the trappers entered a Mohave village only to find it hastily abandoned, a sure sign that the escapee had already been there and warned off the residents.

Fearing the time had again come to "prepare for the worst," Smith ordered his men to take defensive measures. The trappers quickly excavated a rude breastwork along the sloping riverbank and secured their horses in a makeshift pen. Just about then the "little renegade Francisco," Smith's Spanish-speaking Mohave Indian guide, who had run off, hailed the Americans from the opposite riverbank. Smith calmly persuaded Francisco to come across and talk things over. The Mohave informed him that his tribesmen fled out of fear that the trappers had come back to murder them for stealing the horse. Jedediah assured Francisco that he was mistaken; the white men meant to do no killing. "It was true," Jedediah wrote, "I must have my horse but I would not think of punishing the whole of them for the fault of the single scoundrel that stole him."

After the brief council, Francisco departed. A while later the Mohaves drifted back to their village, and some of their leaders promised Smith they would attempt to find his stolen horse. Somewhat relieved, Smith's party recrossed the Colorado and moved downstream about ten miles to camp for a few days at a place where abundant grass would help restore his emaciated mounts. As the end of October approached, Smith was still in the heart of the Mohave country, and still in a quandary over how to proceed.

With his expedition temporarily stalled, Jedediah Smith continued to trade for provisions and again tried to hire a guide. In addition, he improved his time by learning more about the Mohaves. He correctly guessed that they maintained only a rudimentary political organization, for he could not identify "any verry influential chiefs" who spoke for the tribe at large. He noted that Mohave women played a substantial role in village politics, unlike women among the mountain Indians with whom he was better acquainted. Indeed, he wrote, "No Indians I have seen pay so much deference to the women as these,"

This 1850s-era chromolithograph shows a gathering of Mohave
Indians in the vicinity of the Mohave Crossing, where Smith lost
most of his party in 1827. "Camp Scene in the Mohave Valley of
Rio Colorado," chromolithograph from Pacific Rail Road Surveys,
vol. 3. Author's collection.

adding that in their councils the Mohave women "harangue the
Multitude the same as the men."

Some Mohaves requested that Smith attend to a gravely ill
man. As Jedediah put it, the Mohaves seemed to believe that "a
white man could do anything." But by the time he arrived at the
patient's lodge, where more than three hundred Indians were
gathered, the man was already dead. Jedediah then stood by as
several women — presumably wives or relatives — wailed over the
corpse before they placed it atop a pile of wood and burned it,
along with some mortuary offerings. Smith was doubtless one
of the first white men to witness a Mohave cremation ceremony.

Circumstances soon seemed to take a turn for the better. Jedediah managed to hire two guides from "the vicinity of the Spanish settlements," who happened to be runaway mission Indians
from California. And true to their word, the Mohaves located

and returned Smith's horse. With this matter amicably settled, Smith's brigade left the Colorado River and rode away from the Mohave towns in early November, steering westward across the desert in the vicinity of present-day Needles, California.

The Mohave Desert crossing consumed six days of miserably difficult traveling, and the better part of two weeks passed before Smith and his companions reached signs of "civilization" in southern California. Two days were wasted backtracking through "a dry rocky sandy Barren desert" that led nowhere. Then Smith's party passed through a glaring fifteen-mile-wide "salt plain," where a layer of crystallized salt almost one inch thick covered the ground. Horse hooves broke the crust and threw off chunks of the mineral. Picking up a sample, Jedediah brushed the sand from it and pronounced it to be "pure white with a grain as fine as table salt." Beyond the salt plain, Smith's guides found an Indian camp-site featuring holes in the ground filled with briny water. The trappers dug new holes about two feet deep that yielded less salty water for the thirsty men and livestock. Smith's route here paralleled the path of Father Francisco Garcés, who noted some of the same landmarks during his 1770 expedition. Every fifteen to twenty miles Smith's guides led him to little hidden springs. Some were almost too briny to drink, while others were found in what appeared to be dried up riverbeds.

By the sixth day their food supply was nearly depleted, though Smith was sure he had packed enough for at least a ten-day trip. "But," wrote Jedediah, "men accustomed to living on meat and at the same time travelling hard will Eat a surprising quantity of corn and Beans, which constituted our principal subsistence." Luckily, two of his guides were members of the Vanyume tribe, whose people made a habit of burying food supplies in case of trail emergencies. Leading one of Smith's trappers to a cache, they retrieved what looked to Jedediah like "loaves of bread weighing each 8 or 10 pounds." The "loaves" turned out to be a crude form of Vanyume sugar, produced from a type of cane that flourished in the desert. Once again help from Indians kept Smith's party from foundering on the trail.

Three days later Harrison Rogers managed to kill an antelope, welcome fare even if it tasted "quite strong of wormwood." By this time their only remaining Mohave guide had quietly disappeared, but the Vanyumes continued on, knowing that in a few days they would rejoin their families at one of the campsites beside what Jedediah named the "Inconstant River," today's Mohave River. Smith wrote that the channel they followed for several days flowed in "a strong current in places 20 y[ar]ds in width and in others entirely disappeared in the sands."

In mid-November the party arrived at a small Vanyume camp of several lodges. The Indians received the Americans in a kindly manner, offering them acorn and piñon nut mush mixed with some berries. Later they treated the newcomers to a feast of rabbits that they caught by driving the creatures into a long net. Rogers and Smith went hunting and shot two antelopes to add to the feast. The next morning Jedediah distributed a few gifts and the trappers resumed their journey.

Following the path taken by Father Garcés fifty years earlier, Smith descended the West Fork of the Mohave to Summit Valley along an Indian trace that would bring him through the San Bernardino Mountains. The country was definitely changing, and it looked considerably less menacing. Even the air had a fresher feeling to it when the Americans reached the margins of the San Bernardino Valley, a lush place interspersed with gurgling streams, verdant stretches of nutritious grasses, and to the mountaineers' joy, plentiful signs of antelope, bear, and deer.

Around November 20 the trappers walked down a rocky creek bed for roughly ten miles and at last left the mountains behind. In delightful contrast to the grueling desert march on short rations, they discovered "sure evidences of Civilization," including plentiful tracks of horses and domestic cattle. A while later they came upon "fine herds of Cattle in many directions," a sight, wrote Smith:

> that awakened many emotions in my mind and some of them not the most pleasant. It would perhaps be supposed that after

numerous hardships endured in a savage and inhospitable desert that I should hail the herds that were passing before me in the valley as harbingers of better times. But they reminded me that I was approaching a country inhabited by Spaniards. A people whose distinguishing characteristic has ever been jealousy[,] a people of different religion from mine and possessing a full share of the bigotry and disregard of the rights of a Protestant that has at times stained the Catholic Religion.

This passage indicates that Jedediah Smith possessed a passing familiarity with history and was by no means immune to religious prejudice. He would soon test his perceptions and attitudes against a challenging reality, for he was now truly a stranger in a strange land. Mexican California, the land of the Spanish missions, was like nothing he had ever seen, and to his credit, Jedediah managed to adjust to the novel situation in which he found himself.

By November 25 Jedediah's weary men and women had descended the western foothills of the San Bernardino Mountains into a well-watered, "fertile valley extending many miles." The brigade's food supply was completely exhausted, and the Vanyume guides informed Smith that they were still two days from an outlier post of the Misión San Gabriel Arcángel. Smith's famished party soon found themselves threading their way among thousands of well-fed, wandering cattle. The temptation was too much, and Jedediah killed one, though he immediately discovered that hunting half-wild cows required "all the precaution necessary in approaching Buffalo." Finding a brand on the dead cow, Smith stripped off its hide, intending to locate its owner and pay for the animal. Stuffing themselves on fine fresh-broiled meat, the trappers and the Indians lolled contentedly about camp for a day while Smith contemplated his next move.

Jedediah's mind raced as he pondered the disturbing likelihood that the Mexicans "might perhaps consider me a spy[,] imprison me[,] persecute me for the sake of religion[,] or detain me in prison to the ruin of my business." He decided it would be best to "make it appear" to them that dire necessity had forced him to seek relief in California. Then he must convince the provincial authorities that his sole desire was to procure some supplies and quickly depart. With an explanation roughed out, Jedediah and his trappers continued on. Two days later they reached the welcome sight of a "farm house." The lush green land through which they now roamed offered a striking contrast to the "Rocky and Sandy deserts" where they nearly perished several times. Indeed, Smith wrote, the new land "seemed to us [a place of] enchantment," what with its many streams, fine broad savannahs, dense clouds of waterfowl wheeling overhead, and innumerable horses, cattle, and sheep that "rushed wildly across our way."

Every step brought the party closer to "comparative civilization." To Smith this seemed "a pleasure not however entirely unmixed with dred," for he had no idea of how he might be received. The haggard wanderers approached another, larger farmstead, and its mission Indian laborers gaped in silence as the weird procession passed by. Little wonder, thought Smith, that the Indians did not simply take to their heels at the sight of his "ragged and miserable" men, shambling along beside skeletal horses that staggered under loads of "Furs Traps Saddlebags Guns and Blankets."

At last they halted before a pair of rambling adobe-walled farmhouses. An elderly Indian stepped out and politely welcomed them in the Spanish language. Noting their obviously wretched condition, the man instantly offered them a cow. Two Indians leapt on horses and galloped off to fetch a "Bullock." In this country, wrote Smith, it was customary to keep horses "constantly tied at the door Saddled and Bridled and of course ready to mount at a moments warning." He later admiringly credited the Californians as "excellent horsemen," remarking that they were "seldom seen on foot but mount a horse to go even 200 yards."

In true *californio* style, the riders galloped back with the cow in tow, one end of their rawhide *riatas* looped around its horns and the other secured to the high pommel of each man's Spanish-style saddle. At their invitation Jedediah shot the cow and his men butchered it. Apparently, Smith had never seen a *riata*—he called it a "larse"—for he later penned a lengthy passage explaining how Mexican horsemen skillfully threw them to catch cows, horses, and even grizzly bears. They were "made from pieces of strong Ox hide braided . . . 7 or 8 fathoms in Length." Undoubtedly recalling his own frightful encounter, Smith expressed doubt that Mexicans actually lassoed grizzly bears, but the stories were true.

The hospitable old man worked as an overseer at one of the mission's many satellite farms and ranches. He evidently mistook Smith and his sun-bronzed companions for members of some unknown nation of light-skinned Indians, "having no idea that civilized people lived in the direction from which we came." Moreover, these strangers' excellent guns and other exotic items defined them as odd indeed. When Abraham Laplant initiated a halting conversation in Spanish, the old man concluded that at least one of them qualified as *gente de razón* ("rational people"), a culturally loaded term long employed to differentiate Spaniards from Indians. The overseer suggested that Smith, who admitted he was "in the dark as to the manner in which I should conduct myself," ought to apprise the resident priest of his arrival. Smith took this cue to pen a concise missive to the Franciscan Father José Bernardo Sánchez, who only recently had been named director of the sprawling Misión San Gabriel Arcángel.

A mission Indian dashed away on horseback to deliver Smith's note to Sánchez, and within an hour a Mexican army corporal rode up with the priest's reply in hand. Slipping from his saddle, the soldier proffered Smith a handful of "Segars" and congratulations that his party had "escaped the Gentiles and got into a christian country." Sánchez's letter, composed in Latin, proved entirely incomprehensible to Smith, who wrote, perhaps with a rare glimmer of humor, "[I]t seemed that we were not likely to become general correspondents." With Laplant's help, Smith was made to understand that Sánchez meant for him to report to the mission headquarters.

On November 27, after placing Harrison Rogers in charge of the trappers, Smith and Laplant mounted borrowed horses and set off for the mission, accompanied by the corporal and another soldier. They arrived at "a Building of ancient and Castle-like appearance" all too soon, for Jedediah was still at a loss as to how best to explain himself to the priest who greeted him. After dismounting, he fidgeted nervously for a few moments, but the priest gently took him by the arm and steered him through the old mission's pleasantly cool halls and into a quiet reception room. Father Sánchez ordered Smith some bread and cheese and a tumbler of rum, which Jedediah sipped "to please the Father but much against my own taste." Though he was not exactly a teetotaler, Smith was never fond of ardent spirits.

Jedediah's awkward attempt to convey an explanation for his sudden appearance proved less than satisfactory, so Sánchez suggested that they send for an American who lived nearby and spoke fluent Spanish. This American, a fellow named Joseph Chapman, had a checkered career—including a brief stint as a pirate—that had landed him at Monterey in 1818. By 1821 Chapman operated a gristmill for the mission, and since he possessed other useful skills, he had become a valued member of the mission community. While awaiting Chapman's arrival, Father Sánchez found temporary quarters for Smith in one of the mission's many rooms. Two hours later the supper bell clanged and a young Indian lad conducted Jedediah to a dining room, where the priest gestured that Smith and Laplant should take seats next to him. Also present were a former *alcalde* (mayor) of Los Angeles named Francisco Ávila, an anonymous mission steward, and another Franciscan who presided over the Pueblo de los Angeles Church, about ten miles distant. After a few prayers, dinner was served, consisting mainly of various meats and "an abundance of wine," followed by a general distribution of cigars. Smith felt ill at ease among the diners, noting it had been "a long time sinc[e] I had had the pleasure of sitting at a table and never before in such company."

The next day the remainder of the scruffy Americans showed up at San Gabriel with their gear, and Jedediah stowed his belongings in his room. Among them was a pistol that he had lost on the trail shortly before reaching the mission and that he asked Harrison Rogers to retrieve. When Rogers and Smith attended a late dinner that night, Rogers noted appreciatively that he was introduced to the two priests "over a glass of good old whiskey." Afterwards the corporal who commanded San Gabriel's tiny presidial garrison went about collecting all the trappers' guns. The reason, he explained, was to protect their weapons from careless handling by overcurious residents. Most of Smith's Americans probably carried fine flintlock rifles that differed in appearance and quality from the rusty smoothbore *escopetas* commonly used in early California, with their outsized Spanish-style lock plates and exposed mainsprings. But the corporal's excuse failed to satisfy Smith, who suspected the weapons confiscation was "influenced by a motive verry different from the one assigned."

Despite a dawning realization that he had been placed under house arrest, Smith spent the following day wandering about the mission complex. He must have gazed in appreciative wonder at the expansive fenced and irrigated fields that produced wheat, peas, beans and corn, and at the extensive vineyard. The mission also boasted apple, peach, pear, olive, and fig orchards, and an orange grove of some four hundred trees. Several thousand acres of rich grassland supported huge cattle and horse herds. Rogers estimated the mission's cattle herds at more than thirty thousand head, with "Horses sheep Hogs &c in proportion." The high walls of the massive, adobe-built, crenellated mission church with its imposing bell tower and numerous ancillary structures likewise presented an impressive castle-like sight. Smith toured the church and its adjacent presidial guardhouse, as well as storerooms, Indian quarters, a soap factory, shops for blacksmithing, carpentry, and barrel making, and a weaving shop, where Indian women loomed fine brightly colored woolen blankets.

Jedediah Smith and fifteen men and two women had completed the terrible desert crossing. Over a roughly thirteen-hundred-mile march they had experienced no violent clashes with Indians, they lost nothing but some livestock, and all of them made it safely from Bear Lake to California. Smith and his

This circa-1828 sketch of the Misión San Gabriel Arcángel, by American trader Alfred Robinson, was made about one year after Smith was detained for the second time in California. "View of the Mission of St. Gabriel." Courtesy of the Bancroft Library, University of California, Berkeley.

companions had accomplished something that no white men, and probably very few Indians, had ever done before. And yet California was merely a temporary stopping point; Smith was eager to resume his journey in order to reach the 1827 rendezvous at the appointed time. Jedediah Smith was about to find that getting out of California was in some respects even more demanding and frustrating than getting into California had been.

CHAPTER 5

Jedediah Smith and the Californios

MISIÓN San Gabriel Arcángel was one of the richest and most important of California's twenty-one missions. Initiated during the 1770s under the Spanish regime thanks to the tireless efforts of Father Junípero Serra, the Franciscan missions of Alta California were created to draw in and instruct thousands of recently converted Indians, called neophytes. Spain's colonization of the Western Hemisphere had long relied upon a process of gradually converting the "heathen" to Christianity and at the same time commandeering their labor. Less warlike than inhabitants of many regions in New Spain, the Indians of southern California proved relatively easy to subdue. In 1820s California, a few thousand Mexican soldiers, settlers, priests, and government officers retained at least nominal control over a far superior number of Indians.

Established in 1771 as the fourth California mission, San Gabriel Arcángel was relocated after four lackluster years and then entered a florescent era of enormous prosperity. It was severely damaged by an earthquake in 1812, and a lengthy rebuilding project was nearly complete by 1826. During the 1820s roughly one thousand Indian laborers resided in and around the vast mission complex, working on farms and ranches, in winery and distillery operations, or in one of the many craft shops. Among the missions, San Gabriel ranked first in farm produce and second in livestock holdings.

For five decades the California missions enjoyed material abundance and robust state support, but their fabled tranquility would be plunged into disorder a few years after Mexico won independence in 1821. Jedediah Smith's visit to one of the greatest missions occurred during the twilight of its glory years. Indeed, the wheels of wrenching change were already in motion. Governor José María Echeandía, with whom Smith would be obliged to deal at length, had come to Alta California only recently, late in 1825. Echeandía arrived bearing orders from the Mexican government to secularize the missions, place the priests under stricter state control, and initiate a program of land distribution to the mission Indians.

Such a policy was bound to engender discord among government officers, civilian settlers, and priests whose comfortable lifestyle (some labeled it decadent and luxurious) depended almost totally on labor exacted from legions of neophytes. As it turned out, continual political and fiscal chaos in Mexico and ecclesiastical resistance to the secularization program in California hamstrung effective implementation of the new policy well into the 1830s. The California missions continued to dominate the lives of thousands of Indians until shortly before the Mexican-American War broke out in 1846 and the U.S. Army captured the province.

Even at the time of Smith's detention, priests found it no easy matter to keep the missionized Indians under their "mild control." Runaways had long posed a continual, if low-intensity, threat to the Mexican priests' ability to maintain a viable labor force. Many mission Indians fled to California's Central Valley, seeking refuge among the "wild" interior tribes, and neither priests nor soldiers ever developed the wherewithal to curtail this nagging problem. The secularization program was eventually implemented, but the outlook for California Indians remained grim. By the early 1840s most of the missions' lands had fallen into the hands of non-Indians. This was mainly because widespread, systemic political and economic corruption resulted in large blocks of land being granted to well-connected civilians, while many individual Indians' land allotments were seized at the instance of the secular creditors who had driven them into debt.

The mythic "golden age" of the californios, whose ranchero lives were supposedly languid, gay, and peaceful—a fantasy

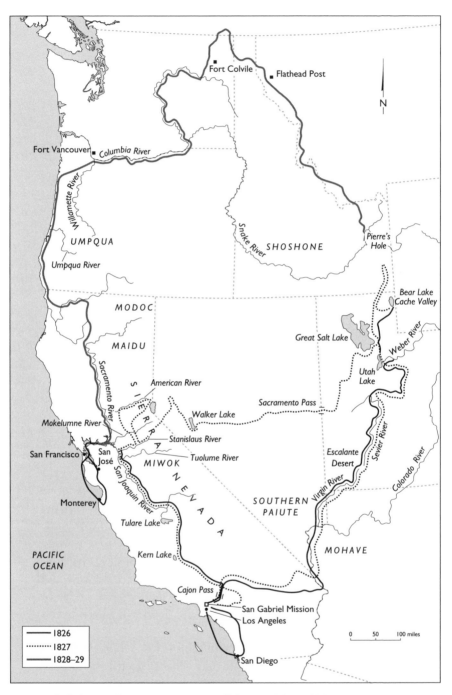

Jedediah Smith's West Coast expeditions, 1826–1829

faithfully recreated by latter day Los Angelenos in numerous "historical" pageants—was in reality a dreadful and devastating experience for the southern California Indians. Many more of them died than were born each year under the missionary priests' administration. Indians who misbehaved or rebelled faced severe whippings and other punishments. Franciscan priests aimed to eradicate aboriginal languages and customs, supplanting them with a simplistic version of Catholicism that somehow, they hoped, would "civilize" Indians. Even as the hide and tallow trade boosted California's economy in the 1820s and 1830s, life for the mission Indians did not improve. Ironically, bad as all this was for California Indians, their plight worsened after the United States seized California and the gold rush began.

Jedediah Smith commented on some of these issues as he learned about the missions. Of the California Indians he noted, "[T]he fact is certain that verry few have availed themselves of the privilege of the [Mexican] revolution," ignoring the fact that practically no Indians in the United States benefited from the American Revolutionary War, either. Father Sánchez informed him that "but few white men" dwelled in the vicinity, and "no white women had ever come there to live." Smith observed that the neophytes were "kept in the strictest order[,] being punished severly for the most trifling offence or neglect," adding they were often "whipped like slaves."

On their second day at the mission, Smith and Rogers's midday meal consisted of "Mutton Beef Chickens Potatoes Beans and Peas," along with "a glass of Gin and some bread and cheese." "Wine in abundance," Smith added, "made our reverend fathers appear to me quite merry." The next day was Sunday, but neither Smith nor Rogers attended mass, fearing that their Protestantism "might not be agreeable to the Catholics." Later that day they were invited to a wedding ceremony. Ashamed to appear in their greasy, worn-out buckskin clothing, they tried to demur, but their gracious hosts would accept "no excuses." (At about this time Rogers possessed nothing but "a leather hunting shirt, Blankett Pantaloons two shirts, p[ai]r of socks, shoes and red cap.") After dinner and a musical performance provided by

A Russian artist, name unknown, made this sketch circa 1816 of
mission Indians playing a popular gambling game. Mission priests
disliked such practices, as well as many other Indian traditions. "Jeu
des habitans de Californie," or "Game of the Natives of California."
Courtesy of the Bancroft Library, University of California, Berkeley.

about a dozen violin-playing Indians, Smith asked the corporal
if an additional room might be found to ease the overcrowding
in his men's quarters. The corporal acceded to Smith's request,
and then Jedediah asked permission for his men to prepare food
for themselves instead of having their "provision ready cooked."
No doubt the spicy Mexican dishes—Smith described one meal
as a "hash highly seasoned with peper"—wreaked intestinal
havoc with Americans who were unaccustomed to such fare.
This, too, was allowed.

    At about this time Smith and Rogers drafted a map of their
travels and presented it to the priests. For the next few days the
Americans awaited the arrival of Mr. Chapman. When Chapman
appeared at the mission, he was accompanied by three men. One
was an American named Capt. William Henderson, master of

the brig *Olive Branch*, and another was his clerk, a Scotsman named James Scott who seemed the ablest translator. Also present was one Francisco Martínez; Smith described him as a "Royalist" supporter of Spain's King Ferdinand who had fallen on hard times and come to California, where the Franciscans were reputedly the king's "secret friends." But Governor Echeandía had not yet arrived from San Diego, about 150 miles distant, so nothing could be accomplished. Martínez offered Smith some advice, and it was not encouraging. He warned that the governor had no appreciation for the ways of business, that he would be insensitive to the fact that lost time meant lost money, and that he would likely detain Jedediah for a "long time."

On December 8 the corporal called upon Smith, bearing orders to conduct him to San Diego for an interview with the governor. Fortunately, an American named Captain William H. Cunningham, master of the Boston vessel *Courier*, turned up at an opportune moment. Like the seamen whom Richard Henry Dana immortalized in his classic memoir *Two Years before the Mast* (published in 1840), Cunningham was engaged in the lucrative California hide and tallow trade. For the past six months he had been "exchanging Dry goods[,] Groceries and hardware for hide and Specie" in San Diego, and while there he learned of Smith's plight. He spoke excellent Spanish, was well connected, and "manifested the most friendly disposition and a willingness to render [Smith] all the assistance in his power." When Jedediah departed the next day to visit the governor, the captain was by his side. With Smith and Cunningham rode the interpreter Laplant and a presidial soldier to guide them—and to keep a close watch on Smith. They also took a *remuda* of spare horses.

While en route they wended their way through vast cattle herds belonging to the Pueblo de Los Angeles, and "some thousands of wild horses." So plentiful were horses, the corporal informed Smith, that residents sometimes rounded up surplus stock, enclosed them in large pens, and after culling the best among them, left the remainder to starve to death. Expressing his "pity for the noblest of animals dying from want in the midst of fertile fields," Jedediah considered the practice "disgraceful."

After riding twenty-five miles, the party pulled up at a ranch belonging to Don Tomás Yorba, where they dined on spicy Mexican food accompanied by "Tortios" and wine. Before the meal a small boy offered a heartfelt prayer that Smith thought more devout than those he heard back at San Gabriel. "Some of the learned fathers," Jedediah quipped, "might learn the air of devotion if not the substance from this little boy." Later that evening Don Tomás arrived and offered them accommodations. Instead of staying the night, the travelers borrowed fresh horses and departed. Seven hours later they reached Misión San Juan Capistrano, about twenty-five miles away. Situated only one mile from the coast, this mission was less impressive than San Gabriel and housed fewer Indians. The mission steward prepared hot chocolate (a favorite beverage among *hispanos*) for his visitors, but also offered the Americans some tea. Smith preferred coffee, noting that the Mexican mistakenly believed that "we are verry fond" of tea. He also found it odd that his host ground tea in a coffee mill, which suggested that "they do not make much use of it."

Saddling fresh mounts selected from the mission's herds, the party proceeded to the coast, turned south at a decrepit farmstead, and rode several more miles to Misión San Luis Rey, where they spent the night. Smith thought the recently whitewashed mission church looked even more handsome than San Gabriel. Departing on the morning of December 11, they rode through hilly country for about thirty miles and by evening reached the presidio at San Diego. Jedediah learned that he would meet the governor on the following morning, and he was permitted the "Liberty to choose" a place to spend the night. An American whom he had just met, Capt. William Dana of the ship *Liberty* (also from Boston), immediately invited Smith to stay with him. A good many Americans came and went through the port of San Diego, and they would prove to be some of Smith's most useful allies in the frustrating weeks ahead.

In Jedediah's opinion, San Diego presented a dilapidated appearance, with its buildings "somewhat like the Missions but lower and much decayed." Still, there was something lovely about its sweeping view of the deep harbor bounded by twin peninsulas and the blue ocean that stretched to the western horizon. San Diego's civilian populace numbered about two hundred souls, though the nearby mission Indians added considerably to the local population and its economy.

While Jedediah uneasily awaited his audience with Governor Echeandía, he reviewed the papers that chronicled his expedition's progress so far. Not only did Smith keep a journal, he evidently drafted several maps along the route as well. Around December 12 Smith had his first interview with the governor. After concisely summarizing his travels and tribulations, Jedediah mentioned that he required supplies in order to continue his journey. Echeandía made an indefinite response and informed Smith that "some days" would pass before he could convene a meeting with other officials to review the case. The governor offered Smith some new clothing to replace his tattered buckskin hunting shirt and a place to stay, but Jedediah preferred to accept Captain Cunningham's invitation to lodge aboard the vessel *Courier,* anchored in the harbor about three miles from the governor's presidial residence. In the meantime, Smith penned a letter to his clerk at San Gabriel requesting that Rogers forward eight fine beaver skins to San Diego. He hoped to lubricate his dealings with Echeandía by presenting Mexican officers with luxurious furs to use for trimming their cloaks.

Several days later Smith was again summoned to the governor's office. Echeandía brusquely insisted that Jedediah hand over his maps and journal as well as the trade license signed by William Clark. Thus began an anxious time for Smith, who later complained with calculated exaggeration to Joel Poinsett, a U.S. diplomat, that he found himself "detained day after day and week after week." According to Jedediah's interpretation, Echeandía was capricious and dilatory, seemingly incapable of making any decision on his own. Meantime, with his stranded men at San Gabriel eagerly anticipating good news, Jedediah fretted over the "ruinous effect" a prolonged detention might have on his business and the "gloomy apprehensions" of his two partners, who had heard nothing from him for several months.

After perhaps two weeks of intermittent negotiations, Jedediah won the governor's permission to leave, but not by the route he planned to follow. Jedediah wanted to head north toward the Columbia River, claiming he desired to "arrive as soon as possible on the territory of the United States." Rejecting this idea, Governor Echeandía ordered Smith to leave California by the same route he used to enter it. Fortunately, the governor had decided not to send him to Mexico City or somewhere else for adjudication of his case; instead, he offered Jedediah a deal that might get both of them off the hook. In exchange for a certificate of good character and a financial bond signed by the captains of the *Courier,* the *Waverly,* and the *Olive Branch,* Echeandía would issue Smith a passport and a permit to purchase such supplies as he required to make his way out of California. Echeandía also forbade Smith to make any more maps. As for the governor, he doubtless counted himself lucky to be shed of his unwelcome visitor without enmeshing himself further in needless bureaucratic entanglements.

Echeandía evidently refused to loan Smith horses for his return trip to San Gabriel, and by this time Smith already considered the governor an irritating and contrary individual. Smith's friend Captain Cunningham rescued him by offering a berth on the *Courier* from San Diego to San Pedro, the closest port to the mission. Jedediah reached San Gabriel on January 10 to find his men "all well." He received a cordial welcome from Father Sánchez, who offered him whatever assistance the mission could provide. Smith and Rogers set about purchasing sixteen horses at the "Parbalo" (Pueblo) of Los Angeles, some of them from their new friend, Francisco Ávila. A day later Rogers set one of the blacksmiths to work forging a branding iron bearing the initials "JS" to mark the newly purchased stock. When Jedediah departed from San Gabriel a week later, his entourage included forty-eight nearly wild horses.

Harrison Rogers had stayed busy during Smith's absence, and not quite everything had gone well with Smith's men. Rogers fell ill after arriving at the mission but found time to compose letters for some of the illiterate trappers, to be sent back home aboard one of the American vessels anchored in San Diego harbor. On December 1 the priests requested that the American blacksmiths, James Reed and Silas Gobel, be permitted to make them a "Bare Trap." Smith acquiesced, but for some reason that very evening he gave Reed a flogging for "impertinence."

On December 14 the priests asked Rogers to let the blacksmiths make them a second "large trap," this one intended to catch Indians who sneaked into the priests' orange grove to steal fruit. On that day, as on several others, wrote Rogers, "friendship and peace prevail with us and the spanyards." It could be that Rogers had expected that peace would *not* prevail and was surprised that it did. Perhaps this was because, as he told his diary, the trappers were "contintious and quarrelsome amongst themselves and have been ever since we started the Expedition." Riotous behavior and belligerent temperament characterized many mountain men, and some were downright unmanageable as employees. Their forced inactivity while detained at the mission probably helped transform petty disagreements into aggravated assaults.

James Reed, for one, was something of an ill-tempered man. On January 6 Rogers wrote, "Some of the men got drunk." Among the inebriates was "our Blacksmith James Reed," who got into a brawl with Daniel Ferguson. When a couple of Mexican soldiers intervened, more trappers charged in and one of the soldiers struck Arthur Black. Hearing the ruckus outside, Rogers dashed into the yard and ordered his men to desist, noting later in his diary that the melee had come close to "terminating with bad consequences." Later that same day, while Rogers supped with Father Sánchez, the still-drunk Reed reeled in and rudely demanded more liquor. Rogers warned him off, but before leaving the room Reed gulped down some wine from a decanter that stood on the table.

Jedediah Smith and Harrison Rogers were genuinely religious Protestants. Like practically all Americans, both men harbored prejudice toward Catholics, especially Spanish and Mexican Catholics. To be sure, theological hostility had sharply divided

European Catholics and Protestants for hundreds of years and much blood had been spilled in bitter denominational warfare. By the early nineteenth century differences in religious opinion rarely caused war, but they did fuel a cultural antagonism that played an important role in U.S.-Mexico relations. Even more important were the roles played by economic competition and U.S. territorial designs on the Pacific coast. Smith and Rogers found ample opportunities to reexamine, and to some degree modify, their assumptions about "spanyards" during their detention among the Mexican Californians in 1826–27.

Smith and Rogers both found Father Sánchez hospitable, generous, and likeable, but their journal entries sometimes betray less rosy opinions. For instance, while acknowledging that Sánchez "evinc[ed] the most benevolent regard for my welfare," in practically the same breath Smith snidely remarked that some of the mission's overseers, favored "half-breeds" who received a "limited education," might in some instances "with strict propriety apply the name of father" to the priests. If this were true, it would be neither the first nor the last such case for Catholics, or other Christians for that matter. For his part, Rogers accounted Father Sánchez a "very fine man, and very much of a Gentleman," but then remarked in harmony with Smith that the mission fathers treated Indians like "compleat slaves in every sense of the word."

On December 14 Father Sánchez queried Rogers "for the first time" about his religious principles. Rogers frankly declared that he was "brought up under the Calvinist doctrine" and did not believe "it was in the power of man to forgive sins," and then listened as Sánchez explained that "when he was in his church and his robe on … [he] had the power to forgive any sin … openly confessed to him." Rogers later registered his opinion that the priests (and their parishioners) seemed to embrace the "form" rather than the "substance" of faith, and he lamented the fact that the Catholics played cards on the Sabbath. On New Year's Day, Rogers treated Father Sánchez to a religious address on the early history of missionaries, but his diary does not reveal whether he delivered his homily in English or had it translated into Spanish.

Not until January 15 did Rogers enter the mission church, where he viewed several life-size "molten Images" and noted disapprovingly that the church also served as a "sugar Factory." A week earlier he attended a "great Fandango" that lasted all night. Unlike his fellow trappers who often found Hispanic and Indian women charming and alluring, Rogers considered the women at the dance "very unchaste … [and] very vulgar in their conversations, and manners." He must have been near his wit's end when "one came into my lodgings last night and asked me to make here a Blanco Pickaninia, which being interpreted, is to get here a white child—and I must say … I was a shamed, and did not gratify her … seeing here so forward I had no propencity to tech here." Little wonder that he was "very impatient" for Smith's return.

Despite his general reservations about hispanic Catholics, by the time Harrison Rogers left San Gabriel he had developed an abiding affection for Father Sánchez. "Old Father Sanchius," he wrote, "has been the greatest friend that I ever meet with, with all my Travels, he is worthy of being called a christian as he possesses charity in the highest degree…. I ever shall hold him as a man of God." When Smith and Rogers bid farewell to the priest on January 19, Sánchez presented each of them with a fine new blanket and offered Rogers "a cheese and a gourd filled with ogadent," his rendering of "aguadiente," meaning brandy or liquor.

Far less fond were Smith and Rogers's memories of Governor Echeandía. This is mainly attributable to the unfortunate circumstances of the Americans' situation; they were, after all, obviously illegal aliens in California. Indeed, if truth be told, they well merited the suspicions of duly delegated authorities. When the governor examined Jedediah's license, maps, and other papers he wondered why an American hunter would need to draft maps of the country. Smith rather lamely retorted that he made maps only "to assist … in traveling," adding that they must "of necessity be very incorrect as I was destitute of the means for making celestial observations." Not surprisingly, Smith and Rogers grew resentful over what seemed to them Echeandía's dilatory management and disposition of their case.

Becoming more impatient with Echeandía as days turned into weeks, Jedediah complained that his fate "depended upon the caprice of a man who appeared not to be certain of any thing … and [was] only governed by the changing whims of the hour." He lamented that he had been "harrassed by numerous and contradictory expedient and ruinous delays until about the first of January." It is worth recalling, however, that Smith had not turned up at Misión San Gabriel until the last week of November and several more days had elapsed before he first made contact with Governor Echeandía. Smith's "delays" seem less outrageous if one admits the novelty of his appearance and the lack of precedent to offer Mexican officials guidance in such a case. Even after he received his passport and permission to purchase horses and supplies, Smith grumbled that these arrangements "might have been done in a few hours or might as well have been left undone."

Smith and his men and women, including two or three mission Indian guides, rode out of San Gabriel on January 18, but it was a rocky beginning. They made less than a half-mile before most of their refractory horses and mules stampeded, scattering gear and losing a dozen tanned hides (another gift from Father Sánchez) over a ten-mile run. Rounding up delinquent livestock that persisted in running off and trying to break the worst of them to saddles necessitated a week-long delay at Santa Ana, one of the mission's outlier farms. It was not until around February 1 that the brigade finally got back into motion.

Three days' travel brought them to the vicinity of San Bernardino, another mission satellite community, where they spent a few days butchering and drying meat and collecting peas, corn, and wheat for their journey—all courtesy of Father Sánchez, who gave them at least eight packsaddles as well. Smith then purchased several more skittish horses that required breaking before they would tolerate packs or riders. His men also busied themselves building, repairing, and rigging pack and riding saddles. In the flurry of activity, Daniel Ferguson found an opportunity to disappear in order to avoid continuing with the expedition. Though Rogers noted that the presidial corporal promised to apprehend the deserter and send him on his way, he commented, "I expect we shall not see him again." A week or two into February 1827, after rounding up some horses that still displayed a marked propensity to wander off, the trappers at last bid farewell to San Bernardino and rode away from the mission settlements of Mexican California.

Smith retraced his inbound path through the San Bernardino Valley for only a few days before deviating from the specifications of Echeandía's exit visa. Persuading himself that he had complied sufficiently with the governor's orders, Smith shifted course toward the northwest and continued to travel through Mexican territory. After crossing the snow-dusted San Gabriel Mountains into Antelope Valley, he followed the Mohave River some miles, possibly to the vicinity of present-day Victorville. There he met a few runaway mission Indians, one of whom he engaged as a guide.

Crossing the Tehachapi Range via Tejon Pass, Jedediah and his party continued northwest until they came to a lake bordered by extensive mud flats thick with tules, or rushes. Spaniards named it Tulare Lake but it is now called Kern Lake, after Richard Kern, an artist who accompanied the explorer John C. Frémont in the 1840s. Near this lake, Smith recorded the first American descriptions of the Joshua tree—he called it a "dirk Pear tree" because its sharp elongated leaves reminded him of knives or porcupine quills—and the acorn woodpecker, which he dubbed the "Provident woodpecker" because it habitually pecked holes into oak trees and stuffed them with acorns.

The next day, as Smith and his companions picked their way along the mucky lakeshore, they surprised some Yokuts Indians, who took fright and hastily shoved off in rush canoes. Smith's guide persuaded them to return, and Jedediah hired a Yokuts guide who spoke a little Spanish. The party continued about fifteen miles to make camp in a wooded spot beside the Kern River. Several Yokuts visited camp, sprinkled Smith "from head to foot" with downy feathers to symbolize friendship, and told him of a river to the north where beavers lived. His interest piqued, Smith discharged his mission Indian guides and hired a Yokuts to lead him northward.

On the following morning Smith's party and their new guide threaded their way through a landscape honeycombed with holes and burrows that rendered traveling difficult, especially when horses sank into the soft earth "up to the [k]nees." Smith suspected that lizards made the holes, but in reality they housed legions of ground squirrels. That night they encamped beside another lake, today called Tulare Lake. Brackish swamps hemmed the shores, and numerous "Boggy Islands" dotted its broad surface. The brigade was running low on provisions, so Jedediah and his party visited a nearby Wowol Yokut village where about three hundred Indians lived in mat-covered, willow-framed lodges.

Smith made a ceremonial greeting, then offered some trade goods for roasted fish and a supply of grass seed the Yokuts made into a mush. After resting among the friendly Yokuts for two days, the Americans moved northward to a new campsite. That evening a severe wind lashed the lake, causing a rapid rise that forced the Americans to move to higher ground. During the next few days the party proceeded northward, dodging the marshes that marked the sluggish Kaweah River's entrance into Tulare Lake. They camped near a band of Yokuts who lived on the Kaweah's north bank.

At about this time Smith banished one of his men, a trouble-maker named John Wilson. Wilson's "seditious disposition" had already caused Jedediah to dismiss him in San Bernardino. In an October 26, 1827, letter that Smith wrote to Governor Eche-andía while detained in California for a second time, he explained that he had initially fired Wilson "in consequence of his cursing my self and every thing else." Mexican authorities refused to allow Wilson to remain in California, so he continued to travel with the brigade but Smith dropped him from the pay-roll. At the Wowol village near Tulare Lake, Wilson's insubordi-nate behavior again infuriated Smith, and a few days later he felt "forced to discharge him." Banishment might have been a death sentence for Wilson had not Jedediah hired two Indians to con-duct the malingerer back to the "upper settlement of California." When Jedediah returned to California several months later in

1827, he would again encounter Wilson as well as the deserter Daniel Ferguson.

Paralleling the eastern margin of Tulare Lake, Smith's party proceeded north, crossing first the Tulare River and then the Kaweah River. Taking stock of the land, Smith found "verry fine" soil that produced excellent grass, with prairie and woodland "mingled in pleasing variety." He made camp in a "fine little grove of timber" and sent out some hunters who managed to kill two antelopes, a welcome change from dried meat and grass-seed mush.

Remaining two days at this pretty campsite, Smith learned that a good beaver stream lay a day or two ahead. Having adopted a policy that maximized the utility of Indian informants, Smith discharged his former guide and hired another Indian more familiar with the immediate vicinity. Jedediah Smith possessed an innate instinct for geography, but he also profited greatly from the wisdom of the Indians he consulted or hired as guides. Virtually all the explorers of North America would have found their work nearly impossible had it not been for the advice and assistance of countless Indians.

On February 28, thanks to his guide, Smith's men commenced trapping on the Kings River, one of several rivers that tumble out of the Sierra Nevada into the eastern San Joaquin Valley. Within ten days they cleaned out the available beavers along the river and moved up the Kings to the San Joaquin River. Several other streams fell into the San Joaquin River, and Smith was fast approaching one that he would dub the "Appelaminy," today called the Stanislaus. A web of streams made the San Joaquin Valley a well-watered place that offered excellent grazing, but Smith traveled it during springtime, when rainfall and snowmelt flooded its broad wetlands and swamps. Rain, mud, and high water impeded the brigade's progress, but plentiful stocks of antelope, elk, and wild horses temporarily eliminated Smith's recurrent food shortages.

Impressed with the variety of wildlife he observed, Jedediah paid special attention to the "birds of passage." His diary lists geese, brants, herons, buzzards, various ducks and hawks, pigeons, and "2 or Three kinds of Eagles." He also encountered a "verry large Bird which I supposed to be the Vulture or the Condor," undoubtedly North America's largest bird, the California condor. Jedediah again noted with approval the "most excellent grazing country" that one day would support "many fine farms." Smith saw very few Indians after arriving at the San Joaquin, but he later learned that most of the local tribes had been forced onto the missions at San José and Santa Clara.

Smith spent half of April investigating the Sierra Nevada foothills to find a route across the massive range that he called "Mount Joseph" in honor of his friend Father Sánchez of San Gabriel. "On leaving my partners," Smith recalled, "it had been my intention to return at the expiration of my falls hunt or if this was found impracticable by the 1st of July of the following year[,] 1827." Sublette and Jackson had heard nothing from him for seven months, and if he was to meet that deadline he must "begin making arrangements for marching Eastward toward the Rendezvous in the Mountains which I then looked on as a home." But as Jedediah moved northward, the mountains grew even bigger, attaining "a most tremendous heighth." Plunging into the sky far above the snow line, their summits were lost in the clouds. The Sierra Nevada posed what seemed an insurmountable barrier, but Jedediah had to attempt a crossing. Even with this daunting prospect in view he could not help but admire their "unsurpassed grandeur and Sublimity."

The little brigade proceeded eastward fifty miles up the Stanislaus and fell upon the Calaveras River. Smith dismissed a former neophyte Indian guide he had hired at the Stanislaus and hired a new guide, a Spanish-speaking runaway whom he found among the Mokelumne tribe. A division of the Northern Miwok nation, the Mokelumnes inhabited several dirt-lodge villages in the Sierra Nevada foothills. Smith's guide escorted the Americans down the Calaveras River to the Mokelumne River. Here Smith met with an unfortunate loss. A horse missed its footing while fording the turbulent Mokelumne and was swept away, taking with it twelve irreplaceable beaver traps. While Smith wasted a day in futile attempts to recover the precious traps, his new guide made off with two more horses. That evening Jedediah observed about a dozen Indians on a hilltop, armed with bows and arrows, but after he met with them and tendered a few presents they left him in peace.

Despite occasional friction and a few threatening moments, Smith and his companions had thus far managed to get along peaceably with the Indians they met, but the situation now began to change. The Northern Miwoks were never "pacified" by Spaniards or Mexicans, and bitter experience taught them to beware of intruders. They would have seen little reason to distinguish the Americans from their Hispanic enemies. The Miwoks' behavior made Smith increasingly fearful and wary as he traveled through their country. Unfortunately, the actions he took prefigured a sequence of events that culminated in a bloody—indeed disastrous—confrontation in southern Oregon more than a year later. Smith and his men's ill-advised behavior was bound to cause trouble as they moved deeper into California's Indian Country.

While Jedediah searched for a path over the mountains, he also attempted to establish communication with the Miwoks. When he happened upon some Indians he described as "wild," he and another man chased down a couple of women in order to "convince them of our friendship." As he handed them beads and sewing awls and signaled that he meant them no harm, several warriors burst out of hiding "close at hand … with intentions apparently not the most friendly." Smith and his companion quickly returned to their camp. Later that day Smith got ahead of his brigade and paused in a pretty grove of trees to await their arrival. Noticing a lone Indian watching him, Jedediah became apprehensive but motioned to the man to come forward. When the Indian approached, "chatting and making many signs," Smith suddenly realized he was "nearly surrounded by a considerabl[e] party" and immediately spurred his horse in the opposite direction. In a darkly humorous passage, Smith noted that he "left my sociable friend to converse with those that could better understand him." From this point on, Jedediah Smith took no more chances with strange Indians. His anxiety over the need to hasten to the rendezvous was compounded by palpably growing tensions between his people and the Miwoks.

The next day brought the Americans to the Cosumnes River, which Smith called "Indian River," reflecting his mounting concern. Even so, evidence of "considerabl[e] Beaver sign" induced his men to set some traps. Cries of alarm soon rang out downstream, and some trappers rushed into camp to tell Smith that two men had barely escaped an Indian ambush. Dispatching Arthur Black upstream to warn the other trappers, Jedediah prepared his men for a fight. By the time the "closely pressed" trappers reappeared, Smith had secured the horses, posted a double guard around the camp, and ordered his men to keep their mounts saddled and ready to ride. Angry Miwoks gathered on the far shore of the swift and unfordable Cosumnes, and Smith regretted that "the indians gave us no opportunity to punish them."

At day break after a restless night, Smith and six men set off to collect the traps they left behind when the alarm was raised. They found but few, for "a good many had been taken by the indians." At this moment the angry trappers again spotted Miwoks across the river, and one rifleman took a long shot that felled an Indian. This was the first time during the expedition that Smith or one of his men deliberately killed an Indian, but it would not be the last. (In spite of the violence, a few days after Smith started across the sierra, a "Mackalumbry" [Mokelumne] chief named Te-mi arrived at camp to return a stolen horse and several traps. The traps were "broken in pieces by the indians," but Smith's men restored some to working order.) Quickly decamping, Smith's party rode a few miles upstream and forded the Cosumnes. They followed it northward about twelve miles to its confluence with the American River, a broad, rapid stream about one hundred yards wide that Jedediah would name the "Wild River" when he returned a year later.

With the prospect of serious trouble looming, Smith decided he must attempt to cross the Sierra Nevada. He glimpsed hundreds of Maidus, but they seemed "wilder than antelopes" and whenever his brigade appeared they went "running and screaming in every direction." To his dismay, with his every northward step the Indians "became more numerous." Turning east, Jedediah left the American River to search for a viable pass. For two frustrating days his men bush-whacked through the high country but found no pass. In the meantime, fearing that the Maidus might attack at any moment, Smith decided to take violent measures that seem darkly out of character.

Twice already the Maidus had "collected in great numbers" around his party, and both times Smith tried "by every means" to persuade them that he posed no threat. But then he became convinced that the Indians interpreted his efforts only as signs of weakness, and that the Maidus thought his men's rifles were "solid sticks which we could only use in close contest." With his customary forbearance again exhausted and finding himself "pressed so closely and in such numbers," Smith led his men to a defensible spot where they might "make a stand." After a final attempt to calm the Maidus failed, he watched in growing alarm as Indians began to surround his position. "Seeing what must be the inevitable consequence," wrote Smith:

> I determined to anticipate them in the commencement and wishing to do them as little harm as possible and yet consistent with my own safety I ordered 2 men to fire (of course not the most uncertain marksmen). I preferred long shots that it might give them the idea that we could kill at any distance. At the report of the guns[,] both men firing at once[,] two indians fell. For a moment the indians stood still and silent as if a thunder bolt had fallen among them then a few words passed from party to party and in a moment they ran like Deer.

From a modern-day perspective, Smith's preemptive strikes seem tantamount to premeditated murder, but he lived in circumstances that few people today can imagine. All mountain men, Smith included, believed that defending their property was every bit as important as defending their lives. And like most Indians, the trappers embraced an "eye for an eye" ethic that mandated retribution for perceived offenses. To the trappers' way of thinking, the Indians' theft or destruction of traps and their menacing behavior fully justified an immediate application of deadly force.

After the Maidus scattered, Jedediah's first impulse was to take his whole brigade over the summit. Leaving the scene of the killings, the trappers moved into the high country, where a forest of pine, oak, and hemlock cloaked the shoulders of the rugged sierra. Three nights later they made camp in three feet of snow. Below the snow line the men had seen signs of deer, but around the campsite no game stirred. Smith heard only the "lonely sound" of a male "Ruffled Grouse" drumming somewhere in the woods.

The following morning found Smith and his company trudging a dozen more miles through soft, ever-deeper snow that made "the prospect of proceeding verry doubtful." As Smith's men and women staggered along in a ragged line behind him, one man informed Jedediah that the weaker horses were starting to give out. They were nowhere near the summit. Jedediah now faced a dilemma, and a critical decision. If he pushed his brigade onward he would wind up abandoning most or all of the horses, and the attempt to traverse the summit might still mean death for some of his companions. On the other hand, retrograde motion would only place him in dangerous proximity to the "highly exasperated" Maidus, who he feared would "surround our little party and kill us with clubs." His spyglass revealed no pass to the north, but if he retreated south and turned eastward near San Gabriel, he could not possibly reach the rendezvous on schedule.

"These reflections," Jedediah wrote, "were passing rapidly through my mind as I stood on a high Peak a mile in advance of my party." Everywhere he gazed he confronted "high rugged Peaks ... covered with Eternal snow." Peering eastward he saw a "frozen waste extending rough and desolate beyond the boundaries of vision," and it warned him to come no closer. Looking down to the west, as if from a cloud, he saw distant forests, waterfalls, and rivers where no living creature stirred. But then Jedediah caught a "transient glimpse" of the little brigade whose lives depended on the decision he alone must make. In this extremity, grimly contemplating life and death, Smith turned to his tattered diary and scribbled a few lines that provide a rare, flickering illumination of his innermost thoughts.

In the midst of a "freezing desolation" that he reckoned ought forever to "keep a man from wandering," Smith's mind was filled with thoughts of "home and all its neglected enjoyments of the cheerfull fireside of my father['s] house ... of the Plenteous harvest of my native land ... of joyous bustle and of busy life." Nostalgic memories, he wrote, "thronged in my mind to make me feel more strongly the utter desolateness of my situation." How was it possible, he wondered, that "creatures of choice" would willingly "follow fortune through such paths as these." A humble home, he mused, "could give us all that is attainable and fortune could do no more." And yet Jedediah Smith, more than most men, was compulsively driven to make good, to achieve economic independence and the admiration of his peers. For these fleeting goals he was willing to risk his neck over and over again.

"Surely of all lives," he admitted with a hint of stubborn pride, "the hunters is the most precarious, we endure all the extremes of heat and cold[,] hunger and thirst[,] our lives and property are always at hazard. When we lay down[,] our guards must be placed our Rifles by our sides and our Pistols under our heads ready to spring up at once from a restful sleep." As if embarrassed at entertaining such thoughts, Jedediah ended his soliloquy with an apology: "I did not indulge in these reflections longer than I have been employed in writing them and they are here as they existed in that hour of trying fortune and will be remembered as long as I live."

Jogged back to hard reality, Smith knew that only "immediate and powerful exertion" would save him and his companions. He resolved to lead his brigade back to the Stanislaus River, leave most of his people encamped there, and take just two men with lightly packed horses over the mountains and on to the rendezvous. Then he would return to the Stanislaus, collect his cohorts, and renew his "endeavor to learn something of this new and unfortunate country."

Rejoining his party, Smith led them back to the vicinity of the previous night's camp. The next day they continued down the slopes to a campsite with abundant grass to recruit his "fatigued and starved horses." Along the way he noticed one "Peak that seemed to rise far above any other part of the Mt. . . . the Giant of the scene." To this lofty crag, now called Pyramid Peak, Smith "had the vanity to attach" his own name. With no food to be had at the new campsite, his men and women killed and ate a colt. After two day's rest they proceeded southward along the flanks of the sierra below today's Placerville, avoiding their former path, which might have placed them within reach of the Maidus. Traveling down the Cosumnes River for two days, they found a favorable location in Pleasant Valley and established a camp.

During this portion of the trek, Smith did encounter more Maidus or Miwoks, but no violence ensued. Twice he stumbled suddenly upon a few Indians whose first response was to dash off, but each time Smith managed to detain one or two. After handing out a few gifts to demonstrate his peaceable intentions, he exchanged more trade goods for the pounded-acorn mush that was a dietary staple among many California Indians. Smith's unquenchable curiosity impelled him to examine storage cribs containing three to four hundred bushels of acorns as he passed by small villages of a few huts, and he noted that the Indians cooked their mush by dropping red-hot rocks into clay-lined pits filled with water and hulled acorn flour.

By the time Smith and his company reached the lower Cosumnes River, they had subsisted for six days on little more than the colt and a lone beaver that someone caught. Once established at a new camp, however, his men again set traps and the next morning retrieved several beavers that yielded valuable skins and meat that proved "much better than the flesh of the poor colt." Reviewing his failed attempt to cross the mountains, which cost six horses and about a week's time, Jedediah grudgingly admitted to his diary that he had "learned one thing which I did not know before[—]that I must sometime be turned back."

While returning to the Stanislaus, Smith's brigade crossed the swift Cosumnes River only three miles from where they recently killed several Maidus. (The shooting that took place before the Americans' ascent into the high country was actually the second time Jedediah had issued an order to shoot Indians. In the first instance, a few days earlier, as many as five Indians had been killed.) There in midstream, the potential for calamity that always hovered around mountain men suddenly became real. A horse carrying most of their ammunition lost its footing on a slippery rock, and the rope securing it to the next horse snapped. The horse was carried downstream, where it drowned and sank in a pool. Knowing the contents of the dead animal's pack, Smith dreaded this "terrible blow." If the ammunition was lost, so was the brigade's ability to hunt. Worse, Jedediah's men would be deprived of the firepower that enabled them "to travel among hostile bands feared and respected."

Smith said nothing, for premature bad news might demoralize his men, who were unaware of the loss. Instead, he dispatched two trappers downstream to find the horse. Smith knew that "unless kept down by a heavy load," a drowned horse would "rise to the surface in from 10 to 30 minutes." Sure enough, by the time his party completed the river crossing one of the searchers spotted a horse's foot oscillating above the roiling current. By a stroke of good luck the animal's pack was jammed in the rocky bottom, preventing a total loss. Smith sent a good swimmer into the river to tie a rope around the dead horse, and the other men dragged it out of the turbulent rapid. Upon examining the pack the delighted trappers found their lead safe; even better, a "good leather sack" safeguarded nearly thirty pounds of irreplaceable gunpowder.

The brigade pressed on and Jedediah noted with relief that "there was not an indian to be seen." It was now early May, and the time had come for a renewed assault on the sierra. The brigade headed south for a few days, retracing their route past the Mokelumne and Calaveras rivers, then halted at the Stanislaus. Moving upstream, Smith selected a campsite "with the intention of remaining several days in order to make the necessary preparations for my journey across the Mt to the Depo."

While encamped, some of Smith's men pressed beaver skins into packs and cached them for later retrieval. Others killed game and prepared dried meat, shoed some horses, and cut hay to feed the livestock that Jedediah would take across the mountains. Smith instructed Harrison Rogers to establish a safe, long-term campsite and to place a note at the cache with directions to the new camp so he could find it when he returned. Smith advised his clerk that if he failed to show up by September 20, 1828, then Rogers should "consider me dead." In that event, Rogers must make his way to a Russian American Fur Company post at Bodega Bay, some eighty miles north of San Francisco, or to Fort Ross, another sixteen miles to the north, where he would purchase supplies and try to reach the rendezvous on his own. If the necessary supplies were unavailable then he was to sell everything he could, make camp on the seacoast, and await "an opportunity to ship to the Sandwich Islands [i.e., Hawaii] and from thence to the United States."

Leaving his "small but faithful party" on May 20, Smith set out with Robert Evans and Silas Gobel. They drove six horses and two mules packed with about sixty pounds of dried meat, some hay, and camp gear. Three unnamed men followed with extra horses in case any livestock broke down early in the trek. Smith and the five men followed the Stanislaus for about sixty miles, and after three days of hard traveling the extra men turned back toward Rogers's camp. Jedediah intended to follow either the Stanislaus or the Mokelumne to its source and then cross to the eastern slope of the Sierra Nevada. As they broke trail into the high country, the snow deepened from four to eight feet, but cold air crusted its surface so their horses only sank six or eight inches into the snow.

On the afternoon of May 25 a blizzard struck. That night "the storm increased in violence and the weather became extremely cold," so the men went nowhere the next day. Smith remembered it as "one of the most disagreeable days I ever passed." Roaring wind and driving snow made it almost impossible to kindle a fire. The temperature plunged so rapidly that two horses and a mule "froze to death before our eyes" and were soon buried beneath snow. Jedediah almost yielded to a horrid premonition that his party had been "marked out for destruction." Perhaps Smith or the others prayed for deliverance from their peril, for on the next morning he gratefully wrote, "He who rules the storms willed it otherwise and the sun of the 27th rose clear upon the gleaming peaks of the Mt St Joseph." Jedediah would never forget that awful night.

Struggling onward the next morning through fifteen inches of new snow made travel "verry fatiguing," but after a dozen miles Smith, Evans, and Gobel finally gained the summit, and in the far distance Jedediah glimpsed a sunlit plain. Descending thirteen miles through gradually thinning snow they at length found themselves in a fine valley with plenty of grass. Even so, one "good horse" had to be left behind, and Jedediah discovered he had again lost a pistol. Crossing the sierra by tracing the Mokelumne to its sources adjacent to Ebbetts Pass, the three weary men followed Kinney Creek northward and made camp "about 100 yards from a high and steep bluff." May 28 was meant to be a day of rest, but at noontime the travelers snapped to attention when a dozen yelling Washoe Indians appeared at the edge of the bluff. Angered but not intimidated, the defiant trappers stood their ground. Gathering "a great many large rocks," the Washoes sent them hurtling down the incline toward camp and then unaccountably departed.

The next few days' travel took Jedediah's party over Wheeler Pass (named decades later by a military explorer) and down Cottonwood Creek to today's Walker Lake, fifty miles closer to the rendezvous. Smith and his men were the first Americans to visit the lake that John C. Frémont would name in 1845 after his guide, a former mountain man named Joseph R. Walker. During this leg of the trek Smith surprised "two squaws," one of whom was so terror-stricken that she rushed at him brandishing a root-digging stick, displaying "such an expression of fear I had never before seen." Jedediah attempted to calm the woman, but away she ran, her shrieks ringing in his ears until they were "lost in the distance."

Skirting the south end of Walker Lake, Smith found signs of horses and familiar Indians, for he had again reached Southern Paiute country. When he approached a lone lodge the inhabitants scurried off, so Smith helped himself to a few fish, leaving some "small presents in their rooms." Continuing on, he encountered some Paiutes fishing with "nets verry neatly made with fine meshes." He offered more presents and the Indians seemed "verry friendly." Assuming that he was relatively safe, Smith went two miles farther and made camp.

At about ten o'clock that evening, Smith awoke to the thunder of many horsemen galloping past his camp toward the nearby fishing spot. Jedediah and his companions speedily piled up gear and prepared "for extremities." Two Indians approached the trappers' camp with intentions unknown, but seeing the trappers were awake they walked in and seated themselves. When Smith offered a pipe, the two Indians brusquely refused to smoke with the white men. Suddenly dozens of Indians infiltrated the camp with "Bows strung and their arrows in their hands." The intruders began "talking loud and harsh" and kept moving from one quarter of camp to another. Smith attempted to defuse the ominous situation, but when he offered presents to their "principal character," the man turned away in disdain. Jedediah would have opened fire on the Indians then and there had his livestock been secured, but he held back, hoping "there was a possibility that they might not commence." Any aggressive act would have fatal consequences, but Smith remained "in readiness to beat them off or sell our lives as dear as possible." Two tense hours later the Indians kindled a fire and agreed to smoke a pipe with the newcomers. With Indians literally sleeping, or perhaps feigning sleep, alongside Smith and his two men, Jedediah "kept a verry close watch during the remainder of the night." Aware that he had come within a hair's breadth of certain death, he concluded that the Paiutes were "not unanimous for the massacre" only because too many of their own warriors would likely be killed.

On the next morning the Paiutes seemed friendly enough. When Jedediah asked them if water could be found to the east, they replied in the affirmative. Smith observed a number of "Buffalo Robes[,] knives and Spanish Blankets," which suggested "some communication with the indians on Lewis's River and with the spanish indians." Taking the Paiutes' advice, Smith, Evans, and Gobel hastened eastward twenty miles but found no waterhole.

This was sufficient to confirm Jedediah's suspicion that the Paiutes "intended to deceive me and send me where I might perish." Eight months earlier he had penned a nearly identical comment about the Mohaves. After a thirty-mile trek on the following day, Smith at last found water and made camp, but not before he had to abandon still another broken-down horse. Fortunately, the animal was only three miles back and the men found it the next morning. They made only a few miles that day before camping in Soda Spring Valley, near Luning, Nevada.

It was now the first week of June, and time was running out if Smith hoped to reach the rendezvous on schedule. But with his horses "much fatigued," he made only halting progress through an exceedingly barren land, pausing an entire day to recuperate at an oasis that offered "tolerable good" grass and water. Smith discovered that the best campsites generally lay at the foot of the "High Rocky Hills," punctuating the otherwise desolate wastes of central Nevada. By this time Smith's men and livestock had about reached the limits of endurance. Provisions had dwindled to almost nothing and game was practically nonexistent. The few Indians they met eked out a meager living at the edge of starvation and had little to spare for strange passersby.

On June 10 Smith encountered a Paiute man and two women, but when he tried to communicate with them they seemed "too stupid or wilful" to comprehend his signs. Still, he traded a single beaver skin from them before continuing on. Later that day another horse gave out and was abandoned, doubtless furnishing some Paiutes a welcome dietary supplement. The few surviving horses were in such bad shape that Jedediah and his companions walked most of the time. Shortly after sundown the three wanderers noticed a campfire winking in the distance.

Making for it, they found a "Squaw and 2 children" traveling alone across the desert. The Indian woman generously shared what little water she had, and then Jedediah "for the first time saw scorpions prepared to eat," though he could stomach none himself. That night a welcome rain fell, refreshing their dehydrated horses and leaving a few puddles from which the men drank the next day. Daily rations for Smith's party were down to just four ounces of dried meat for each man. Five days went by with no fresh meat except a hare that Jedediah shot. Meanwhile, they were tortured by the sight of distant antelope and deer that capered safely beyond the range of their guns.

On June 16 the famished trappers bolted down the last crumbs of their dried meat. They had been on pathetically short rations for twelve days. One horse, with only its forefeet shod, had become "so lame in his hind feet as to be unable to travel ... his hind feet were worn to the quick." Jedediah killed the suffering beast and Gobel and Evans dried "the best of his meat." Emaciated horseflesh made poor fare, but the Americans were "hungry enough to eat almost any thing." Smith and his enfeebled men crossed the Shell Creek Range and entered Spring Valley. Having stumbled onward for two waterless days, Robert Evans dropped by the trailside on June 17, unable to continue. Just then about fourteen Indians appeared. They let Smith know that water was nearby and offered to assist the strangers. The Indians accompanied Jedediah to the spring, and one of them carried back to Evans a small kettle of water that saved his life.

The Indians gave Smith two small ground squirrels and showed him how to prepare a kind of "water rush," which he judged to be pleasant tasting. For canteens Jedediah carried three cow horns that he filled with water at "every opportunity." He noted that he "seldom drank more than half a pint before they were exhausted[,] for neither of my men could do as well without water as myself."

On June 19 the three wayfarers advanced fifteen miles, crossing Sacramento Pass and moving along the eastern flank of the Snake Mountains. During the day's trek they picked up some wild onions that "made the horse meat relish much better." The next day they trudged another twenty miles, and at night came upon a water hole. The snow-laden peaks that interrupted the otherwise dreary landscape provided practically the only source for grass or water in "this inhospitable land," and they were "to this plain like islands of the Ocean." Jedediah suspected that the "short distance from the sandy base [to] the snowy region" offered "evidence of the great elevation of this plain."

During the following two days Smith's party crossed paths with more Indians, a few of whom possessed iron arrow points and glass beads, but when Jedediah tried to acquire information as to the direction of the Great Salt Lake, he got nowhere. He made several attempts to communicate using sign language, but the Indians merely imitated his gestures "as nearly as possible." Somewhat miffed, he disparagingly noted that all the Indians he had met since departing Walker Lake—mostly Paiutes—were "the same unintelligent kind of beings.... They form a connecting link between the animal and the intellectual creation." When a curious Paiute fumbled with the double trigger of Smith's rifle, Jedediah fired it into the air, undoubtedly to demonstrate the gun's mysterious power. The terrified man stood stock still and his companions fell to the ground; then they all fled at the outlandish noise. Stymied in their effort to gather useful information, Jedediah and his men moved on.

June 21 found the trio in present-day Utah, on the muddy shore of a small salt lake. When they attempted to pass through an especially swampy spot, one of the horses became hopelessly mired. After a fruitless effort to extricate the animal Smith decided to kill it, since their meat supply was again exhausted. They butchered the horse, but the growing weakness of the men and their horses made it impossible to take away more than "a quarter of his flesh." By the end of the next day's twenty-five mile hike, the landscape looked familiar enough to suggest that Jedediah was nearing his destination. He had finally reached the southern margin of the Great Salt Lake Desert, and probably made camp on what is now called Thomas Creek. On June 23 they filled their water horns and moved on, making a waterless camp that night in mounting gloom and foreboding.

Jedediah roused himself "verry early" the next morning and clambered up a steep hill to take his bearings, hoping to discover signs of water. He saw nothing but "sandy plains or dry Rocky hills" stretching away for fifty miles, but he dared not tell his discouraged, worn-out men the bitter truth. Instead, he said he had seen "something black at a distance near which no doubt we would find water." While Jedediah walked ahead peering toward the horizon, another horse gave out. Sending one man back "to take the best of his flesh," Smith continued through aggravatingly soft sand that slipped away under his every footstep, vainly seeking water. After a while he halted to await Evans and Gobel, who had fallen behind.

When they showed up, Smith did his best to bolster their flagging spirits, but in his heart he admitted that "the view ahead was almost hopeless." As a midsummer sun blazed down upon the dehydrated men, the sand grew so hot that walking became practically unbearable. By late afternoon they could advance no further, so they took shelter under a lone cedar tree that clung precariously to a sandy hillside. There the men scraped out shallow troughs—like graves—and lay down in dappled shade "for the purposes of cooling our heated bodies."

An hour later they moved out, shambling along until about ten o'clock in the evening, when they paused for rest. In the extremity of their suffering even the comfort of sleep was denied, for as Smith wrote, "tormented nature made us dream of things we had not." Like other moments when his life seemed to hang by the slenderest of threads, Jedediah contemplated the folly of his ambition. "How trifling," he mused, "were all those things that hold such an absolute sway over the busy and prosperous world. My dreams were not of Gold or ambitious honors but of my distant quiet home[,] of murmuring brooks[,] of cooling cascades."

Their situation worsened the next day. By mid-morning Robert Evans again collapsed in the pathetic shade of a stunted tree, "being able to proceed no further." Sometimes leaders of men face the awful responsibility of having to abandon one man in order to save others, and such was Jedediah Smith's lot on this day. "We could do no good by remaining to die with him," he wrote, "and we were not able to help him along, but we left him with feelings only known to those who have been in the same situation and with the hopes that we might get relief and return to save his life." In stark desperation Smith and Gobel staggered on. Just three miles later, to their "inexpressible joy," they stumbled upon a spring. Gobel fell into the pool and began gulping down water, and even Smith drank without regard for the possible unpleasant consequences of overfilling his belly.

Before bending to drink at the spring, Smith happened to glance backward. In the distance he noticed two Indians moving toward the place where Evans lay helpless. Moments later he heard two gun shots but could not tell if they were meant as signals or if Evans had been assaulted. After refreshing himself for a moment he got to his feet and saw a smoke plume rising from Evans's location. Hastening back with a few pieces of dried horse meat and a small kettle filled with water, Smith found his man "far gone[,] being scarcely able to speak." The Indians had disappeared, but Evans managed to croak out, "[H]ave you any water?" Jedediah passed the kettle and Evans swallowed "at least 4 or 5 quarts," then begged for more. Smith helped Evans return to the spring, where they camped to recruit their "wearied and emaciated bodies" and Jedediah cut thin slices of horse meat and spread it on the ground to dry.

On June 26, as Smith, Gobel, and Evans trudged northward through Skull Valley, Utah, they happened upon an Indian family, who seemed "somewhat alarmed but friendly." When Smith indicated by signs that his men were hungry, the Indians offered to share some antelope meat. Jedediah was elated when he heard them speak "like the snake Indians." Further inquiry disclosed that they were "Panakhies from Lewis's River," meaning Bannocks from the Snake River. This was good news indeed; not only were these Indians from a familiar tribe, but Smith had reason to hope that he was close to his destination. The Bannocks told Smith that buffalo were plentiful a few days' march to the northeast, though Jedediah could learn nothing from them regarding the direction of the Great Salt Lake. After encamping that evening, Smith scrambled up a rocky slope and saw in the distance "what appeared to be a large body of water."

The following day, after ten miles of travel past many salt springs and across the Stansbury Mountains, the three Americans crested a ridge, from which they "saw an expanse of water Extending far to the North and East." It could be none other than the Great Salt Lake. This "joyful sight" Smith could "scarcely believe."

His men's spirits immediately lifted. Though they still had miles to go to reach their "depo," they knew they would "soon be in a country where we would find game and water." The land was not merely familiar to these men; it represented a return to comfort and comparative safety. Smith's arrival in the Salt Lake Valley elicited "feelings known to the traveler who after long and perilous journeying comes once again in view of his home." A few lines later Smith repeated the analogy, noting that he had "traveled so much in the vicinity of the Salt Lake that it had become my home of the wilderness." Temporarily energized, the trio marched fifteen more miles and camped at a spring. Joyful feelings, however, could not eradicate the men's need for food and rest. Jedediah saw some antelope but failed to get off a shot at them, and he knew he and his men still faced some hard traveling.

When the three trappers reached Utah Lake, south of the Great Salt Lake, they found its outlet flooded "a considerable distance from the channel." Two to three feet of water covered the river bottom, which was thick with bullrushes and cane grass. The main channel, about sixty yards wide and swollen by snowmelt, rushed along at a great velocity. Smith decided to attempt a crossing of what is today called the Jordan River. He and the others cut bunches of cane grass, lashed them into bundles, and assembled a flimsy but effective Indian-inspired raft to carry their equipment. First, however, Jedediah had to swim the remaining horse and mule across the torrent—no simple task considering his debilitated condition.

Upon returning to where his men waited, Smith tied a cord to the raft, took the opposite end in his teeth, and all three men plunged into the river. Neither Gobel nor Evans were able swimmers, so they clung to the raft. The trio were "swept down a considerable distance" before they managed to crawl onto land. Jedediah was "very much strangled," an understatement indicating that he had nearly drowned. To top off this misadventure, the mule and horse got stuck in thick mud near the shoreline, and none of the men had strength enough to unpack goods and gear and free the animals. The exhausted men kindled a small fire, dined on scraps of dried horse meat, and tried to sleep.

On the morning of June 29, Smith and his men extracted their animals from the slimy muck and spread goods out to dry in the sun. Though they were "verry weak and worn down with suffering," the three men decamped at about ten o'clock and trudged fifteen more miles. That afternoon Smith wounded a bear but it escaped, so the men had to make do with a few scraps of horse meat. In camp that evening there may have been hopeful murmurs that their privations might soon end, though Smith noted that "men suffering from hunger never talk much but rather bear their sorrows in moody silence which is much preferable to fruitless complaint."

Despite their suffering, the men could take comfort in the knowledge that they were again on the trail they had taken almost a year earlier when they set out for the unknown southwest. Breaking camp early the next morning, Jedediah forged ahead in hopes of killing a deer, for he noticed signs that some were in the neighborhood. He managed to shoot one but the wounded deer ran off, leaving a telltale blood track. When Smith approached the deer, it seemed "nearly dead," so he stooped down to pull it into a better position for butchering. To his amazement, the beast sprang up and dashed away. Smith was "vexed" at himself for not shooting the deer twice, and his men seemed very discouraged.

Luckily, Smith again located the deer and severed its hamstrings to prevent another escape. Within minutes bloody venison sizzled over a fire. Smith, Gobel, and Evans "employed ourselves most pleasantly in eating for about two hours ... with a relish unknown to a palace." Their sudden deliverance from starvation left them "as well satisfied ... as we would have been in the possession of all the Luxuries and enjoyments of civilized life in other circumstances." Smith added, "These things may perhaps appear trifling to most readers but let any one of them travel over the same plain as I did and they will consider the killing of a buck a great achievement and certainly a verry useful one."

So invigorating was their repast that after trekking twenty-five miles on the following day along the northern margin of Utah Lake, Smith noted simply, "Nothing material occurred." On July

2 Smith's party at last reached their cache and happened across a large contingent of Snake Indians, comprising about two hundred lodges. When the Snakes informed him that many trappers were gathered at Bear Lake and they were themselves en route to the same destination, Smith gladly agreed to accompany them. On July 3 Smith hired a Snake guide and borrowed a horse, then dashed ahead to the rendezvous, which he and his men reached at about three o'clock that afternoon. "My arrival," he wrote, "caused a considerable bustle in camp[,] for myself and party had been given up as lost. A small Cannon brought up from St. Louis was loaded and fired for a salute." Of the eight horses and mules he led out of California, only two survived. Like Smith and his companions, they were "mere skeletons" when they reached the rendezvous. Despite the myriad hazards and difficulties they endured, Jedediah, Gobel, and Evans arrived just two days later than he had predicted—an astonishing feat.

And so ended Jedediah Smith's pathbreaking venture across the Great Basin to Mexican California. Smith, Evans, and Gobel were the first men to record a crossing of the Sierra Nevada. He and his companions had suffered extraordinarily, but they learned much about the strange, dangerous, and starkly beautiful land hitherto known only to Indians. Some of the glaring emptiness that dominated maps of western North America long after Lewis and Clark's expedition could now be eliminated.

This was a great accomplishment, and a proud moment for Jedediah Smith, but he had little time to spare for celebration. Several critical questions remained unanswered. How had his partners fared in his absence? Where did the company books stand with reference to profit or loss? And finally, what was the fate of those men he had left behind in California with the promise of a speedy rescue? Smith was not a man to renege on a commitment, but the thought of retracing that dismal trail must have been sobering indeed.

CHAPTER 6

"The Folly of Men in Power"

AS spring turned to summer in 1827 and Jedediah Smith neared his destination, the Rocky Mountain beaver trade was in the midst of rapid transformation. Smith learned of some of these developments when he reunited with his partners at the rendezvous. Ashley and Henry had retired, and Smith, Jackson & Sublette were beginning to generate success that would threaten the HBC's grip on the western trade. But rising competition among the Americans promised to destabilize the system that Ashley inaugurated, which amounted to a temporary monopoly. The ensuing changes would reconfigure not only the fur trade but the future of the entire Pacific Slope.

In the autumn of 1826, while Smith led the first Southwest Expedition to California, David Jackson's party trapped through southwestern Idaho, and William Sublette's brigade worked the Snake River and Henry's Fork toward Jackson's Hole and the Grand Tetons. Jackson's and Sublette's brigades harvested enough beaver fur to justify dispatching William Sublette and "Black" Harris to Saint Louis with a second order for goods from Ashley, as noted in the previous chapter.

The 1827 rendezvous took place at Sweet Water Lake, now Bear Lake, on the eastern Utah-Idaho border. At the rendezvous, Jackson and Sublette delivered a fine haul of fur to Ashley's man James Bruffee. The partners had ample credit to purchase goods for another year, even though Smith's packs of beaver fur remained cached on the trail or in California with the men he left behind. At that moment, Smith, Jackson & Sublette was the best-organized outfit in the Rockies, but it was powerless to prevent the robust competition that soon threatened its dominant position.

From 1822 to 1826 William Ashley's most serious competitors were HBC men, and like Ashley, they were in the early stages of investigating the little-known interior northwest. For several years George Simpson, John McLoughlin, Alexander Ross, and Peter Skene Ogden strove to bring order, economy, and profitability to their operations in the Columbia-Snake region. Like Ashley's men, they acquired much useful geographical information and developed tactics well suited for the brigade-based trapping system. In the interim, the HBC policy of making the Snake River Plains a "fur desert" allowed the company to keep prices for goods high and to hold its engagés in economic thralldom under contractual obligations in a region largely free from competition. But in 1824 Ashley's men, and Johnson Gardner in particular, began to undermine HBC power by seducing engagés with promises of cheaper goods and higher fur prices.

To some degree, the successive partnerships of Ashley & Henry, Ashley & Smith, and Smith, Jackson & Sublette controlled the prices of goods and furs in the Rocky Mountains. But as more trappers from New Mexico ventured into the Salt Lake Valley and beyond, some hatched their own schemes to pack goods to the rendezvous. The Columbia Fur Company likewise sought access to the central Rockies and after 1827 became a powerhouse as Astor's Western Department. Even as several well-funded competitors threatened to break into the mountain trade, trappers at the lower rungs of the fur trade business ladder nursed growing discontent with Smith, Jackson & Sublette's high prices for goods. Their sole-provider deal with Ashley benefited Smith, Jackson & Sublette in the short run, for there would be no competition at the 1827 rendezvous. Free trappers might sell furs to any buyer, but as the partners' hirelings, engagés were required to hand over their furs in exchange for an annual wage. With no rivals to drive down prices, Smith, Jackson & Sublette stood to reap a tidy profit.

Before arriving at the 1827 rendezvous, a Pennsylvanian named Daniel Potts spent the previous autumn and winter with William Sublette's brigade, trapping in the vicinity of the spectacular geyser basins near Yellowstone Lake. At Bear Lake he posted a letter in which he described the trappers' plight. "There is poor prospect of making much here," he lamented, "owing to the evil disposition of the Indians, and the exorbitant price of goods." Gunpowder sold for $2.50 a pound and lead was $1.30 a pound. Coffee, sugar, and tobacco all cost $2.00 a pound, while vermillion and pepper went for $6.00 a pound, and a three-point woolen blanket cost $13.00. Average horses sold from $150 to $300 each, equivalent to a good year's wage back in the states. The best horses cost as much as $500. Potts lost three horses to Indian thieves within a year, one of which was "a favorite Buffalo Horse." These naturally talented and specially trained "buffalo runners" were highly prized and commanded extravagant prices. Calculating his livestock losses at no less than "four hundred and fifty Dollars," Daniel Potts added dourly, "this you may conclude keeps my nose cllose to the grind stone."

Potts's complaints about the cost of goods were not groundless, but Smith, Jackson & Sublette's prices reflected more than avarice alone. William Ashley's agreement to supply them goods pegged gunpowder at $1.50 per pound, lead at $1.00 per pound, and vermillion at $3.00 per pound; three-point blankets cost them $9.00 apiece. Markup on these and other Smith, Jackson & Sublette goods ranged from 50 percent to better than 100 percent. Their agreement with Ashley also stipulated that he would pay $3.00 a pound for beaver fur, the nominal price at which they bought it in the mountains. And then there was the $1.12 per pound that Ashley collected for marketing the furs.

Much of the partners' profits came from markups on the goods they sold in the mountains or at the rendezvous. They could expect no better opportunity to eliminate their debt and turn red ink into black than they found in 1827, with a handsome fur harvest and not a single competitor in the field. Profits, pricing, and competition were important issues for merchants engaged in the mountain trade, but the rising number of beaver hunters in the Oregon Country generated substantial international friction, too. HBC field men and directors observed with growing consternation the increase in American activity. At the same time, Mexican and Californian officials grappled with disturbing rumors about Jedediah Smith and his intentions.

When reports of the Americans' rendezvous and trapping operations reached HBC men at Fort Vancouver, Spokane House, and elsewhere, they waxed wroth at the likelihood of energetic opposition. Thanks to the meddlesome Americans and their inexpensive goods, HBC managers had already lowered prices for some goods and boosted employees' salaries. By January 1828 Peter Skene Ogden became acutely aware of American competitors, for a number of his freemen were trading with the Americans. He knew the Americans' goods cost more than his own, but he also knew they offered nearly twice as much value per pelt. Ogden somehow learned that Smith, Jackson & Sublette "made a gain of twenty thousand dollars" during their first year of operation. With no competitors about, he added, "they sold their goods one third dearer than Ashley did, but have held out a promise of a reduction in their prices this year [1828]."

Late in 1827 Mexican officialdom in California had likewise become alarmed about Smith's activities when they received reports about a foreign "army" prowling through their land. The confusing reports were evidently based on garbled references to the 1827 rendezvous and to the trappers' camp on the Stanislaus. Authorities in Mexico City were painfully aware of their inability to prevent alien fur hunters from operating beyond their reach along the Pacific Slope, but fiscal and political chaos in the heartland meant that the peripheries would be ignored. As a result, Mexican sovereignty had very little meaning north of San Francisco. Still, Californian officials suspected that Jedediah Smith and his fellows were up to no good and forwarded to their superiors whatever details they had of Smith's illicit activities. Unaware that he was at the center of these gathering storms, Smith prepared to redeem his promise and rescue the trappers he left in California.

With the 1827 rendezvous winding down and the trappers sobering up, Smith, Jackson & Sublette launched their campaign for the coming year. Sublette's men would trap through the land of the Blackfeet and attempt to open trade with them. Jackson may have made a round trip to Missouri to collect trade goods for 1828, and he possibly spent the winter at Bear River. Smith planned to return to California, rejoin his men, and trap and explore the country from San Francisco to the Columbia River before heading for the 1828 rendezvous at Bear Lake.

Jedediah Smith recruited and recorded the names of another eighteen men for a second Southwest Expedition. The faithful veteran Silas Gobel volunteered again. So did Robeseau, the "Canadian half-breed" who dropped out from the 1826 expedition. Toussaint Maréchal, Gregory Ortego, and François Deromme were newcomers to the mountains. Isaac Galbraith and Thomas Virgin had been Ashley men since 1824, and the remainder had at least some field experience. "Ortego" (Ortega) was listed as a "Spaniard," probably meaning a Mexican. French Canadian volunteers included Deromme (probably a misspelling of Desraume), Joseph Lapointe, Maréchal, John Relle, and John B. Ratelle. "Polette Lambross" (i.e., Lambroise) was identified as a "mulatto." Anglo-Americans named Henry Brown (nicknamed "Boatswain"), William Campbell, David Cunningham, Thomas Daws, Joseph Palmer, Charles Swift, and John Turner completed the trappers' roster, but Smith's party again included at least two mixed-blood or Indian women. A few dogs also accompanied the trappers.

When Jedediah Smith left "the Depo" on July 13, 1827, he meant to collect his men encamped at the Stanislaus River and "then proceed further in examination of the country beyond Mt. Saint Joseph and along the sea coast." He expected "to find Beaver, which with us hunters is a primary object," but he also confessed that he was "led on by the love of novelty ... which is much increased by the pursuit of its gratification." Recalling the hardships he endured while crossing from the Sierras through the sandy wastes of western Utah en route to the rendezvous, Smith decided to return to California by the same route he used in 1826.

Over the next six days Smith led his brigade south from "the Little Lake" (Bear Lake) to Bear River, then southwest to Weber

River. Following the Weber until it made a bend to the southeast, Smith turned southwest and crossed a divide that brought him to Utah Lake where he found a large encampment of Utes. He traded goods for sundry items and two additional horses, and the Utes told him that several months earlier they had met some starving trappers passing eastward toward Taos. Smith made his way to the Sevier River, where he detected horse and mule tracks that seemed to confirm the Utes' tale. Upon reaching the Beaver River he encountered more of the "wild" Indians he met in 1826. This time they appeared in even larger numbers but behaved in a friendly manner. Smith succinctly noted, "In this time nothing worth relating occurred."

Mindful of the difficulties of traveling down the Virgin River canyon, Jedediah struck out overland from the Santa Clara River and crossed the mountains to the Virgin River. During several days' travel he saw only one Indian, who seemed quite "wild" and stuck "as close to Rock as a Mountain Sheep." Smith passed several burned lodges, a corn field, and some "works for making the sugar or Candy of which I have before spoken," but he saw no more Indians.

Pausing briefly to restock his dwindling supply of salt at the cave he had visited in 1826, Smith continued down the Virgin toward its confluence with the Colorado. He was again in the Mohave country, not far from the familiar river crossing. After fording the Colorado he reached the first Mohave settlements and halted for a day to rest his men and livestock. When some Indians wandered into his camp, Jedediah wrote, they appeared "as friendly as when I was there before."

While encamped on the bank of the Colorado near present-day Needles, California, Smith again encountered "Francisco," his Indian interpreter from the previous year. Smith "made a present to the Chiefs," swapped a few jaded mounts for fresher Mohave horses, and purchased some corn and beans. Francisco informed Smith that a band of "Spaniards & Americans from the Province of Sonora, by way of the Gila," had recently passed by, but a quarrel had divided them. Some headed up the Colorado, and perhaps others had left the tracks Smith saw on the

Mojave Raft.

This illustration from the 1850s shows the same type of crude but effective cane-grass raft that Smith and his men used in 1827. "Mohave Raft," line engraving from Pacific Rail Road Surveys, vol. 3. Author's collection.

Sevier River. Jedediah Smith may have pioneered a route across the southwestern desert, but within just a few months other trappers also prowled for beavers in that dreary land. Indeed, a trapping party that included George Yount, Ewing Young, and James O. Pattie had clashed with the Mohaves in the fall of 1826. After killing several Mohaves, the trappers hanged their corpses in trees.

The Mohaves' outwardly peaceable demeanor evidently convinced Smith that he had nothing to fear from them. He would pay a terrible price for his misjudgment. On the morning of August 18, most likely, Smith's brigade prepared to cross the Colorado. After stowing guns and supplies in cane-grass rafts, possibly loaned by the Mohaves, some of the trappers commenced swimming the rafts across the river. About half of Smith's men, both women, and all the horses remained on the bank near the village. Jedediah later recalled that the Mohaves "in large numbers and with [the] most perfect semblance of

This circa-1855 image shows the densely forested bottomlands bordering the Colorado River at the Mohave Crossing. "Rio Colorado Near the Mohave Villages, View No. 2," chromolithograph from Pacific Rail Road Surveys, vol. 3. Author's collection.

peace and friendship were aiding the party to cross the river." When the rafts reached midstream, the Mohaves raised a war cry and attacked the white men on the beach with arrows, clubs, and rocks. It happened with breathtaking speed.

Smith and eight men managed to get their rafts across the river, but not without a fight. Thomas Virgin suffered a serious head wound from a club-wielding Mohave before Jedediah's raft reached the other shore. The white men looked on helplessly as the Indians murdered their companions across the river and some men on the rafts. Within seconds ten trappers lay dead, and the two Indian women were taken captive or killed. Nine survivors stood on the sandy beach and watched the Mohaves furiously hack and club their unfortunate comrades. Only the river separated them from the yelling Indians, who undoubtedly meant to finish them off as well. Among the dead were Brown,

Campbell, Cunningham, Deromme, Lambross, Ortego, Ratelle, Relle, Robeseau, and poor Silas Gobel, who had already endured much suffering in his travels with Jedediah Smith.

The Mohaves now possessed all of the trappers' horses and most of their weapons, ammunition, and trade goods. Smith's papers and journal were gone as well, though he would later reconstruct his travel narrative. Some commentators in Smith's time and later have suggested that the Mohaves attacked his party at the behest of Mexican authorities who advised the tribe to allow no more Americans into California. Perhaps so, but it seems far more probable that the Mohaves' recent conflicts with other "American" trappers persuaded them to punish the next ones that came their way. A tribal tradition suggests that that the violence may have been sparked by disagreements over payment for the Mohaves' assistance.

The survivors had no time for mourning or even for a moment's contemplation. It must have seemed that time stopped while Smith's dying companions' screams rang in his ears, but the slaughter consumed no more than a few minutes from start to finish. A quick glance showed his men in possession of only five guns, a little ammunition, their butcher knives, and about fifteen pounds of dried meat. They also had a small pile of now-useless trade items. Meanwhile, Mohave warriors gathered on the distant shore, and some began to swim across the river. "I was yet on the sand bar in sight of my dead companions," Jedediah wrote, "and not far off were some hundreds of Indians who might in all probability close in upon us and with an Arrow or Club terminate all my measures for futurity."

Mastering his grief and rage, Smith swung into purposeful action. While five riflemen temporarily cowed the approaching Indians, Smith directed the other three men to heave whatever goods would sink into the Colorado and strew the rest across the sand bar in the faint hope that Mohave plunderers would squander precious moments picking through the jettisoned goods. Then Smith hastened his men away from the scene of the massacre. A few minutes later he saw that the Mohaves had nearly encircled his party in the open desert. If the circle were closed, they were dead men for certain. Reversing course, Jedediah and the others dashed back toward the river, desperately searching for cover that offered a defensive position. Spotting a stand of small cottonwood trees crowding the riverbank, he and his men ran for it.

Unsheathing their knives, they hacked down the little trees to make a clearing, then heaped the saplings into a simple perimeter breastwork. Each man lashed his butcher knife to a cottonwood pole "so as to form a tolerable lance." Then the trappers awaited the impending attack that must, Jedediah thought, "in spite of courage[,] conduct[,] and all that man could do terminate in our destruction. It was a fearful time."

Smith preserved his composure, just as he had in 1823 during the fight with the Arikaras on another sandbar by another river. This time, however, he saw no way out; his men possessed few guns and scant ammunition, and they could expect no reinforcements. Nine men with only five rifles among them lay huddled behind a preposterous sapling barricade facing what Smith calculated to be "four or five hundred indians whose hands were yet stained with the blood of their companions." "Some of the men asked me," wrote Jedediah later,

> if I thought we could be able to defend ourselves. I told them I thought we would. But that was not my opinion. I directed that not more than three guns should be fired at a time and those only when the Shot would be certain of killing.... Seeing a few Indians who ventured out from their cover within long shot I directed two good marksmen to fire. They did so and two Indians fell and another was wounded. Uppon this the Indians ran off like frightened sheep and we were released from the apprehension of immediate death.

Once again, good fortune stayed death's hand when it reached for Jedediah Smith. Once again, his cool-headed leadership and characteristic instinct for survival permitted him to seize an opportunity that another man might have failed to grasp. The Mohaves temporarily held back, nursing their wounds and contemplating their next move. Smith and his men awaited nightfall and then slipped away undetected into the gloomy desert. By then Smith had devised a plan. "After weighing all the circumstances of my situation as ca[l]mly as possible," Jedediah wrote, "I concluded to again try the hospitality of the Californians. I had left with my party on the Appalaminy [the Stanislaus] a quantity of Beaver furr and if the Governor would permit me to trade, and I could find any person acquainted with the value of furr, I might procure such supplies as would enable me to continue my journey to the north." Whatever he may have thought of his previous experiences with the californios, it would be better to be mistreated there than to stay and die where he was. Besides, California offered the only opportunity to acquire supplies and rejoin his men encamped at the Stanislaus River.

The disconsolate men trekked westward all night and came upon a spring the following morning. Sweltering desert heat and the fact that they possessed woefully inadequate water containers persuaded Jedediah to rest his men at the spring until evening, and they again stumbled through the night. By morning Smith had lost his bearings. Ascending a nearby hill, he recognized no landmark. After pointing his men in the right direction, Jedediah took one man, a "good walker," and set out ahead in search of a spring. Within a mile or two Smith and his companion found another water hole. Sending his assistant back to fetch the others, Jedediah rested briefly to alleviate his "incessant anxiety and fatigue."

After recovering his equanimity, Jedediah climbed another hill, and this time he discerned his former route about five miles to the southwest. The men rested at the spring until night fell and then marched through the entire night and much of the next morning before reaching another waterhole. Smith and his men paused briefly and then started across the "Salt Plain" that he had traversed in 1826. For several days they staggered from spring to spring, suffering fearfully from dehydration. Smith's wrought-iron constitution again enabled him to go without water better than his nearly delirious men. They gained a modicum of relief by chewing leaves of what Smith called a "Cabbage

Pear," a "verry juicy" plant "frequently found growing on the most parched and Barren ground."

Urging his debilitated men forward, Jedediah discovered a tiny, almost invisible spring amid drifting sand at the edge of the salt desert. Two men had collapsed a few miles back, so Smith once again filled a "small kettle" with water and dispatched a man to deliver it. After the stragglers arrived, the trappers rested a while and trudged into the night. Happening upon the same campsite where Smith's men had dug little wells in damp sand the year before, they paused for a few hours' sleep. Another day's travel brought them to the Mohave River, which was even drier than it had been in 1826. Even in such wretched circumstances, Smith's curiosity compelled him to ponder the natural processes of floods and evaporation that produced the "beautiful encrustation" he found in the "Salt Plain."

The next day, after marching eight miles along the dusty riverbed, Smith spotted a pair of horses near a few Indian lodges. Deciding he must have the horses, he roped them and found their Indian owners. In what may have been a forced exchange, he persuaded the Indians to take a small collection of "cloth, knives, Beads, &c." for the animals and for "grass candy and some demijohns [baskets] for carrying water." In the next day or two the trappers acquired two more horses from some Vanyume Indians and set out for the "Gape of the Mountain," Cajon Pass, which took them across the San Bernardino and San Gabriel ranges.

Jedediah Smith and his bedraggled mountain men descended the southern slopes of the San Bernardino Range during the final week of August 1827. When they came across a herd of cattle at one of Misión San Gabriel's satellite ranches, they instantly killed three. After gorging themselves on as much meat as they could stand, they dried the rest. The harrowing trek from the massacre site at the Colorado to the mission region had consumed ten days.

According to Smith's journal, the dried meat was provender for the journey he intended to make "through the Barren country Between Bernardino and the Appelaminy." Smith clearly intended to dodge California's mission and presidio settlements altogether and hasten northward toward the camp on the Stanislaus. Perhaps his conscience spurred him to dispatch an Indian with a note to inform the mission's overseer that he had taken the cattle. A while later the overseer rode into camp and presented the men "such little Luxuries as he had." Jedediah accepted an invitation to spend the night at the man's farmhouse, and the next morning the overseer brought several fresh horses to Smith's camp. Jedediah traded some "things we had brought on our backs from the Amuchabas [Mohaves]" for nine horses.

While at the overseer's house, Smith penned a note to his former benefactor Father Sánchez at Misión San Gabriel Arcángel. In it he explained why he again came to California, apologetically declined to visit the mission, and mentioned that he must leave two men at the mission. Thomas Virgin had not recovered from the head wound he received at the Mohave Crossing. Isaac Galbraith, a free trapper who wished to go no further, offered to care for Virgin while he convalesced. Smith would leave Virgin with a good horse and instructions to rejoin him at or near San Francisco as soon as he was sufficiently mended. Smith also requested Sánchez to inform Governor Echeandía of his arrival and departure. With these matters settled—or so he thought—Smith prepared to depart for the Stanislaus.

After resting for five days, Smith and his men set off for the trappers' encampment on the Stanislaus. Hurrying along, they managed to keep ahead of the squad of Mexican soldiers dispatched from San Diego's presidio with orders to apprehend them. Retracing his 1826 route, Smith reached the camp safely around September 18, two days ahead of the date on which he had promised to return. Jedediah's knack for maintaining a travel schedule over an enormous and rugged country and under such trying circumstances seems downright uncanny. Unfortunately, Smith's troubles in California were far from over. Instead of beating a hasty retreat from inquiring Mexicans, he would soon be caught up in another lengthy detention. But for the moment he rejoiced in the pleasure of rejoining his comrades, who, as Jedediah wrote in masterly understatement, had become "somewhat anxious for my return."

Of the eleven men he left the preceding year, only two had deserted. The trappers on the Stanislaus had passed a "pleasant summer, not in the least interrupted by Indians." But their relief at greeting their bourgeois was tempered by the sad news he conveyed. "I was there," wrote Smith, "by the time appointed but instead of Bringing them the expected supplies I brought them intelligence of my misfortunes." Still, the mountain men had reveled in California's gentle climate, and they got on well with the neighboring Indians, who "appeared to be verry honest, having at no time manifested a disposition to steal, and [were] entirely friendly." The Mokelumne leader named Te-mi was a frequent guest in camp, bringing the trappers "grass seid [sic] meal, currents and raspberries &c, and they in return loaded him with meat . . . a most acceptable present." Smith fondly remembered Te-mi, who made good his promise to restore a stolen horse and also returned "7 or 8 of the traps lost in Rock River." The trappers had also received one visit from "a party of Spaniards" from the missions, who had heard about the Americans' camp from visiting Indians. Initially at least, the Mexicans "appeared satisfied with the reasons Mr. Rogers gave for his being in the country."

Jedediah organized his men into trapping parties, then set off with three companions and a couple of Indian guides for Misión San José, some seventy miles west. Smith left no explanation for why he risked placing himself again at the disposal of men for whom he had so much contempt. It appears, however, that he had already decided to purchase many horses and sell them at the rendezvous, and perhaps felt he needed to clear the way to buy livestock from the californios.

Smith's first venture to California and its settlements may have been somewhat accidental, but after the "Mohave massacre" he had no choice but to revisit the coastal settlements before proceeding northward. The unprecedented appearance of the Americans from the eastern desert in 1826 had obviously caught

Governor Echeandía and his minions off guard, and they were no doubt relieved when the trappers departed in February 1827. Just a few weeks later, however, the governor began receiving disturbing reports. Visiting Indians told him about the foreign trappers encamped on the Stanislaus River, and some of the news seemed to implicate the Americans in illegal military and diplomatic operations. In September 1827 Echeandía learned that when Smith and his haggard survivors returned to California, they failed to notify proper officials. By then Echeandía also knew Smith had ignored his orders and departed California by a route of his own choosing. Amid mounting suspicions, the governor had by this time been gathering intelligence on Smith for months.

In March 1827 Echeandía was informed that John Wilson, the trapper whom Jedediah had banished for insubordination two months earlier, had passed through Monterey and turned up at San Francisco. The governor ordered Wilson's arrest and interrogation. San Francisco's presidial commandant, Lt. Ignacio Martínez, locked Wilson in the *calabozo* (jail) at the end of March. During questioning, Wilson claimed he had been on his way to the Columbia River to rejoin Smith, but Martínez concluded that Smith had left Wilson behind as a spy to examine "all that his companions could not see."

During another examination at Monterey in mid-May, Wilson told the *juez fiscal* (customs officer) Juan José Rocha that he and Smith had been at odds for months, and that he only continued with Smith because there was no other way to get back to the United States. He had left San Gabriel with Smith's party in January but at Tulare Lake his horse fell on him, injuring his chest and causing him to cough up blood. An Indian guide conducted Wilson to Misión San Miguel, where he mended. Upon leaving the mission, Wilson traveled north, only to be arrested at San Francisco. Evidently unaware that Jedediah had taken a different route, Wilson told Rocha that Smith intended to purchase supplies from the Russians near Bodega Bay and head for the Columbia River. Rocha also questioned Daniel Ferguson, the deserter who remained in the vicinity of San Gabriel when Smith's brigade departed. Identified as a twenty-seven-year-old

Irish shoemaker, Ferguson claimed ignorance of Smith's route or intentions, but said that Smith's principal reason for coming back to California was to obtain horses.

Unfortunately, a marked increase in the number of mission Indian runaways—including a mass exodus of four hundred Indians from Misión San José in mid-May 1827—coincided with rumors that American trappers were agitating disorder among the interior tribes. The priest at San José, Father Narciso Durán, believed the Americans were guilty of exhorting neophytes to flee his mission. Aware of Durán's allegations, Jedediah sent an explanatory note to the priest shortly before leaving for the 1827 rendezvous. Durán received Smith's letter from a pair of runaway mission Indians named Amaranto and Narciso. Amaranto also possessed a letter from Smith commending him as a "friendly native" and "well disposed man." Both Indians may have worked as guides for Smith after he met them near the Stanislaus River. Father Durán forwarded Smith's unopened letter to Lieutenant Martinéz, who in turn delivered it to Governor Echeandía.

At about the same time, five runaway Indians from the San José and Santa Clara missions returned to San José. Upon interrogation, they claimed that the Americans encamped among the Mokelumnes had many weapons and were making a map. When officials assessed this new, albeit unsubstantiated, information in light of what they already suspected, their worst fears seemed confirmed. Smith had indeed gathered information about the province's military strength and resident populace and about mileages between some missions and the seacoast. He also expressed interest in buying horses and cattle, and he attempted to trade furs from some of the mission Indians. The intruders' questionable behavior during a period of unrest among mission Indians led Mexican officials quite naturally to conclude that they were dangerous troublemakers.

All of this persuaded the governor to issue an arrest warrant for Smith and instruct Lieutenant Martínez to apprehend him. Martínez dispatched Sgt. Francisco Soto with two dozen soldiers to the camp on the Stanislaus. When Soto arrived in the first week of June, Smith was already en route to the 1827 rendezvous, so the sergeant confronted Harrison Rogers with a list of charges, drawn up by Capt. Luis Antonio Argüello, a former governor of California. Addressing his letter to the "Commander of the American Expedition of the East," Argüello vigorously chided the Americans for their many indiscretions.

Argüello noted that the provincial government was "astonished" that American interlopers meddled in the affairs of a territory over which they had no jurisdiction. They had committed "hostile acts," thumbed their noses at duly constituted officials of California and Mexico, and asserted authority over Indians who were "well satisfied with the law that incorporates them into the Mexican nation." Argüello alleged that the trappers had commissioned certain Indians as "captains with insignias" and had drawn "surveys" of the land. Mexico would not tolerate such "insults" in blatant disregard of international law. But Sergeant Soto had no orders to arrest all of the trappers, and Smith had already left; instead, Argüello's letter served as a warning that the Mexican government would soon "put its complaints before your government."

Mustering all his charm, Rogers demonstrated his grasp of practical diplomacy. Tearing a sheet from his journal, he penned a reply on June 3, 1827, writing "in an open prairie, on my [k]nee, where the wind and dust are blowing." Casting himself as a "poor, misfortunate man, in poverty," Rogers disavowed any seditious intent. "No sir," he wrote Argüello, "Believe me, that all reports you have heard from the Indians are down right lies." He merely fed Indian visitors who happened by his camp, and he recruited none to serve American interests. "Struck with astonishment" to learn that "Indians had raised such reports," he offered to come in and "stand trial without opposition." Rogers closed his exculpatory missive with news that Smith was even then "hunting a pass across the mountain," and he signed the letter as "your strange but real American friend and humble servant." Two days later, Sergeant Soto returned to Misión San José. His commander advised the governor that in Soto's opinion the Americans had not incited Indians to flee from the missions.

Yet Argüello remained suspicious that the foreigners might still cause trouble with mission neophytes. Despite Soto's assessment, Argüello feared that the "shameful and cowardly" Americans were "scoundrels who came [to California] with no other intention than to explore our possessions" for some nefarious purpose. Captain Argüello remembered only too well the mission Indian rebellion that he had helped to suppress while he temporarily governed California in 1824.

His reluctance to accept Rogers's assertions at face value is not surprising. Though he admitted in a letter to the governor dated June 6, 1827, that most of his fears had "dissipated completely," he intended quietly to pursue his investigation of potential collusion between Americans and mission Indians. A month or two after receiving Argüello's note, Governor Echeandía sent the entire dossier on Smith to Mexico City, hoping the matter would die quietly and spare him from more trouble on account of Jedediah Smith. In this conceit the governor was sadly mistaken.

During September 1827, while Jedediah Smith journeyed to the Stanislaus, authorities at San Gabriel questioned Isaac Galbraith and Thomas Virgin as to Smith's intentions and whereabouts. The trappers told their interrogators that Smith was no spy, that he lacked the instruments necessary for mapmaking, and that they wanted only to rejoin Smith at Fort Ross or Bodega Bay and head homeward via the Columbia River. Two days after Jedediah arrived at his men's camp, he decided he must visit Misión San José, spin a convincing yarn for the Catholic priests there, and persuade them to assist him. Before he left he told Rogers that if he failed to return in short order, the clerk should take his men to the Russian American Fur Company's trading post north of San Francisco. Then Smith, Abraham Laplant, James Reed, and Joseph Palmer saddled horses and rode seventy miles to Misión San José. Jedediah's "last and only resource" was to "try once more the hospitality of the Californians."

When the trappers arrived at the mission on September 23, they were in for a nasty surprise. Their horses were confiscated and the Americans were ushered into "a dirty hovel which they called a guard house." The arrest evidently originated with Father José Viador, the director of the nearby Misión Santa Clara, who harbored considerable dislike for Americans. Smith wrote that when he entered the mission, the two priests, Father Viador and Father Narciso Durán, "appeared somewhat confused by my sudden appearance and could not or would not understand me when I endeavored to explain the cause of my being in the country.... They would neither put me in close confinement nor set me at liberty." For the next two days he received no provisions from the priests, but thanks to the "kindness of the old overseer" at the mission, he and his men did not go hungry. In yet another wry passage, Smith noted that Father Durán seemed to think that "two or three days was nothing for a heretic to go without eating."

Jedediah Smith learned that an American named William Welch who was fluent in Spanish lived at the Pueblo of San José, so he requested Welch to pay him a visit. With Welch interpreting, Smith tried once more to converse with Father Durán, but the close-lipped priest said only that Smith must await the arrival of a military officer from San Francisco. When the presidial commander, Lt. Ignacio Martínez arrived, he brusquely informed Smith that he was to stand trial under charges of illegally claiming land near the San Joaquin River. At a preliminary hearing Martínez produced an Indian witness against Smith. Recognizing the Indian as a visitor to his Stanislaus camp, Jedediah began grilling him on the details of his allegations, but nothing substantial emerged. Martínez soon lost patience with the Indian and, Smith wrote, "instead of punishing me as the father [Durán] desired Sentenced the Indian to a severe flogging, which perhaps he did not deserve."

Smith told Lieutenant Martínez that he wished to travel to Monterey to see the governor, but the officer replied that he must remain confined at San José until the governor sent for him. Still, Smith gained permission to exchange elk hides, deer skins, and beaver skins for guns, powder and lead, tobacco, clothes, and other goods in preparation for departure from the province. He was also permitted to purchase more horses and mules to add to the sixty-odd animals he had already acquired around San José. He even persuaded Martínez to allow two blacksmiths, most likely James Reed and Joseph Palmer, to forge a few beaver traps.

Despite these concessions, Jedediah's requests for a speedy resolution of his case fell upon deaf ears, and he impatiently marked time for about four weeks. On October 27, 1827, Smith urgently requested Echeandía to convene a hearing, and a few days later four soldiers came with orders to take him to Monterey. In the meantime, Smith had made contact with two Bostonians, Captain John Cooper, who had married a local woman and lived in Monterey, and Thomas Park, a clerk aboard the vessel *Harbinger*. Cooper promised to follow Jedediah to Monterey and offered "any assistance in his power" while Smith waited on Echeandía.

A three-day ride brought Smith and the squad of soldiers to the provincial capital, where Jedediah was incarcerated without the benefit of a meal. Captain Cooper brought some food the next morning and then accompanied Jedediah to the governor's office. When Echeandía began speaking in Spanish, Smith interrupted to inform him that he must have an interpreter. Echeandía sent for William Hartnell, a multilingual Englishman who did business along the coast. With Hartnell's assistance Smith tried to explain his situation to Echeandía, but the governor's responses seemed to be "distinguished by the same traits as those that Marked his character when I saw him at San Diego," namely, arbitrary contrariness and vacillation. Still, the governor granted Smith liberty to walk about the town until their next meeting. During one of his strolls Smith ran across his former companions Daniel Ferguson and John Wilson. Both men appeared eager to remain in California.

At length Governor Echeandía summoned Jedediah to a second interview. It did not begin auspiciously. The governor wondered why anyone would choose to return to California over the tortuous desert route instead of the more direct path across the Sierra Nevada. (Obviously, the governor had never tried crossing the mountains.) He upbraided Smith for failing to notify him when he reentered California, but Jedediah retorted that he had posted a letter to Echeandía through Father Sánchez at Misión San Gabriel in September. Then he reminded Echeandía that his October 26 letter from "Mission St. Joseph" summarized the past year's travels and difficulties.

That letter began with the deadpan comment "it will undoubtedly surprise you to hear that Jedediah S. Smith is at this place." In it Smith asserted (more than little disingenuously) that he had tried to leave by the same route he followed into California "but the Mountains hung covered with Snow, were impassible and I was obliged to go northwardly." He recounted his conflicts with Indians, noting "they shot some arrows at some of my men and I killed some of them," but he feared his trappers were too broken-down to risk taking the whole party over the mountains. Instead, after losing some horses in one attempt at crossing the sierra, Smith "concluded that the only method by which I could save the lives of my Men would be to take two men and endeavor to slip through the Indians undiscovered." He mentioned that he reached the rendezvous (unwisely referring to it as "Camp Defiance") and then headed back toward California, only to lose ten men and two "half breed" women at the Mohave Crossing. He finished by requesting permission to buy supplies and livestock, hire two or three men to help manage the horse and mule herd, and to have Virgin and Galbraith sent to him so they could all leave together.

Governor Echeandía did not "appear satisfied with [Smith's] explanation" and remarked that "it was altogether a misterious business." He thought it might be best to send Jedediah Smith to Mexico City for further interrogation. In that event, he must pay his own way, and two or three months might go by before a Mexican vessel made sail for Acapulco. Outraged, Smith concluded that Echeandía had been "placed in power to perplex me and those over whom he was called to govern." Smith thought it ludicrous that the governor "should seriously talk of making a man take himself at his own expense to prison," adding, "I plainly told him that on such conditions I would not go."

William Hartnell, "whose opinion seemed to pass with the Governor for law," came up with a novel solution to this quandary. According to Hartnell, under English maritime law four masters of vessels in a foreign port could constitute an ad hoc committee and empower a temporary consular agent to adjudicate matters in such emergencies. He obliquely suggested that perhaps the Americans also had such a law. Though they were not "perfectly satisfied of the legality of the proposition," four American ship's captains proved willing to undertake the unusual measure on Jedediah's behalf.

One more hurdle remained. Governor Echeandía ordered Smith to write a letter requesting his men to turn themselves in at Monterey. Jedediah informed him that his trappers were nearer to San Francisco than to Monterey, and the governor "remarked that they might go in there." But when Echeandía had the letter translated, he thought it "hinted at the treatment" Smith received and seemed to suggest that Harrison Rogers ought to ignore the order. Smith admitted as much in his journal, noting that his veiled warning would be "sufficient for Mr. Rogers" to head for Bodega Bay instead of San Francisco. The governor insisted that the trappers present themselves at San Francisco. Jedediah believed that Echeandía was fearful of precipitating a shoot-out with the Americans, for there were "some terrible stories in circulation about the shooting [i.e., marksmanship] of my men," and "it was said they were sure of their mark at any distance." Echoing this theme, after meeting Smith at Monterey, a British naval officer of HMS *Blossom* wrote that each of Jedediah's men was "necessarily a good shot with his rifle[,] performing as we were told the feat of William Tell frequently for pastime."

When Rogers and the other trappers arrived at San Francisco in the first week of November, he sent Smith a letter apprising him that they were camped "at a spring not far from the Precidio" and had been "well supplied with Beef Corn Beans &c." Meanwhile, in order to buy provisions, Jedediah arranged to unload his remaining furs—1,568 pounds of beaver and ten otter skins—to a Boston ship captain, John Bradshaw, at the bargain price of $2.50 a pound. The sale netted Smith $3,940, a paltry showing for two years' work but enough to meet his immediate requirements. Echeandía once again spoke of sending Smith to Mexico City, but when Jedediah informed him he had already sold his furs and completed arrangements for departure, the governor relented "with some little hesitation."

By November 12 Captain Cooper had been named a consular agent by the four sea captains. After further rounds of frustrating negotiations, a bond was drawn up that contained several stipulations. In exchange for a "free and safe passport" out of California, Smith promised to leave speedily and to make "no hostile excursion" and "no trip toward the coast or in the region of his establishment south of the 42nd parallel." He would be permitted to purchase guns, ammunition, 100 mules and 150 horses, and sundry provisions before departing, and he must follow "the road from Mission San Jose by way of Carquinez Straits and Bodega." At Monterey on November 15, Jedediah Smith gave his residence as "Green township in the state of Ohio" and, with Rufus Perkins (Captain Bradshaw's supercargo) as a witness, pledged "the sum of thirty thousand dollars for the faithful performance" of the mandates in the bond that he and Captain Cooper signed.

Later that day Smith boarded Captain Bradshaw's ship, *Franklin,* for the voyage to San Francisco, and he was seasick for the entire unpleasant three-day journey. Upon landing on November 17, Smith presented his passport to Capt. Luis Antonio Argüello and greeted his men sequestered within the presidio. The next day his furs were stowed aboard the *Franklin* and he set about purchasing goods and livestock. On November 22 he and Captain Bradshaw were invited to dine on the British sloop HMS *Blossom*, but Smith was too busy dealing with Governor Echeandía to attend. The following day he prepared to off-load his gear from the *Franklin,* and that evening he supped with half a dozen captains aboard the vessel. Doubtless he relished the meal with his countrymen, but after dinner a stiff gale obliged the company to remain aboard the ship. Making the best of their situation, the seafaring men stayed up most of the night

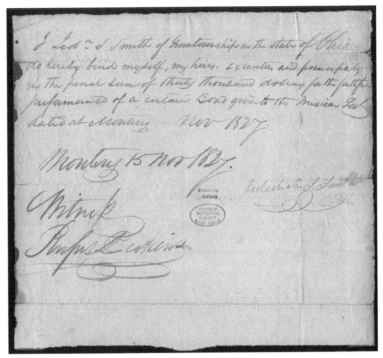

Bond signed by Jedediah S. Smith and Rufus Perkins at Monterey,
California, in November 1827. Smith's thirty-thousand-dollar bond
was equivalent to about 150 years' labor for the average Missouri
working man in the 1820s. William Sublette Papers, courtesy of the
Missouri Historical Society, Saint Louis.

drinking bottle after bottle of wine. Jedediah took some part in
the bibulous carousal but wrote—characteristically—that the
affair had been "contrary to my wish."

Finding it impossible to complete his preparations for departure at San Francisco, and with his horses "nearly starved"
because of scanty pasturage, Smith persuaded Captain Argüello
to allow him to take his men about forty miles down the penin-
sula to San José. In spite of their lingering mutual mistrust, on
November 26 Argüello kindly permitted Smith to pasture his
stock at his own sheep ranch at San Lorenzo, not far from San

José. Ironically, at about the same time Jedediah "spoke with great acrimony of his long and unjust detention" to William Smyth, a British expeditionary artist. Smyth served under Capt. William Beechey, a famed polar explorer whose vessel, HMS *Blossom,* was then anchored in San Francisco Bay.

On November 27 Smith's men were on their way to San Lorenzo while he rode ahead to the Pueblo of San José. Accompanying him was an Englishman named William R. Garner who had deserted from a whaling ship about two years earlier. Jedediah had recently hired Garner to exchange two horse-loads of goods for more horses at Monterey. At San José, Smith located the house of his former interpreter William Welch, where he was to receive "the payment of [a] draft of 200 Dollars on him from Mr. [Rufus] Perkins." Welch was away but had left word that Jedediah could collect the sum at Misión Santa Cruz, thirty miles distant. After hiring a man to find Welch, Smith and Garner continued on to Misión San José. With Garner interpreting, Smith persuaded Father Durán to allow James Reed and Joseph Palmer use of the blacksmith shop for a week to repair guns. The priest also agreed to house Jedediah in one room and his men in two other rooms. Some of Smith's trappers arrived at the mission later that afternoon, but they had abandoned several exhausted horses on the trail. Smith sent Garner back to the pueblo to buy replacements for the lost horses.

By November 28 most of the trappers were assembled at the mission, though many horses and mules had either run off or been stolen. Smith dispatched two men to collect any new horses that Garner had purchased, and he fretted about Welch's unpaid draft. Just then Captain Bradshaw rode up to the mission with some supplies for the priest and Smith. He told Jedediah that he would cover the bill but that the coin was aboard his ship near the north end of the bay. On December 1 Smith and the captain rode to San Pablo and Jedediah hired a small boat to ferry him across the bay. By ten o'clock that evening he was on his way, but high tide and severe winds forced the shallop to shelter in the lee of a small island, and Smith did not board Bradshaw's vessel until dawn. Captain Bradshaw was detained on shore until late the following night, and Jedediah finally received his money on the morning of December 4. Hastening back to San José, Smith found that Harrison Rogers had driven the livestock into the mission's plaza to safeguard and brand them. Rogers told Jedediah that all but five horses were accounted for.

Smith's men spent the next day baling goods for the trip, and on the following day, perhaps, Isaac Galbraith arrived from San Gabriel. Galbraith had no news of Thomas Virgin. For the next week Smith and his men guarded horses, prepared bags of jerked meat, and collected camp gear. Jedediah found time to attend mass, where he enjoyed another musical performance by Indian neophytes, the orchestra mustering "12 or 15 violins 5 Base viols and one flute." His men constantly watched and counted livestock, but every day they had to chase down more runaways.

On December 13 Thomas Virgin finally arrived. After several weeks of recuperating at San Bernardino he had been transferred to a San Diego prison cell, where he was sometimes left without food, enjoined not to speak with anyone, and "abused in almost every way." On December 5 Governor Echeandía had released him and sent him on to San José. It was a happy reunion for these men, hardened as they were to danger, privation, and death. Jedediah wrote only that he "was quite glad to see the old man again." Virgin told Smith that the young mission Indian who was jailed while Smith was at San Gabriel had been sentenced to be shot, but Father Sánchez, "influenced by his own good feelings and his promise to [Smith], wrote to Mexico and procured his pardon." Jedediah's conversation with Thomas Virgin convinced him that he had "good reason" to believe that the Mohaves had been instructed by the Mexican government to "kill all Americans coming in from that direction."

Capt. W. A. Richardson, a trader at San Francisco, secured Smith an interview with Paul Shelikov, who ran the Russian American Fur Company's post near Bodega Bay. Shelikov provided a letter of introduction and informed Smith that the company factor at Fort Ross would sell any goods he might require after leaving San Francisco. After another exasperating week of watching his trappers round up recalcitrant livestock, Smith asked the mission director's permission to move his camp to Captain Argüello's sheep ranch at San Lorenzo, where "there was plenty of grass and a pen in which I could shut up my horses & Mules."

Jedediah Smith left San José with 250 to 300 horses and mules. Having paid about ten dollars for each animal, he anticipated a roughly 500 percent profit from their sale, presumably to trappers at the next rendezvous. Smith evidently wanted to continue trapping beavers on Mexican land, collect his men at the Stanislaus, move his large herd of livestock to the rendezvous, and explore northern California more or less simultaneously.

By Christmas Eve his men were en route to their new quarters and Jedediah set out with Abraham Laplant for San Francisco and a final round of discussions with Captain Argüello. One of the captain's children died on Christmas Eve, so nothing could be accomplished until the following day. Christmas Day passed unnoticed in both Smith's and Rogers' journals. On December 26 Jedediah Smith locked horns for the last time with "Don Lewis" Argüello.

During two interviews the captain stated he had orders for ten soldiers to escort Smith out of California, and that he must ford the Sacramento River (Argüello referred to it as the "Buenaventura") "near its entrance into the Bay of St. Francisco." The mouth of the river was broad and turbulent, so Smith asked permission to go upstream to find a safer crossing for his men and horses, but Argüello would not hear of it. Governor Echeandía had ordered Argüello to see that Smith departed within one month and that he followed a prescribed route. This was at the moment impossible, Smith argued, since the only available boat was in disrepair and the water was too rough for rafts. Argüello refused to alter the governor's orders, and Smith sarcastically suggested that the captain had better furnish a boat. Argüello responded that he had no boat and told Smith he "must wait until the Gen'l could be advised of the situation of things and give further instructions."

To Jedediah's way of thinking, this was the last straw. He was spending money daily instead of making it; his hired men's labor was being needlessly squandered; he had already suffered enormous losses in men killed and in stolen gear and goods; and now for a second time he endured an aggravating round of meetings with obdurate officials. Murmuring acquiescence, he left the interview "with a determination fixed to take my own course without waiting for their tardy Movements which the situation of my finances would not permit." British mariner James Wolfe, who got the story from the artist William Smyth, recorded that when Smith's cavalcade departed San Francisco on December 26, 1827, it "consisted of 16 men well armed and mounted, with about 60 horses to carry baggage ... presenting rather a formidable appearance." According to Wolfe, Jedediah "seemed to think very lightly of his trip across the continent."

As he had done on both expeditions to California, Jedediah Smith recruited eighteen men for his impending venture into northern California and Oregon. Some were veterans of the 1826 trip, including Harrison Rogers, Arthur Black, John Gaither, Emmenuel Lazarus, Peter Ranney, Abraham Laplant, Martin McCoy, John Hanna, and John Reubascan (possibly a mistaken reference to Robeseau, who was supposedly killed at the Mohave River, but the identification is uncertain.). Seven of the eight survivors of the August 1827 Mohave Crossing slaughter continued with the expedition. They were Charles Swift, Toussaint Maréchal, Thomas Virgin, John Turner, Joseph Palmer, Joseph Lapointe, and Thomas Daws. Richard Leland, a young Englishman, joined Smith's party in California. One French-Canadian member, "Pombert," was either hired in California or may have been with Smith's 1826 expedition. Last to join would be an Indian youth they called "Marion," whom they more or less kidnapped months later in Oregon, shortly before the brigade arrived at the Umpqua River.

Jedediah Smith's journal is often annoyingly imprecise, and nowhere is this more evident than in his vague account of how he left the San Francisco Bay area to begin what ought to be called his "Northwest Expedition." But his course must have been shaped in conformity with the dictates of California's interior river systems. Two great rivers bisect the Central Valley, and both empty into San Francisco Bay. Out of the alpine north

This sketch of the mission at Yerba Buena (later San Francisco) was made in 1826 by William Smyth, an artist who served aboard Capt. William Beechey's HMS *Blossom*. The artist was acquainted with Jedediah Smith. "The Mission of San Francisco, Upper California." Courtesy of the Bancroft Library, University of California, Berkeley.

flows the Sacramento, taking in its course several streams that tumble out of the Sierra Nevada, the most important of which are the Feather and the American rivers. From the south flows the San Joaquin. Its main feeder streams include the Kings, the Chowchilla, the Merced, the Tuolumne, and the Stanislaus. Both rivers flow into the easternmost extension of the broad delta of San Francisco Bay. The Strait of Carquinez, which Smith was ordered to cross, divides the main bay from its eastern estuary. The search for the Buenaventura, Captain Argüello's name for the Sacramento, had consumed a good deal of William Ashley's time in 1825 with no palpable results. Jedediah Smith likewise pondered the possible existence of such a useful river, and he meant to determine if it was the one he was ordered to cross on his way out of California.

Smith knew that Captain Argüello had led a "party of discovery" about three years earlier "up the principal Branch of the

Buenaventura or Piscadore." But he dismissed the "indolent" Mexicans' expeditionary efforts as at best half-hearted, since they supposedly mistook his snow-bedecked "Mt. St. Joseph" for one made of "Chalk," and Smith knew better. He also scoffed at their estimate that it lay about six hundred miles from San Francisco, recalling from his own exploration that it was "not over 250 m[iles] from San Francisco to the place where the river leaves the Mount St. Joseph."

Jedediah Smith certainly had an agenda, and as long as he had a say in the matter, no Mexican official was going to disrupt his plans. Though generally considered a fair and honest man, in California Smith developed a rationale to justify more than a little dishonesty. Guarded in his dealings with Mexicans at all times, he rarely allowed himself to speak openly on any topic. He never lost sight of his self-interest, and he was something of a nationalist and a cultural supremacist.

Jedediah routinely dissembled to Governor Echeandía and Captain Argüello and was less than forthright with some of the mission priests. After Smith violated Echeandía's orders about leaving the bay area via the Strait of Carquinez, Captain Argüello unburdened himself in a letter to the governor on January 2, 1828. Venting his spleen over his unpleasant discussions with Smith, the captain complained of the Americans' deceits and of their contempt for Mexican laws and policies. Smith and his men, he wrote, were "not grateful for the favors given to them" and they "mock[ed] the authorities." Argüello asserted that Smith failed to pay "import duties and other taxes" when he purchased goods from Captain Bradshaw's ship *Franklin*, and that Smith did not repay a personal loan of forty pesos. (There is, however, evidence that Smith left $176.69 with "Guellermo Gardinier" to pay a 15 percent duty on roughly twelve hundred dollars' worth of goods that he carried to San José.) The captain ended by insisting that Smith and his fellows had insulted Mexican honor, adding that he mistrusted the motives of all Americans who "live among us in the guise of mediators." Argüello rightly suspected that Smith and his mountain men would do as they pleased and go their own way, trapping illegally as they went.

Two days after leaving San Francisco, while his men were "engaged in breaking mules" at Misión San José, Jedediah had written to Echeandía and Argüello to inform them of his intentions. On the same day Jedediah wrote a letter to the chief American diplomat in Mexico City, Joel R. Poinsett. A year earlier Smith had written to Poinsett to explain that after he and his partners bought out Ashley he had crossed a "Country of Starvation" before arriving at Misión San Gabriel. In his 1826 letter Smith had described Governor Echeandía as "very much of a Gentlemen but very Suspicious." At Echeandía's request, Jedediah explained, he had turned over all his papers, but the governor, "instead of thanking me for the information … and assisting me to pass on about my business," detained him until he became convinced that Smith was no spy. Now, following his second detention in 1827–28, Jedediah was less willing to mince words with Poinsett, though he remained mindful that he was dealing with a diplomat. Observing that his firm was "duly authorized … to hunt and trade on lands claimed by the United States, (West of the Rocky Mountains)," he neglected to mention that his party trapped many beavers in northern California—clearly no part of the United States.

After summarizing his adventures and misfortunes since August 1826, Smith defended his method of dealing with Echeandía. Several discussions with Echeandía produced "no effect," for the governor doubted his sincerity. Some of his men had been cruelly mistreated, and he was forbidden to hire more men even though several Americans wanted to leave with him. He finished by noting Argüello's refusal to extend the time allotted him for leaving California. When Argüello said he must first receive permission from the governor, Smith was "intirely destitute of money," and that explained why he wrote to Echeandía and proceeded on his way "without waiting for an answer."

The letter to Poinsett provides additional evidence of Smith's willingness to stretch the truth if it served his purposes. Jedediah claimed that when he left the California settlements in January 1827 he retraced his route "about two hundred and fifty, or three hundred miles directly back," but heavy snow in the mountains forced him to find a new route. This assertion was not quite true. On the other hand, Jedediah felt he had good reasons not to comply with orders. The British seaman James Wolfe heard second-hand that Jedediah had been "treated as an already convicted criminal, and put in close confinement," while his trappers "also were confined in the Praesidio of San Francisco." Little wonder, perhaps, that Smith found his grievances sufficient to justify ignoring the law and violating his bond.

In April 1828 the government at Mexico City delivered minister Poinsett its own interpretation of these matters and charged the Americans with deliberate trespasses on Mexican soil. The Americans' rendezvous site at Bear Lake lay about fifteen miles south of the 42nd parallel and was thus inside Mexico, though it is doubtful that anyone knew its true position. More to the point, the Mexican government claimed that some Americans at the rendezvous negotiated an informal peace treaty between the Snake and Ute nations in order to boost trade with both nations. The garbled account that Mexican officials heard persuaded them that the treaty had been made by a "general of the United States of North America" leading a small army accompanied by five wagons and three cannons. The treaty was allegedly signed at a "fort" four days' journey "beyond the lake of Timpanagos." This charge was obviously based upon Jedediah Smith's 1826 "treaties" with the Utes and Snakes. The Utes, at least, had long been considered to be under Spanish and then Mexican oversight. The Mexican complaint further stipulated that "five-and-twenty [Americans] separated themselves to go into the Californias," another oblique reference to Smith's brigade that returned to California after the 1827 rendezvous.

Considering Smith's evaluation of his treatment by the Californians, it is scarcely surprising that he decided to ignore both the letter and the spirit of his agreement with Echeandía. Smith rarely expressed anger in his journals, even when the most shocking catastrophes befell him, but he made plain his dislike for the governor and the generality of Mexican officials when he groused to his journal about how he was "much perplexed and harassed by the folly of men in power."

CHAPTER 7

The Northwest Expedition from California to the Umpqua River

JEDEDIAH Smith's journal distinguishes his 1828 journey from San Francisco to the Oregon Country with no particular title, but it was not merely a continuation of his Southwest Expedition. Indeed, the Southwest Expedition technically encompasses only the 1826 venture to California, and Smith's 1827 trek should be considered as a "Second Southwest Expedition." But Smith's 1828 trek to the Columbia River was itself a singular achievement. As the first documented overland journey from California to Oregon, it merits consideration as an entirely separate undertaking.

In its objectives, circumstances, and experiences, Jedediah Smith's Northwest Expedition markedly differed from his California expeditions. Instead of confronting thirst and heat in a desert environment where few Indians dwelled, Smith and his companions struggled through rain, floods, mud, and dense forests. Encounters with Indians were much more frequent and more generally violent than had been the case in their marches across the desert land. Unlike the trek through California, travel through jointly occupied Oregon posed no legal problems, and Smith's brigade trapped almost continually from San Francisco to the Umpqua River. The only non-Indians Jedediah met were HBC men, and unlike the California officials, they had no difficulty understanding exactly why he came to Oregon. In all three treks Smith's fascination with exploration played a leading role, but in the latter two expeditions devastating Indian attacks resulted in the deaths of most of Smith's companions.

From January to June of 1828 Jedediah's brigade slowly worked northward through California into Oregon. Their journey took them from the San Francisco Bay area eastward into the Great Valley near modern-day Modesto and northward past the sites of Stockton, Sacramento, Yuba City, Chico, and Red Bluff. They trapped numerous streams that flowed westward from the Sierra Nevada and spent many weeks prowling through rugged, thickly forested foothills and mountains. They wandered through what later became famous as gold rush California's "mother lode country." Near present-day Redding they veered northwest through the Klamath Range toward the seacoast. After weeks of extremely challenging travel through dense rain forests, they came to the Pacific Ocean in the vicinity of today's Crescent City, California. By midsummer, when Smith's brigade had almost attained the Columbia River, disaster overtook them.

On December 30, 1827, with a steady rain churning the ground into thick mud, Jedediah Smith and his men departed from San Lorenzo, about halfway down the eastern shore of the great bay. The brigade rode north, then turned east and crested the hills overlooking the east side of San Francisco Bay and camped near what is today Concord. Continuing eastward for two more days, they covered about forty miles to reach the San Joaquin River.

On January 2 Smith's brigade camped beside the San Joaquin. In preparation for crossing the swollen river the next day, his men built log rafts for their gear and a rough livestock pen and chute. Driving several bucking horses and mules at a time from the pen through the narrow chute, Smith's trappers swam them across the river "without the loss of any," wrote Jedediah, "contrary to my expectations." On the following morning some men hunted for beaver sign while others constructed two bull-boats to use while setting traps or crossing streams. Exultant over his departure from the California settlements, Smith celebrated his return "to the woods, the river, the prairae, the Camp & the Game with a feeling somewhat like that of a prisoner escaped from his dungeon and his chains." Strange though it may seem, Jedediah Smith preferred the uncertain and perilous trapper's life to one in a land he described as "a fine country[,] pleasingly varied by prairae and woodland."

Rain fell almost every day, inundating the riverside lowlands, but Smith's men resumed trapping operations. Each trapper ordinarily managed six traps, but with only forty-seven traps and eighteen men Smith probably divided the traps among a half-dozen skilled trappers. The rest busied themselves hunting elk, stretching and drying beaver skins, repairing saddles, maintaining the camp, breaking mules to carry packs, and keeping track of roughly three hundred half-wild mules and horses. Over the next two weeks Smith's men harvested about one hundred beavers along the San Joaquin River, in violation of his agreements with Echeandía.

On January 16 Harrison Rogers and two hunters came into camp with a pair of "Machyma" Indians of the Miwok nation. One of them was the "principal chief" of a village that Jedediah visited on the upper Calaveras River a year earlier. Smith handed out a few presents to his visitors, and they accepted his invitation to accompany him to Bodega Bay, a side trip that did not materialize. The next morning two of his "Canoe trappers" arrived to inform Smith that the river had burst its banks a few miles below camp and flooded the land. Trapping beavers was out of the question, so Jedediah decided to drive his herd to the Mokelumne River. First, they had to ford the Calaveras River.

Jedediah directed two men, "Reed & Pompare [Pombert]," to continue trapping in a bull-boat and then set off with the rest for the Mokelumne. At Smith's first attempt to get his livestock across the Calaveras, some sank to their bellies in the thick mud and got stuck fast. The men extracted them from the muck and set up camp. On January 19 the brigade slogged ten miles through "verry miry" terrain and camped at a better place for fording the river. Smith's men spent the next day constructing another pen and chute and getting horses, mules, men, and gear across the river. With so many animals crossing the river, the far shore quickly became a giant punch bowl of thick mud. Smith's men chopped down saplings and brush and built a sort of ladder that enabled the livestock to climb out of the river and up the steep bank. Then they felled bigger trees to bridge the river and carried their baggage across. Jedediah and another man each shot at grizzly bears they saw prowling around the camp, but they did not kill them.

By January 21 Smith's brigade reached the Mokelumne and set up camp. The land was so sodden that "horses sank at every step nearly to the [k]nees." The next morning four "Canoe trappers" in bull-boats returned to camp after several unproductive days of searching for beavers. They told Smith they had seen "a great many Indians but found them friendly." Later that evening Jedediah discerned "a good many" close to his camp, but when he hailed them they disappeared. On the following morning several Miwoks entered the camp. With their food supply exhausted, Smith's men gladly traded tobacco to their visitors for three "fine salmon[,] some of which would weigh 15 or 20 lbs." One man soon killed a deer and meat was again available, but the men found so few signs of beavers that setting more traps would be pointless. Meanwhile, a heavy rain fell on the already saturated land and the river made another rise. Smith had been planning to ford it and move downstream on the opposite shore, but the river had its way and he stayed put.

On January 23 more Indians visited the camp. Among them Smith recognized some who had been "so hostile" the year before. Now, however, they all seemed "quite friendly," and he passed out gifts of tobacco and sugar. One troubling incident took place, and Jedediah's response reflects his growing intolerance of what he perceived to be Indian aggression. One Miwok said he wanted to travel for a few days with the Americans. He was "quite naked," so Smith loaned him a blanket. That night he absconded with it. Snatching another Indian who "called himself a Chief," Smith detained him until the blanket was restored. From Jedediah's point of view, he was only safeguarding his property, but his ill-advised seizure of a leading man unquestionably angered the Indians, who probably thought the blanket small compensation for the game the trappers and hunters killed in their land. Indeed, from now on Smith and his men would find it increasingly difficult to maintain amicable relations with local Indians. As the handful of white men pushed deeper into northern California Indian Country, far beyond the reach of Mexican authority, their power to overawe the ever-growing numbers of Indians eroded.

The next morning Smith moved downstream a few miles and forded the Mokelumne River. Seven miles farther downstream his men discovered beaver sign and set some traps. While some of the men aired out and repacked damp beaver skins the next day, Jedediah set off with four others to find Reed and Pombert, the "canoe trappers" he had last seen a week earlier. He descended the Mokelumne River a dozen miles, almost to its confluence with the "Main [Sacramento] River," but soggy conditions along the river bottom prevented Smith from locating his men. After posting written messages in visible locations on the riverbank and the trail nearby, he returned to camp. On January 26 his party recrossed the river to visit a Miwok camp of fifty lodges, where Jedediah hired an Indian who spoke some Spanish to help him find Reed and Pombert. After another miserable day searching for the tardy trappers, Smith stayed the night at the Indian village, where he was "treated with great Kindness." Before rejoining his men the next morning, Smith hired six more Indians to look for the missing trappers and invited the village headman to visit his camp.

The month of January ended in a frustrating round of searches for Reed and Pombert and for livestock that caused "considerable trouble" by lagging behind, getting mired, or running off. Smith remarked that the Indians he called "Machalunbrys" (one of several variants he used) possessed a "good many Spanish Blankets & Shirts." Like other northern California Indians, the Northern Miwoks enjoyed acorn mush as their dietary mainstay, they dwelled in mat-covered lodges, and they fashioned a variety of excellent baskets. He also noted, with a hint of condescending approval, that they "did not manifest a disposition to steal which as I have before remarked is no small merit for an Indian." A few days later, however, another Indian made off with a blanket.

On February 4 his Indian searchers brought news that they had spotted Smith's delinquent men a mile or two off. While a few men continued trapping, Jedediah departed with the Indians to find Reed and Pombert, again to no avail. In the succeeding days many Indians came to Smith's camp. Jedediah Smith and Harrison Rogers killed nine elk, enabling them to offer useful gifts to their visitors, who "seemed to want nothing but meat." By February 9 Smith concluded that Reed and Pombert were not lost but had deserted. Reed's fate is unknown, but Pombert returned to California and by 1829 was living at San José. Bad as it was to lose two men, worse still was that the miscreants made off with eleven precious beaver traps, leaving Smith's brigade with thirty-six.

February 12 found Jedediah and his men encamped on the San Joaquin. Its low banks were lined with a narrow grove of ash, cottonwood, sycamore, willow, and a few oak trees, but a morass of wetlands and tules extended as much as two miles beyond the swift, muddy current that spanned about two hundred yards. Jedediah took a moment to admire the "rich[,] chocolate colored loam" and the lush grasses that flourished thereabouts in the rainy season, both foretelling good prospects for future cultivation. Along the river he saw "verry little Beaver but plenty of Otter sign."

During the following week Smith moved camp twice while his men set their traps, gathering an additional fifty beaver skins. On one of those days several Indians seized a trap from Emmenuel Lazarus, and just as they appeared to be closing in on him with murderous intent, some other trappers happened by. They "drove the Indians off and would have punished them had it not been for some miry ground over which they retreated." Despite Smith's reasonably careful forest diplomacy, intended to maintain peace, his brigade's relationship with Indians was turning sour, and the Miwoks had not forgotten that Smith's men had killed some of them in April 1827.

At about this time Smith found himself close to the campsite from which he had set out across the Sierra Nevada the year before. Remembrance of those harrowing days and nights prompted Jedediah once again to question the wisdom of his enterprises. In his journal he reflected on the "vanity of riches and of all those objects that lead men in the perilous paths of adventure," adding that "in times like those men return to reason and make the true estimate of things. They throw by the gaudy baubles of ambition"—that troubling word again—"and embrace the solid comforts of domestic life." But, he admitted, "a few days of rest makes the sailor forget the storm and embark again on the perilous Ocean and I suppose that like him I would soon become weary of rest."

Jedediah enjoyed little repose during the next few days. After a challenging crossing of the American River on February 22, he led his brigade to its confluence with the Sacramento, only to find more "flag Ponds & Lakes" that rendered the ground too muddy for travel. At this point Jedediah and his trappers passed within a few miles—perhaps even a few yards—of the site where Swiss emigrant-turned-Mexican-land-baron John Augustus Sutter would erect a sawmill in 1847, and where the first discovery of California gold would be made in January 1848. But the trappers scanned the water's surface and the riverbanks for beaver sign and took no notice of the glittering flecks of gold that might have winked at them from beneath the rippling current.

That day, blind to the fabulous wealth that lay almost literally under their moccasined feet when they waded across those cobble-filled stream beds, Smith and his men passed several Maidu Indian lodges, deserted save for "two squaws, one too old to run away and the other blind." As the terrified women "made signs for us to go away," Jedediah offered them an awl, a few scraps of woolen flannel, and some fish that his men commandeered from one of the lodges. Thereupon, as Smith remarked, "they altered their tone so much as to invite me to sit down." While resting, he pondered his next move. By this time he had abandoned any idea he may have entertained of visiting the Russian post near Bodega Bay.

"I hardly knew what course to pursue," he wrote, "for it was impossible to travel North and useless to travel up the [American] river on which I was encamped for there was no beaver in that direction." He decided to cross the "slou" by stretching the bull-boat skins he carried onto new frames and assembling another log raft. Perhaps his Indian guides directed him to a regularly utilized ford. The first logs that came to hand, he wrote, "appeared to have been hewn many years since and used for the same purpose to which I applied them." Possibly, these hewn logs were artifacts left by a passing North West Company or HBC brigade, for Smith found no evidence of axes in any of the nearby Indian lodges he examined. During the next two grueling days, his party advanced less than four miles. The bulk of one day was consumed in rafting everything across two "slous" only forty yards apart, and the omnipresent thick mud "made the country quite impassible for horses."

On February 26 a tragic event took place that signaled further deterioration in Jedediah Smith's dealings with northern California Indians. While Smith was off hunting, two trappers hastened into camp with evil tidings. Toussaint Maréchal and John Turner had been three or four miles from camp checking their traps when they observed some Indians. The Indians fled as soon as the two men hailed them, so the foolhardy trappers simply opened fire on them. Turner killed one man and Maréchal wounded another.

Upon learning of the shootings, Smith "was extremely sorry for the occurrence and reprimanded them severely for their impolitic conduct." But his sole means of punishing the irresponsible men was to "forbid them the privilege of setting traps." Unable to constantly monitor his men, Jedediah was also in no position to flog or restrain such offenders, for they might simply run off and he could ill afford to lose any of them. The next day, as the brigade moved cautiously downstream a couple of miles, searching for a route, Smith stumbled upon an Indian man, whom he "coaxed" into camp and presented with a few gifts in hopes of ameliorating the growing discord.

Unfortunately, by this time a handful of trade goods was not going to assuage Maidu or Miwok grief and anger over the murder of their relatives. On March 1 Jedediah and his men backtracked to a recent campsite, then advanced two more miles downstream to the confluence of the American and Sacramento rivers. Moving along the American River later that day, they came upon a village. Every single resident fled immediately.

Some dived into the river, others leaped onto a raft, and still others scurried for hiding places along the riverbank. Smith's horsemen galloped after the fleeing Indians, overtaking one woman, "who appe[a]red very much frightened." Jedediah offered her a few gifts in order to calm her fears.

Then he hurried forward to where he had seen another female fall down, only to discover a girl about ten years of age, "still laying there and apparently lifeless." To his dismay, when he dismounted he realized she was indeed dead. "Could it be possible," he wondered, "that we who called ourselves Christians were such frightful objects as to scare poor savages to death?" Christians some of them may have been, but these were also large, hairy, filthy, ragged, and fully armed strangers who had already given ample evidence—from the Indians' viewpoint—that they were liable to kill for no good reason.

Jedediah Smith spared but "little time for meditation" over the girl's death, turning instead to the pressing problem of finding a way out of that ill-omened place. But first, he covered the dead girl's body with a blanket and left some other items "to convince the friends of the poor girl" that it had been a sad accident. "Covering the dead" with offerings or gifts, especially in the case of accidental death, was a means by which Indians assuaged grief and prevented corrosive blood feuds, and white trappers learned to emulate the practice. After this tragedy Smith called the stream the "Wild River," to commemorate "the singular wildness of those indians and the novel occurrence" of the girl's inexplicable death. Within a few days two more horses drowned, and the brigade was left with only thirty-one traps. Their provisions were almost depleted, and game was nowhere to be seen.

Over the ensuing four days Smith searched for a way out of the flooded river bottom while his men set traps and hunted. Every time they approached an Indian village the inhabitants ran away. At one abandoned village, as Smith rather callously remarked, he appropriated the use of "some lodges which the owners left for our accommodation." On March 7 their food supply was exhausted and the brigade crossed the Sacramento, but when Jedediah went downstream to deliver a few blankets to his trappers, he found them merrily feasting on a large bear. Even "at a distance of 2000 miles from his home," wrote Smith, a hunter might still "enjoy and be thankful for such Blessings as heaven may throw in his way." Bears, as they well knew, were anything but an unalloyed blessing.

On the evening of March 8 Harrison Rogers killed one bear and wounded another. The next morning Rogers decided to finish off the wounded bear, and with him on this errand went John Hanna. A few minutes later Hanna rushed into camp yelling that a bear had mauled Rogers. The two hunters had cornered the wounded bear in a dense thicket when it suddenly lunged at them. Hanna dodged the enraged animal and Rogers managed to fire his rifle once before the grizzly attacked him. When it temporarily desisted, as bears sometimes do after an initial assault, Hanna shot him a second time. Still alive, the grizzly again savaged Rogers. By the time Smith arrived at the site, Rogers lay in a bloody heap, "being severely cut in 10 or 12 different places." Doubtless recalling his own experience, Smith set about bathing his clerk's gashes and "dressed them with plasters of soap and sugar."

Jedediah Smith's best friend among his companions lay mangled. If Rogers was to survive at all he needed careful tending, in which case the expedition would be stalled at an exposed campsite, a dangerous situation that left the brigade more than ordinarily vulnerable to attack. His trappers brought in a few more beaver skins every day, and Smith was unwilling to suspend trapping operations. Only smooth talking, open-handed distribution of presents, and plain good luck could prevent further bloodshed between Indians and Smith's trappers, some of whom seemed incapable of understanding that shooting Indians was a very bad idea.

As Smith dressed his friend's wounds, a number of "entirely naked" Indians gathered on the opposite bank. He coaxed a few into crossing the river by offering them beads, pieces of flannel, and a few hunks of fresh meat. During the next two days more Indians ventured across the river to bring Jedediah "presents of several Bunches of feathers worn on the head," and he in turn offered small gifts to demonstrate his desire for friendship. With Rogers incapacitated, Smith was obliged "to remain at that place for some time." Fortunately, game abounded in this vicinity. Jedediah enumerated a list of animals that included bear, elk, deer, antelope, wolves, beaver, otter, raccoon, swans, geese, cranes, herons, loons, brants, many types of ducks, and "Indian Hens."

On March 10 Smith again dressed Rogers's "verry painful" wounds with "cold water and salve of Sugar and Soap." To promote cordial interactions with the resident Indians, probably Maidus, Jedediah thought it wise to visit their village. On March 11 he crossed the river and was conducted to a village of about fifty lodges, where he took a seat on a mat and "commenced business by giving my presents." Village leaders quietly distributed the gifts according to rank, "giving to some one and to others two or three Beads as their respective merits might claim." The Indians offered Smith some fish nets and food, but he politely declined, expressed his satisfaction with the meeting, and returned to camp.

The council appeared to have gone well. When Jedediah Smith took his leave the Indians "endeavored to cry as a demonstration of their sorrow" at his departure. He saw no evidence that they engaged in trade with white men, commenting that most were "generally naked," though a few sported "feather robes and dresses made of net work," while others wore woven rabbit-skin robes. He remarked that most women wore only "a belt around the waist to which was attached two bundles of bark or flags one hanging down before and one behind in the form of a fringe," though others wore "scanty aprons" of deer skin.

These Indians, possibly from the Wokodot or Pan-pakan bands of the Maidu, lived along the Yuba River, an affluent of the Feather River that flowed into the Sacramento. Smith called it by its Maidu name, "Hen-neet." Noting that "most of the indians of this valley ... wear their hair not more than 5 or 6 inches in length," Jedediah referred to them as "short-haired Indians." Their diet, he wrote, consisted primarily of acorns, along with

"Grass, Pea vines, Roots and what few fish and water fowl they are able to take."

Over the next week Smith's trappers gathered another eighty-five beaver skins along the Yuba River, though Rogers's painful convalescence limited their mobility. On March 15 Smith accompanied some of his trappers across the Yuba, and two days later they ventured about ten miles up the Feather River, which he called the "Ya-loo" after a nearby Maidu village. During his absence from the base camp his men nervously watched a large number of Indians passing along the opposite shore. Their alarm abated a while later, when they saw the Indians returning laden with baskets of acorns retrieved from caches.

On March 19, having detected "but little Beaver sign" along the Feather River, Smith elected to move about five miles up the Yuba River. Beaver appeared more plentiful there, and Rogers was still in no condition to make "a great days travel." That afternoon Jedediah reconnoitered several miles upriver and found a "Creek 20 yards wide running west" that he named "Red Bank Creek." Today called Honcut Creek, its name commemorates a Maidu village that once stood nearby. By this time the rain had let up and the country was becoming "dry and firm and apparently fit for cultivation." Jedediah and a few companions came across two men and one woman tending "some nets set for the purpose of catching Brant." Long cords stretched from the shore two hundred or more yards into the rushes where the birds gathered. Pulling on a single cord triggered three large nets "arranged much like the common pigeon net." Smith stopped for a while and passed out a handful of beads.

As Jedediah huddled with the Indians, his men noticed some brant in the distance and crept closer to kill a few. Firing several times, the marksmen thought for sure they hit their quarry but the water birds continued to float placidly amid the tules. Somewhat frustrated, one man quipped that "his gun must be crooked" but he took another shot and missed again. The chagrined hunters then discovered the targets were decoys "so complete that the deception could not be detected except in verry near approach."

Though he admired the Maidus' skill in crafting fine decoys, Jedediah viewed the northern California Indians with considerable ambiguity. He remarked that these Indians were "numerous[,] honest[,] and peaceable in their dispositions," adding that their land boasted fine soil for planting crops (which the Maidu did not do) "with the exception of 2 or 3 months in the winter when there is too much rain." On the other hand, Smith believed that "a great many of these Indians appear to be the lowest intermediate link between man and the Brute creation." He scoffed at their domestic architecture, suggesting the cause was either "indolence" or "a deficiency of genius inferior to the Beaver."

Many local Indians, he wrote, "live without any thing in the shape of a house and rise from their bed of earth in the morning like the animals around them and rove about in search of food." Even the persistent specter of hunger, he added, "does not teach them providence. Each day is left to take care of itself." Characterizing them as "degraded," "ignorant," and "miserable," he expressed contempt-tinged surprise that they lived meagerly even though they dwelled "in a country where the creator has scattered a more than ordinary Share of his bounties." Smith thought such a richly endowed land ought to "expand rather than restrain the energies of man."

The final week of March found Jedediah Smith busy caring for Rogers, keeping his herd together, seeking a route away from the flooded regions, maintaining peace with the Maidus, and encouraging his men to trap more beavers. On March 24, two weeks after the bear attack, Rogers was sufficiently recovered to hand out some beads and meat to a few Indians who visited the camp. Smith continued his general policy of not allowing Indians to linger in his encampment. At one point when an Indian made "so bold as to venture into camp," Jedediah abruptly signaled that he must leave. In that week his trappers brought in seventy more beaver skins.

As April opened and immense numbers of migratory birds began their long northward flight, Jedediah kept his trappers at work. Beaver were plentiful, though "the numerous Slous interfere[d] much with trapping." On April 1 Martin McCoy and

Joseph Palmer killed a large grizzly bear "in tolerable order." Upon butchering it, they found a stone arrowhead and three inches of shaft embedded in one of the creature's lungs. Apparently the wound had fully healed, encapsulating the broken arrow shaft. Smith handed out some of the bear meat and entrails to visiting Indians, who ate so much that they "were puffed up like Bladders."

From their base camp on the Sacramento the trappers fanned out, taking another seventy beaver skins in the first week of April. On the morning of April 6 about one hundred unarmed Indians came to Smith's camp holding bunches of "green leaves," probably to signify peace. According to his "usual custom," Jedediah welcomed the visitors about eighty yards from his camp. In council he identified their "principal men" and passed out "cotton shirting[,] Beads Awls, and Tobacco." The curious Indians spent the day shadowing Smith's men while they set their traps but "did no further damage than springing a few of them."

April 7 was surely an unforgettable day. For a week the trappers had been working small streams that fed the Sacramento. While setting up camp on the banks of Mill Creek, Smith noticed "considerable appearance of game and particularly bear." That evening he and a few men went out hunting. They shot and wounded several bears, all of which disappeared into nearly impenetrable undergrowth. A few men, Jedediah among them, tracked a "Badly wounded" bear to its hiding place in a thicket so dense that a man on horseback could not enter. Dismounting and stepping forward, Smith spotted a bear and shot him in the head. The bruin collapsed.

Confident that the bear was done for, Smith walked up to it with an unloaded rifle. When he got within a dozen feet of the beast, the man behind him sang out, "He is alive." Jedediah retorted that the bear was most certainly dead, but he failed to notice a second bear lying beside the dead one. A split second later a very much alive bear lunged at Smith "with open mouth and making no pleasant noise." Two desperate leaps later, Jedediah dived head first into the creek. The bear overran the next man in line, doing him no harm, and then "made a furious rush" at a third man, Joseph Lapointe. Luckily, Smith wrote, "Lapoint[e] had … a Bayonet fixed on his gun and as the Bear came in he gave him a severe wound in the neck which induced him to change his course and run into another thicket." Regaining their equanimity, the three men again beat the bushes and killed the bear, wounding still another one.

But there was more. Not satisfied with the hunting so far, or perhaps wishing for safety's sake to rid their immediate neighborhood of grizzly bears, Jedediah and two men mounted horses and trailed the wounded bear. Thinking his quarry was hiding in a certain thicket, Smith circled the spot several times, yelling at the top of his lungs, in order to flush out the creature. Concluding he must have been mistaken, Smith halted momentarily to take a final glance. Just then, in a furious blur of dark fur, white teeth, and murderous claws, "the Bear sprang for the horse." Jedediah instinctively sank spurs deep into his horse, but before it could leap away the bear snagged its tail and held on tight with its powerful paws.

With eyes rolling and nostrils flared, the terrified horse reared and plunged in a desperate effort to escape. This fine horse, Jedediah wrote, "exerted himself so powerfully that he gave the Bear no opportunity to close uppon him and actually drew him 40 or 50 yards before he relinquished his hold." The surprised bear then loped off, and Jedediah, with a hint of humor, pronounced himself "quite glad to get rid of his company on any terms." Smith and his fellow nimrods sauntered back to camp to "feast on the spoils and talk of the incidents of our eventful hunt." Jedediah named the stream on which they camped "Grizly Bear Creek." Such were the reckless capers of the mountain men when life was good.

By April 10 the brigade pushed into the high country near the northern margin of the Sacramento Valley. Some twenty miles to the east loomed the jagged spires of the Sierra Nevada, Smith's "Mt. Joseph." Shallow rock-strewn creeks tumbled down steep mountainsides, and beaver were there for the taking. Jedediah considered trapping his way farther up the Sacramento, but the precipitous mountains enclosing it left no room for a path. Clambering up a rocky slope, Smith took a view of the countryside. He could see the river twisting its way from the northeast through thirty miles of rugged cliffs. Beyond lay heaped-up mountains that seemed "too high to cross at that season of the year or perhaps at any other."

Revising his plans, Smith returned to the river valley and sought a good fording place. On April 11 his men assembled a bull-boat, swam their livestock across the Sacramento River, and encamped slightly north of present-day Red Bluff, California. The next day the trappers found beaver sign too scarce to warrant setting traps. While en route back to camp, Smith happened upon about twenty Indians, who instantly "sprang to their feet and commenced dancing . . . throwing their bodies into every imaginable position." Taken aback, Jedediah thought perhaps the demonstration served as a "charm or a Medicine," or maybe it represented "a mark of respect or the accustomed manner of saluting strangers." Interrupting the ceremony, he handed out a few presents and headed for camp with several Indians following him. Smith motioned them to keep their distance but then distributed some meat, which seemed to please them.

On the following day Smith moved eight miles closer to the "Gap of the Mountain" through which he meant to pass toward the northwest and the coast. During the march more Indians appeared and he gave them part of an antelope that Rogers shot. By noontime the trappers halted to make camp. Smith's men set about drying gear that got wet in a recent downpour and stretching some fresh beaver skins on circular willow hoops. Noticing an Indian man adorned with "wampum and Beads," Jedediah guessed that this tribe was acquainted with the HBC men.

Over the next few days the brigade covered about twenty miles and made camp in a ravine by the bank of a swift-flowing stream about twenty yards wide. Smith and his men gathered livestock and herded them to safety under a steep bank beside the creek. While rounding up horses and mules that afternoon, Jedediah noticed that one of the horses had just been shot in the neck with an arrow. He shouted for his men to secure their horses and "spring to their Guns." Smith and several trappers galloped to the spot where they had seen a number of Wintu warriors "throwing their arrows into camp." Opening fire on the Indians, the trappers felled two, who managed to crawl away. Jedediah himself shot an Indian who "went off leaving much blood behind." The Indians hovered around the camp just beyond gunshot range until night fell and then dispersed. Among the livestock the trappers counted nine horses and two mules wounded, some seriously. Smith calculated that he and his men killed two or three Indians in retribution "for the damage they had done." On the following morning the Americans hastily decamped, putting twelve miles between themselves and their adversaries, or so they hoped. Travel was "extremely bad," and three badly wounded horses had to be abandoned.

The Indians, however, were neither frightened nor so easily outdistanced. Dogging the trappers' heels all day long, they shouted insults from the surrounding hills and at night crept "quite close to camp." Still hoping to avoid all-out war, Smith took a few men and approached within shooting distance of the Indians. Attempting to pacify the angry warriors, he tried to persuade them that despite the previous day's bloodshed he wanted no more trouble. The Indians gesticulated angrily, and some had arrows already notched against taut bowstrings, leaving Jedediah with "no doubt ... of their inclination to be hostile." Then, cleaving to the unforgiving tooth-and-claw mentality of the mountain men, Jedediah Smith and his cohorts began shooting at the Indians, "in order to intimidate them and prevent them from doing me further injury." Two Indians fell wounded, and the rest dashed into the forest, "leaving some of their property on the ground." Smith and his men rushed back to camp and secured their livestock within a hastily built pen.

Prior to these unfortunate events, amounting to two preemptive strikes, Smith himself had shot no Indians in northern California. Despite several troubling episodes in the expedition's dealings with Indians, the trappers had generally tried to minimize bloodshed and preserve a measure of cordiality. But from this day forward Smith and his trappers could never again afford to relax their vigilance. As the overstressed, trail-wracked men grew weaker, their psychological condition also degraded, and a sense of foreboding must have hovered about them. Though Jedediah continued his efforts to maintain peace, conflicts with Indians increased in frequency and intensity.

The next day no Indians were seen, and Smith wrestled with the problem of finding a way out of his dangerous fix. On April 17, sixteen miles of strenuous riding took the party across a snowy mountain ridge to "waters that ran to the North West," and they camped at a small creek. Passing from the upper reaches of the Middle or South Fork of Cottonwood River to the headwaters of Hayfork Creek, which flowed about thirty miles before joining the south fork of the Trinity, Smith's party had reached the western edge of the Sacramento Valley. Near the west side of a divide that separates today's Shasta-Trinity and Six Rivers national forests, they had entered the North Coast Range.

Smith sent men out to reconnoiter the broken, confusing country. When his scouts reported a "practicable but verry rough" pass to the west, Smith elected to try it. April 19 found Smith's brigade still on Hayfork Creek its course narrowly constrained by steep mountains. They camped on a small alluvial flat where another rivulet entered the Hayfork Creek, within today's Hayfork Valley. Trouble soon erupted again.

Not far from his camp Jedediah discovered an Indian lodge. A woman and child managed to run away, but Smith found an old man too feeble to escape and presented him a handful of beads and a bit of tobacco. A few minutes later his men at camp discerned warriors across the river who appeared to be "creeping up to get a shot at the horses." Jedediah Smith and Arthur Black cautiously drew near the riverbank. Making "friendly signs," they invited the Indians to come across for a parley. In response the angry warriors leaped about and set arrows against their bow strings. Smith instantly ordered Black to fire on them, but he missed his mark. As the Indian archers retreated up the hillside releasing their arrows, Jedediah also shot at one and missed.

Across the river a dozen warriors kindled a large fire to create a diversion while others stealthily approached the white men's camp and launched more arrows at the livestock. Smith's men again opened fire on them, again "without success." Around sunset, when the Indians released a third volley of arrows at the livestock, Jedediah and three other exasperated trappers jumped on their horses and gave chase. This time they killed another two Indians and, wrote Smith, "they troubled us no more."

During the past few weeks several horses loaded with gear and traps had drowned or fallen off cliffs. By late April the brigade possessed only twenty-six traps. Meanwhile, Indians continued to closely monitor the trappers' progress. Smith and his companions observed smoke signals from many fires the Indians kindled on the mountainsides. Undoubtedly, the "forest telegraph" broadcast advance warnings of these unwelcome and unpredictable strangers far more rapidly than they themselves could travel. Moreover, each morning more horses turned up lame from scrambling over loose river rock and steep hills, and the brigade's rate of travel suffered accordingly. Jedediah gave his own name to the river they now followed, but it did not stick. Today it is the Trinity River; "Smith's River" flows out of Six Rivers National Forest to enter the Pacific Ocean a few miles south of the Oregon border, at a little town also named Smith's River.

On April 22 the party advanced barely three miles before stopping in a small valley with good grass, today called Hyampom. Throughout the day the trappers heard Indians "yelling on the hills," and they later spied some near camp. When Smith tried to communicate with them they vanished. At dusk a horse guard apprised Smith that more Indians were "close at hand" across the river. Setting off to investigate, Jedediah and another man saw Indians launching arrows at the horse guards from about one hundred yards, too far away to do much damage. A few trappers rushed to the riverbank and "fired several guns[,] wounding one or two of them but killed none dead on the ground." Smith again penned up his livestock and posted guards during the "fore part" of the night, but the weather was cold and the Indians "had but little clothing," so he relieved his men of further duty.

The next day's travel proved extremely galling for horses, mules, and men. While crossing a treacherous mountain pass, the brigade spent four hours advancing a single mile over "exceedingly Rocky and rough" land that "mangled the feet of the horses most terribly." During that dismal march Jedediah took time to marvel at a species of tree "with which I was before unacquainted" and that his European-born men judged to be a "Red Laurel." On April 25 they remained in camp to recruit their worn-out livestock, and Smith's men bagged three deer.

While hunting they came across several ingenious Indian-made deer traps. In the forest, Indians built a long fence of cut tree limbs and brush, leaving a few narrow passages through the barrier. Above each aperture hung a cordage noose set at the level of a deer's head. When the animals passed through the passages, they got caught and either strangled or were dispatched by waiting hunters. Indians as far away as British Columbia and the Yukon fashioned nearly identical traps. The Indians that Smith described as "troublesome" may have been members of the Penutian-speaking Wintu nation. At least one subdivision dwelled on the Hayfork River.

The last days of April sorely tested the endurance of the entire brigade. Smith generally traveled ahead while Rogers rode as a rear guard "to see that things are kept in order." Chasing runaway livestock and trying to hunt in the rough country drained every man's strength. One mule packed with beaver skins ran off but was recovered the next day. Jedediah struggled to make sense of the tangled geography but was hampered by his inability to get a clear view of the rugged mountains that surrounded him. Advancing by fits and starts, on May 3 Smith's fagged-out party reached the Klamath River, which entered the Trinity from the east. For two days Jedediah was "obliged to lay by in consequence of the lameness of my horses," but there was little rest for him or his men. Some trappers dried and repacked damp beaver skins, others hunted and processed deer meat, and Smith and a few men backtracked to collect stray stock.

Adding to their misery were the dense fog and rain that lately enshrouded almost every camp. Perhaps, they hoped, fog offered evidence that the ocean was not far off. May 6 found the trappers camping in the territory of unfamiliar Indians, the Hupa nation. Of Athabascan linguistic stock, they lived mainly along the Trinity River. Hupa lodges, Smith remarked, "were built differently from any I had before seen." Constructed of wide pine planks, the houses were about a dozen feet square with three-foot walls and roofs "shaped like a house."

When Smith saw some Indians paddling a canoe downstream "with a good many Deer skins on board," he hailed them, but they refused to stop. He later signaled to a handful of Indians across the river from camp, and they likewise ignored him. During the next few days' march more Indians appeared, and a few traded deerskins for axes and knives at Smith's camp. Characterizing the Hupas as "quite civil and friendly," Harrison Rogers noted that "the women does the principal trading." The Hupas wore clothing of deerskin tanned with the hair on, and some wore moccasins. Smith counted many Hupa lodges and paid special notice to "a few good canoes" beached along the river.

Jedediah Smith's livestock herd continued to suffer a slow but steady attrition. Each day men hunted for lost horses and mules, finding a few but never all. On May 11 Rogers recorded that several horses, some carrying packs, lost their footing on a steep hill and rolled "20 or 30 feet down among the sharp rocks, several badly cut to pieces with the rocks." Most of the men, wrote Rogers, were "as much fatigued as the horses," and on May 10 one man "lossed his gun, and could not find it." On May 14, wrote Smith, "Two of my horses were dashed to pieces from the precipices and many others were terribly mangled." Unable to proceed, he detailed two men to guard a pile of packs that had to be left behind and spent the following day collecting stray stock and hauling the packs of goods to camp. The two-day halt permitted Jedediah's trappers a much-needed respite from the killing work. Smith sent two men, Maréchal and Turner, to reconnoiter the country ahead.

A few Hupas visited the camp to trade lamprey eels and edible roots for some of the Americans' goods. Rogers presented the Hupas a few beads, and in turn they gave him a "lamper eel dryed," which he could not bring himself to eat. They wanted to trade for knives, but Rogers had none. Smith characterized the Hupas as "very friendly" and permitted several men and "Some of their Squaws" to enter his camp. Rogers thought one woman was "very good featured." On May 17 Smith's scouts reported that the country to the west "was tolerable," and more importantly, "the Ocean was not more than 15 or 18 miles distant." Jedediah decided to change course and head for the sea, abandoning the difficult riverside route. His animals had grown weaker by the day from hunger and so had his men, for the "poor venison of the country contained verry little nourishment."

Leaving the river behind them, Smith's men plunged into the forest, making three miles before they camped "in a small prairae of good grass." The next day they became the first Euro-Americans to encounter one of the coast range's greatest natural wonders, the ancient groves of enormous redwoods. "Some of the Cedars," Jedediah wrote, "were the noblest trees I had ever seen[,] being 12 or 15 feet in diameter[,] tall[,] straight and handsome." With satisfaction, he noted, "I encamped in a prairae with the Ocean in sight." At long last, after months of enervating hardships, he again gazed upon the distant but attainable Pacific. Whatever pleasure this achievement conferred, however, was short lived. Getting through the remaining few miles to the ocean would prove no easy task, and there remained a high probability of further clashes with Indians.

On May 20 Smith dispatched Thomas Virgin and Harrison Rogers, whose wounds were almost healed, to find a route to the coast. The rest of the men butchered and dried elk meat, or endured the daily ritual of searching for strayed livestock. Clawing their way through "steep and brushy" terrain, Rogers and Virgin "got within 80 or 100 yards of the beach" but were too worn out to proceed further. They returned to camp later that night with disappointing news. Making way along the beaches would be "verry bad" because heavily timbered and brush-choked hills fell right to the rocky seashore, leaving practically no room for a trail.

Worse still, Smith's scouts had narrowly dodged death. Some Indians, likely Chilula allies of the Hupas, ambushed Virgin as he guarded the horses while Rogers stalked some elk and a bear. When the Indians loosed a volley of arrows at Virgin and the horses, he took cover in the brush and in turn shot an Indian. Rogers heard the gunfire and then heard Virgin shouting for him to hurry back. Cautiously approaching, Rogers found "an Ind.[ian] lying dead and his dog by him." As the western sky darkened, the two men quietly returned to camp to find a handful of Chilulas or Hupas. Rogers "made signs to them that we were attacked by some of there band ... and we had killed one." The Indians, reported Rogers, "packed up and put off very soon." Not surprisingly, "no indians visited camp" the next day. Well enough, Smith must have thought, since heavy rain and dense fog precluded travel for the next two days.

Brought to a standstill in the labyrinthine forest highlands, and in growing desperation, Jedediah Smith decided to retreat. The brigade backtracked through redwoods, pines, and hemlocks, punctuated, wrote Rogers, by a tangled undergrowth of "hazle, oak, briars, currents, goose berry, and Scotch cap bushes ... and sundry other shrubs too tedious to mention." During a heavy downpour on Thursday, May 22, Rogers penned a brief, poignant prayer that highlights his consternation over the brigade's prospects: "Oh! God, may it please thee, in thy divine providence, to still guide and protect us through this wilderness of doubt and fear, as thou hast done heretofore, and be with us in the hour of danger and difficulty, as all praise is due to thee and not to man, oh! Do not forsake us Lord, but be with us and direct us through."

May 24 found Smith and his men back at their Trinity River camp of a week earlier. Though Jedediah had named the Trinity after himself, for some grim, unexplained reason Harrison Rogers called it "Indian Scalp River." From there the brigade made its way to the upper Klamath. Winding southward just below today's Oregon border, this river makes a westward swing through the mountains and flows northwest to the ocean near Smith's River, California. The Trinity River enters the Klamath at a sharp bend in today's Hoopa Valley Indian Reservation, where the Klamath turns north.

At the Klamath River, Jedediah encountered some Yuroks. After he quieted their fears that he had "evil intentions," the

Yuroks rented him several canoes to ferry his men and "plunder" (as Rogers put it) across the river near the modern town of Klamath. In exchange the Indians received "beeds and razors." The next day Hupas visited Smith's camp in "considerable numbers" to trade more lamprey eels, a hunk of salmon, two beavers, and an otter skin. Rogers noted, "Mr. Smith purchases all the beaver fur he can from them." When the Indians left, however, they filched a beaver trap. It was time to get moving again.

On May 26 the brigade got an early start and advanced about six miles along a ridge before camping on a mountainside "where there was pretty good grass for our horses." The next morning Smith and Virgin left early to survey the trail ahead and blaze trees to guide Rogers and the others. They traveled only three miles before making camp and sending men out to fetch lost horses. That evening a handful of Indians, "inoffensive in appearance and without arms," visited the camp. Smith offered the usual presents and learned that the Indians had "a fishing establishment" on a nearby creek. Over the next two days they advanced only seven miles, blundering through a blanket of fog through which they "could scarce see how to get along the ridge." Late in the evening of the first day, the fog lifted just long enough for the trappers to get "a fair view of the ocean," some twenty miles distant.

The final days of May and the first week of June passed in like manner. Brush grew so thick everywhere that it was nearly impossible to keep track of horses and mules. While the brigade scrambled down a steep slope on May 30, they lost track of some horses and a pack load of gear. Smith's men recovered the horses and gear, but when he opened the pack he noticed that another beaver trap was gone. They had now lost half of their traps. On some mornings the livestock were so scattered that it took more than four hours to collect them. Rounding up strays kept a half-dozen of Harrison Rogers's rearguard men constantly busy. They had, he wrote, "a serious time running up and down the mountains after horses through the thickets of brush and briars."

In the meantime, scouts floundered about in fog-shrouded and brush-clogged mountains, desperate to discover a tolerably decent route. With the men as worn down as the livestock, progress was pitifully slow. Rogers remarked, "we have two men every day that goes a head with axes to cut a road," but even then "it is with difficulty we can get along." June 1 found the mountain men slogging along under a cloudburst, making just three miles over rugged slopes before they camped in a little fern-bedecked bottom. Rogers described the trail conditions that day as "amazing bad" and noted, "all hands very wet and tired." When Rogers and his men pulled into camp, he learned that Jedediah had been "hurt pretty bad" when a mule kicked him. In severe pain, Smith puttered about camp the next day but wrote nothing about his injury.

On June 4 an incident occurred that again elevated the growing tensions between Smith's trappers and the Yuroks and Klamaths. In camp after another punishing day, Rogers traded a handful of beads to some Indians for raspberries and then walked away, leaving the "coloured man by the name of Ransa" with the visiting Indians. A few minutes later he heard gunfire, and Ransa shouted that the Indians had attempted to rob him of a blanket. Ransa said that when the Indians dashed into the brush to snatch up bows and arrows, he shot at them and they ran off.

Ransa's tale excited Rogers's suspicion, for he had seen no weapons among the Indians when he left the spot. The clerk thought that Ransa had "wanted to get some berries and fish without pay," and when the Indians demanded a knife in payment, Ransa had raised a "false alarm" and fabricated a story. Rogers gave Ransa "a severe reprimand" for his ill-advised act but could do nothing to smooth over the situation with the Indians. Jedediah noted that Ransa was "not a good marksman" and had probably done the Indians no harm, but he too suspected that Ransa had lied.

Whatever its details, the affair came at an awkward moment. With game scarce, Smith absolutely had to purchase food from Indians, but that would be impossible if hostilities erupted. The brigade's meat supply was gone; a "few pounds of flour and rice" constituted their only remaining provisions. "Capt. Smith," wrote Rogers, "give each man half a pint of flour last night for their supper." So dire was the food shortage that on June 5, having found "nothing to kill," the trappers "killed the last dog we had along" and stewed it with a few handfuls of flour. Smith traded for a few eels and berries the next day, but such fare did not quiet his men's growling stomachs. A day later they killed one of their young horses, "which," wrote Jedediah, "gave us quite a feast."

On June 7 the brigade remained encamped while some men pressed and packed beaver furs, two others went hunting, and three men rounded up stray animals. When a dozen Indians came into camp, Jedediah exchanged beads for more eels, berries, and mussels, but when the Indians departed they "stole a small kittle belonging to one of the men." Rogers remarked that they "come without arms and appear friendly but inclined to steal."

On June 8 Smith and his companions beat their way through three miles of thorny underbrush. The exhausted livestock were so broken down that the animals could "scarce be forced through brush any more." But the men kept pushing horses and mules forward, and at last they broke free of the thickets. Gone instantly was the murky closeness of clotted shrubbery that mangled men and livestock. It must have seemed as if they had emerged from a tunnel when the infinite expanse of sky and sea burst into view and they found themselves on an ocean beach, "where there was a small bottom of grass for our horses." Steep hills, bare of timber but cloaked with underbrush, fell to the shoreline. The brigade made camp, probably at the mouth of what is called Wilson's Creek.

At intervals up and down the beach the trappers saw well-built Indian houses. When they encountered some Indians, they traded for a "few clams and some few dried fish." Smith sent out hunters, but even "after the greatest exertion" game eluded them. Several men stayed out all night and still found no game. The next morning Rogers and some of his men "hunted hard until 9 or 10 O.C. [o'clock] A.M. but killed nothing." John Gaither wounded a black bear, but it escaped. Every man who thought himself a good hunter searched for prey, and all came up empty-handed. "This," wrote Smith, "was what hunters call bad luck and what we felt to be hard times[,] for we were weary and verry hungry." The destitute men traded more beads for "a few small fishes and clams" and some "cakes made of sea grass and weeds."

Such poor victuals did not sit well with the mountain men. Smith set out again in search of game, and this time he got lucky. He shot three fine elk, "a pleasing sight to a set of hungry men." What a change, he remarked, from "the moody silence of hunger to the busy bustle of preparation for cooking and feasting. . . . [M]en could be seen in ev'ry part of camp with meat raw and half roasted in their hands devouring it with the greatest alacrity." Jedediah thought that "nothing less than twenty four hours constant eating would satisfy their appetites." After they stuffed themselves on broiled elk meat, quipped Rogers, the men appeared "better satisfied than they do when in a state of starvation."

The elk meat was soon devoured and hunger still gnawed at the trappers, so they eagerly purchased more "trifling things" from local Indians. In Smith's view, the Indians were "great speculators," who "never sold their things without dividing them into several small parcels[,] asking more for each than the whole were worth." Some of his trappers traded for "Blubber[,] not bad tasted but dear as gold dust." The strange food, Jedediah wrote, "served but to aggravate our hunger," for elk meat and "nothing else could satisfy our appetites." Still, the Americans' fierce craving for meat had been temporarily allayed. When Indians brought more shellfish to trade the day after Smith bagged his elk, they found "not so good a market for them as they did yesterday."

On June 11 Smith and Rogers roused their men early. By nine o'clock they were ready to get under way. A few minutes after they started hiking up a steep ridge overlooking the sea, someone told Smith that a felling axe and a drawknife were missing. Angered by what he considered blatant thievery, Jedediah took five men and returned to an Indian lodge adjacent to his campsite. There they found only "an old man who pretended to know nothing about them." Taking the old man with him, he walked to other nearby lodges, but at his approach the Indians "ran off." Seizing another hostage, Smith sent the old man to tell his fellow tribespeople that he would release the captive if they brought back the tools. Commencing their own search of the village, the trappers soon found the axe, "covered in the sand under their fire," but they failed to recover the drawknife. Making good on his threat, Jedediah and his men departed with the hostage. The trappers camped a few miles later and erected a livestock pen in case of further trouble with Indians. The drawknife was not returned, and Jedediah realized that keeping a prisoner could serve no useful purpose, so he released the hostage. At the time Smith's party was somewhere between today's Requa and Crescent City, California.

The following week brought more of the same grueling routine: painful trekking, the continual need to kill game, and occasional exchanges of trade beads for food. The week's highlight came on June 15, when Joseph Lapointe shot a gigantic elk. Possibly using a small steelyard that escaped mention in his inventory, Jedediah weighed the dressed elk meat and found that it tallied a whopping 695 pounds. Plagued morning and night by swarms of "muskeatoes, large horse flies, and small knats," the brigade pressed northward into Tolowa tribal land, keeping close to the shoreline at low tide and moving to higher ground as necessity dictated. From June 17 to 20 the trappers remained encamped while Jedediah led a party in search of a trail that offered good grass. On June 19 Jedediah and two men followed an Indian trail over a ridge to a "river 80 yards wide coming from ESE." This stream, today's Smith River, enters the Pacific five miles south of the Oregon border. While crossing the swift-flowing river, Smith's horse lost its footing and nearly drowned before he managed to pull it out on the other side. By June 24 the brigade was encamped at the mouth of Chetco River in Oregon.

Just after sunrise the next morning, the trappers forded the Chetco and moved twelve miles up the coast. When they stopped to camp near a Chetco Indian village at Thoglas Creek, Smith found the village empty of inhabitants. That afternoon he sent two men a few miles back to find a lost mule. After night fell they slipped quietly into camp and informed Smith that when they passed the Chetco lodges some warriors had "sallied out . . . with bows and arrows and made after them, yelling and screaming." Fearing they were on the verge of being surrounded and killed, the trappers escaped across a creek and stealthily returned to camp. Among the livestock rounded up the next morning, Smith discovered two horses with arrows protruding from them. A while later Rogers spotted some Indians in a canoe a short distance off, but he made no attempt to pursue them. That day the trappers covered twelve miles, which Smith judged "the best march I had made in a long time." Two days and another fifteen miles later, the brigade came to the mouth of a "considerable river," the Rogue River. "On each side of the Bay," Jedediah wrote, "were several indian villages but the indians had all run off."

Then Rogers recorded something that Smith—perhaps motivated by shame—did not. Rogers noted that "as usual" the Indians ran away when the trappers appeared, abandoning their "lodges and large baskets." Rogers continued, "we tore down one lodge to get the puncheons [i.e., planks] to make rafts, as timber was scarce along the coast." Soon he observed that Indians had "raised smokes on the north side of the bay . . . for signals to those that were absent, or some other villages, to let them know that we were close at hand." It is no small irony that these trappers, for whom petty pilfering was a sufficient cause for detaining, threatening, and even murdering Indians, seemed willing to destroy an Indian house and steal its timber without a second thought. Moreover, with the "forest telegraph" warning Indians far and wide to beware of such thieves, it is hardly surprising that hostility resulted.

When the Americans rafted across the Rogue on June 28 a dozen horses drowned, making a total of twenty-three horses and mules lost in a three-day period. In the next few days more livestock died from falling down mountainsides or into one of the numerous elk traps that Indians maintained in the area. Despite his problems, Smith found time to describe the traps: "These Indians Catch Elk in Pits dug in places much frequented.

They are 10 or 12 feet deep and much Larger at the bottom than top. They are completely covered over and some of my hunters with their horses fell into one and got out with considerable difficulty." As July opened, the brigade was encamped at the mouth of Sixes River, near today's Port Orford, Oregon. Jedediah remarked that "[f]or many days we had hardly got sight of an Indian and but one had visited camp since my horses were killed." For his part, Rogers appreciated the good potential for ranching in the area: "The country for several days past [is] well calculated for raising stock, both cattle and hogs, as it abounds in good grass and small lakes."

On July 2 Rogers noted, "most of the mens times expired this evening." Their year-long contracts had come to an end. Smith "called all hands and give them up their articles," meaning that he handed over their contracts, thus ceremonially terminating their employment. Immediately, however, he reengaged men to continue with him at one dollar per day to "the place of deposite." The list included John Gaither, Arthur Black, John Hanna, Emmenuel Lazarus, Abraham Laplant, Charles Swift, Thomas Daws, Toussaint Maréchal, Peter Ranney, and Joseph Palmer. For some unexplained reason, Martin McCoy was to be paid two hundred dollars "from the time he left the Spanish country, until he reaches the deposit." This accounts for only eleven men, perhaps because the rest were considered "free trappers." Neither Smith nor Rogers offered further details, and the "coloured man" Ransa was not mentioned.

Jedediah Smith wrote his final journal entry for the Northwest Expedition on July 3. That morning found his brigade camped two miles from the Coquille River. As he rode along the river in search of a ford, he glimpsed Indians paddling a canoe upriver "as fast as possible." He galloped ahead "in order to stop them," and when they realized they could not escape, the Indians beached their canoe and "fell to work with all their might to split it in pieces." Harrison Rogers's journal offers a more revealing account of the incident. According to Rogers, when the Indians "tried to split the canoe to pieces with their poles," Smith "screamed at them, and they fled, and left it, which saved us of a great deal of hard labour making rafts." Once again, Smith decided to commandeer Indians' property whether they liked it or not. Later that day the last member to join the brigade enters the record. Toussaint Maréchal "caught a boy about 10 years old and brought him to camp." Rogers gave him "some beads and dryed meat" and the lad—they called him "Marion"—made signs that when the other Indians fled they left him behind. Young Marion, sometimes described as an "Umpqua slave," would thereafter accompany the Americans.

Rogers's journal is the sole source for details covering the following days. The weather was "warm and pleasant" when the brigade forded the Coquille, repacked their gear, and moved on five miles to camp near a place today called Whiskey Run. The next day, Independence Day, passed with no patriotic celebration. Instead, they trudged nine miles over "pretty bad" terrain, beating their way through more thickets, timber, and "some very bad ravines." On July 5 they encountered some Indians who spoke the "Chinook jargon," a pastiche of Indian words mixed with Russian, English, and French. This was the common trade language of the northwest coast, but rarely heard so far south. The Indians informed Smith that he was within ten days' travel of the Willamette River, "which is pleasing news to us."

For two days the Americans remained in camp to rest livestock, hunt meat, and cut a rough road toward a nearby slough they had to cross. About one hundred Indians—possibly of the Coos or Kuitsch nations—came into camp to trade some fish and mussels. Jedediah noticed that one warrior carried a flintlock gun, "all have knives and tomahawks," and one Indian wore a capote, a simple tailored coat fashioned from a woolen blanket. The presence of such items indicated that the Indians traded with white men. The next day brought many more Indians to camp, from whom Smith purchased "scale and shell fish," berries, and a few furs. Later that night, however, the Americans discovered that the same Indians had "been shooting arrows into 8 of our horses and mules; 3 mules and one horse died shortly after they were shot." Two Indians who served as interpreters informed Jedediah that the animals were killed by a disgruntled man who "got mad on account of the trade he made." On July 9 Smith's party camped at the southern extremity of Coos Bay and planned to cross the Coos River the next morning using borrowed canoes. The vicinity was heavily populated with Indians who seemed willing to trade, but a palpable sense of menace hung in the air.

When Smith spoke to a local chieftain about the recent assault on his herd, he "could get but little satisfaction as they say they were not accessary to it." Seeing so many Indians about and feeling pressured to keep moving, Smith decided it was "advisable to let it pass at present without notice." Meanwhile, he continued to purchase beaver and otter skins at every opportunity. By mid-morning of July 10 the brigade had forded the Coos River. Smith swam an injured mule alongside his canoe, leaving behind two dead horses. All the Indians seemed "pretty shy," but Jedediah shared with Rogers his fear that they "had a mind to attact [*sic*] him from there behaviour." The burned-out company then made camp.

The night passed without incident, and at daybreak the brigade quickly got under way, putting fifteen miles between themselves and the Coos River Indians. With them traveled an Indian guide who spoke Chinook. Smith's brigade was now in Lower Umpqua tribal land. After the Americans made their camp, about eighty "Omp quch" Indians brought fish and berries to trade. They seemed friendly enough but sold their goods "at a pretty dear rate." The weather turned cold and windy. Several trappers were by then at the uttermost limits of endurance, perilously close to collapse. For the past six weeks Peter Ranney had suffered from a painful "swelling in his legs," a possible indication of scurvy.

Perhaps the knowledge that they were drawing closer to the Columbia River cheered the worn-down trappers. Jedediah Smith's journal, always tantalizingly brief, sheds no light on what he or his men thought of their situation at this juncture. Months of unpleasant weather, the terrible struggles along the trail that sapped the brigade's strength, and their rapidly deteriorating relations with Indians must have figured in Smith's calculations that night. Still, the fact that they had made it safely to Oregon would likely have prompted some sense of satisfaction and urged Smith and the others to gather their strength and press on.

Early in the morning of Saturday, July 12, Smith's debilitated brigade forded the Umpqua River near today's Reedsport, Oregon. All their horses, mules, goods, and gear were safely landed by eight o'clock. After repacking their equipment, the men moved eight miles upriver and made camp on the flats beside the broad stream. It was a lovely location, with a sweeping view that even today is comparatively undeveloped. The shores of the Umpqua River were lined with lush bottomland, offering plentiful grasses for the herd. Heavily timbered mountain hummocks clustered along the river's edge, and in the hazy distance to the south other ranges hung in the sky. Harrison Rogers wrote, "The river at this place is about 300 yards wide and makes a large bay that extends 4 or 5 miles up in the pine hills." Unfortunately, Smith and his trappers almost immediately precipitated an ominous confrontation with the Lower Umpquas, sometimes called Kelawatsets.

About fifty Indians stood by while the brigade set up camp, and the white men soon discovered that an axe was missing. Later reports suggested it was the last one they possessed, which undoubtedly added to their anger at its disappearance. Seizing an Indian they suspected of perpetrating the theft, Smith and another man "put a cord around his neck" and bound him, hoping to frighten him into returning the precious axe. The other trappers stood by with guns loaded and ready to fire on the Kelawatsets, but the Indians in camp "did not pretend to resist." Even then, the Americans continued negotiations to purchase otter and beaver skins and some "Pacific rasberrys and other berries." A few tense hours later, the captive admitted the theft and led Smith's men to where he had buried the axe in sand near a camp fire. Smith released the culprit, doubtless hoping the matter was settled and that his blunt lesson in camp etiquette had left the Indians with the desired impression. Smith, Rogers, and the others evidently did not notice that their prisoner was a Kelawatset chieftain who was much aggrieved.

On Sunday morning, wrote Rogers, Smith's party "made a pretty good start" and followed the bay shore eastward about four miles. They probably camped on the west bank of what is today called Smith's River (the second of that name) near where it joins the Umpqua. Rogers remarked that their path was "quite mirey in places." Some of the men extracted horses from belly-deep mud and cut brush and timber to lay down crude bridges for livestock to pass over the worst sloughs. Adding to their difficulties, a "considerable thunder shower" fell later in the morning, and rainfall continued at intervals throughout the gray day. Once again, after Smith's party made a sodden camp about sixty Kelawatsets came in and traded "15 or 20" beaver skins as well as elk meat, tallow, and a few lamprey eels. Indians informed Jedediah that a few days' march up the river would bring him to an easy divide that separated the Umpqua drainage from that of the "Wel Hammett or Multinomah" River.

Monday, July 14, dawned clear, the previous day's rainfall having temporarily drained the clouds. Smith decided to take a couple of men up the Umpqua to find a ford for their livestock that avoided the marshes through which they had struggled for the past two days. After warning Rogers to permit no Indians to enter the camp, Smith left him in charge and set out in a borrowed canoe with John Turner, Richard Leland, and a Kelawatset guide.

Despite Smith's admonition to exercise extreme caution, for some reason Rogers failed to prevent a great many Kelawatsets from entering the camp. Maybe he assumed that they could be trusted because they traded with HBC men. Perhaps they were simply too numerous to be cowed by a handful of worn-out mountain men. Perhaps, too, the Indians sensed that they had the advantage over the white men. Several trappers were obviously suffering from sickness, and all of them were in terrible physical condition. Within a few minutes nearly two hundred Indians had gathered in knots around Smith's fifteen trappers. Some were cleaning and recharging weapons that got damp during the night's rainstorm. A handful of men were eating breakfast, and a few others were only just waking up. Suddenly, at a preconcerted signal the Kelawatsets swarmed over the totally unprepared Americans. The attack came with lightning speed and staggering ferocity.

Wielding axes, knives, and clubs, the Kelawatsets commenced murdering Jedediah Smith's trappers. Shrieks of pain and terror echoed briefly across the placid waters and the Americans were annihilated. The killing probably took only a minute or two. Some men died while still wrapped in their blankets. For others, life flickered a few moments longer. Facing certain death and schooled in the harsh classrooms of Rocky Mountain life to "sell their lives dearly" when in a hopeless "fix," a few trappers grappled with their assailants. But they must have known in those awful seconds that they stood no chance of escape. Just one man, Arthur Black, managed to get away. He would be the only white man to provide an eyewitness account of the bloodbath. Though neither Rogers nor Smith ever noted the presence of women, Indian testimony recorded long after the event indicated that Smith's brigade included two Indian or mixed-blood women, both of whom survived the attack.

Smith and his comrades had by then completed their reconnaissance and were paddling downstream in mid-river when their camp came into sight. A moment later they heard an Indian yelling something in his own language from the riverbank. Their guide suddenly shifted his weight and jerked the canoe topsy-turvy. He managed to snatch Smith's rifle before he disappeared under the current and swam off to the east bank. Ducking a hail of musket balls and arrows, Smith, Leland, and Turner pushed away from the capsized canoe and desperately swam for the opposite shore.

Perhaps as they crawled onto the riverbank and took cover among the bushes they heard the last shrieks of their dying fellows, though the killing may already have ended. Jedediah and the others stealthily ascended a low promontory and squinted across the river at their campsite. Only a little while earlier it had been alive with their comrades, filled with the horses, mules, and packs of fur that meant Smith's arduous work might finally pay off. Now all they saw was a hellish chaos. Howling Indians slashed and mutilated the trappers' corpses, then stripped them of valuables and rummaged through the company's gear. The livestock must have been milling about, snorting and jumping, recoiling from the stench of fresh blood and the corpses of men. Never again would Smith greet old Thomas Virgin or his trusted clerk and friend, Harrison Rogers, or the other companions with whom he had shared such suffering and privation during two immensely challenging years.

At some point along the trail, Rogers had scrawled a few poignantly hopeful lines on the front wrapper of his tattered journal. Perhaps Smith had seen and appreciated them. But if he recalled his friend's words at this unbearable moment, they must have seemed a hideous mockery. "When young in life and forced to guess my road," Rogers had mused,

And not one friend to shield my bark from harm,
The world received me in its vast abode,
And honest toil procured its plaudits warm.

Fifteen members of Smith's nineteen-man brigade lay dead. All his prudence, wisdom, and leadership had availed naught. All those dearly gained furs, mules, and horses seemed forfeit. Even though each of Smith's trappers willingly accepted the risks of his hazardous occupation, the death of so many must have tortured Jedediah.

But if he and his fellow survivors expected to see another sunrise, they could not spare a single moment trying to analyze why the disaster had befallen them. Painful recriminations over how things might have been done differently could be indulged later, but the immediate imperative was to get themselves safely away from the Kelawatsets. Then they must walk northward toward the Columbia River and head east to seek refuge and succor at the HBC's Fort Vancouver.

CHAPTER 8

From the Umpqua Massacre
to the End of the Trail

OF Jedediah Smith's difficulties on the trail to Fort Vancouver there is scarcely any record. Brief summaries of the attack and its aftermath, however, appear in two letters he penned on December 24, 1829, at "Wind River, East side of the Rocky Mountains." Writing to William Clark on behalf of Smith, Jackson & Sublette, Smith dispassionately noted, "The Indians who made the attack were very numerous; they entered the encampment and massacred the men with their knives, axes, &c. Mr. Smith then made his way to Fort Vancouver." In a second, more personal letter to his brother Ralph, Smith wrote, "[I]n July 1828 fifteen men, who were in Company with me lost their lives, by the Umpquah Indians." Smith's sketchy and inadequate information sheds precious little light on what happened or, more important, what had caused the catastrophe.

A handful of other sources fill in some of the gaps. Smith's letter to Clark listed only ten men who were "Killed at Umpquah," but his October 1830 letter to Secretary of War John Eaton offers a better count. The fifteen murdered men were Thomas Daws, John Gaither, John Hanna, Joseph Lapointe, Abraham Laplant, Emmenuel Lazarus, Toussaint Maréchal, Marion the "Indian boy," Martin McCoy, Joseph Palmer, Peter Ranney, Harrison Rogers, Charles Swift, Thomas Virgin, and "one other," most likely the black man named "Ransa." Neither Smith nor Rogers mentioned the presence of women with the expedition, but an Indian informant early in the twentieth century alleged that women were present at the Umpqua camp. "The entire Smith party got massacred except 2 women," he testified, "one of whom became the wife of the Coos chief, and the other the wife of the Umpqua chief."

Arthur Black was the first survivor to stagger into Fort Vancouver, almost two hundred miles from the Umpqua River battle site. On the evening of August 8 he appeared outside the fort's gates with some Tillamook Indians. Physically exhausted and emotionally overwrought, Black could scarcely speak. Roused by the commotion, Chief Factor John McLoughlin ordered the gates opened. A while later Black recovered sufficiently to explain his sudden appearance. At that point, he believed he was the sole survivor "of 18 men, conducted by the late Jedediah Smith." As the fight began, Black said, two knife-wielding Kelawatset warriors had tried to seize his gun. Refusing to relinquish the weapon, Black suffered lacerations on his hands as the Indians slashed at him. When a third warrior swung an axe at Black's head, he twisted sideways and took a glancing blow on his back. Letting go of his rifle, he dashed into the forest. As he ran for his life, he caught a glimpse of Indians killing Thomas Virgin. He saw several Indians in a canoe pursuing a man in the river that he thought was Thomas Daws, and still others hacking at a trapper with axes. After making his getaway, Black wandered to the coast and headed north. Upon reaching the Tillamook country, 120 miles north of the Umpqua River, he was stripped of everything save for his trousers, but at length he met a kindhearted Indian who conducted him overland to the HBC post.

McLoughlin listened to Black's woeful tale and early the next morning "sent Indian runners to the Willamette chiefs, to tell them to send their people in search of Smith and his two men." He promised the Indians they would be well paid if they brought any Americans to the fort but warned that if "any Indians hurt these men, we would punish them." He then mustered forty "well-armed men," and just as the search party made ready to leave the fort at about noontime the next day, Smith, Turner, and Leland showed up in as sorry a condition as Black.

Like Black, Smith and his companions had stealthily made their way to the seacoast after the Umpqua disaster; they then

This image shows the Hudson's Bay Company's Fort Vancouver as it appeared circa 1855. Here the HBC men offered Smith shelter during the winter of 1828–29. "Fort Vancouver, W. T.," chromolithograph from Pacific Rail Road Surveys, vol. 12, book 1. Author's collection.

traveled 150 miles north to a Tillamook village, where they persuaded guides to escort them to the HBC fort. At the moment that Smith arrived, McLoughlin and his men had nearly completed preparations to dispatch a large and well-equipped HBC brigade under the veteran field man Alexander Roderic McLeod, traveling southward to trap the Umpqua region and continue into California. McLeod and Smith departed on September 6 with revised orders that called upon him to collect as much of Jedediah's property as possible and to ease tensions with the Indians in the HBC's territory.

In the interim, Chief Factor McLoughlin immediately dispatched a preliminary search party commanded by Michel Laframboise, who had first come to the Pacific coast in 1811 with the Astorians. Two days after Jedediah Smith left Fort Vancouver with McLeod's brigade, Laframboise arrived with news that he had discovered no evidence of other survivors. He reported that Smith's property was scattered far and wide, most of it

probably beyond recovery. Within a few days Laframboise left
the fort again to rejoin McLeod's brigade and deliver letters the
chief factor wrote to Smith and McLeod.

Jedediah Smith surely wanted to recover his possessions, but
he also had volunteered to help punish the Indians. He evidently
suggested to the chief factor that it would "confer a favour on
your humble Servant to allow him and his men" to kill some
Kelawatsets for revenge. McLoughlin diplomatically informed
Smith that it would be imprudent to pour oil on this particular
fire. "I conceive," he wrote, "in our intercourse with such bar-
barians we ought always to keep in view the future consequences
likely to result from our conduct." He believed that further violence would only jeopardize other travelers, adding, "it would
be worse than useless to attempt more than our forces would
enable us to accomplish." He finished by advising Smith that
McLeod "knows best whether we can effect any good," and
therefore, "he will decide on what is to be done."

John McLoughlin was by no means insensitive to Smith's
plight. He wrote McLeod that he was "extremely sorry to find
… that Mr. Smith's affair has a more gloomy appearance than I
expected," and remarked, "either we must make War on the
Murders of his people … or drop the matter entirely." Accepting
the necessity of preventing "the perpetuation of such atrocious
crimes," he thought the best means of doing so was to persuade
the Indians to restore the "illgotten booty now in their possession." Assuring McLeod of his complete confidence, McLoughlin left it to his field man to determine his own course of action.

From early September through early October McLeod's
brigade cautiously moved southward. Along the way they
learned that Smith's goods and livestock had been distributed
among several nations. Lower Umpquas (Kelawatsets), Upper
Umpquas, Willamettes, and perhaps others now held portions
of the stolen gear, and they feared reprisals. By September 21
McLeod received a report that the Kelawatsets, "elated with
their late success," had offered the other Umpquas "large presents" in order to recruit them in common cause against the
white men. October 9 found McLeod's men camped at the

Umpqua River, and the next day he sent an invitation for the local chiefs to parley with him at his camp. On Saturday, October 11, three months after the killings, an Umpqua chieftain and a dozen warriors came into camp with eight horses bearing Smith's brand. On that day for the first time the Indians gave their version of the causes for their assault on Smith's party.

The Umpqua headman, called "St. Arnoose" and "Starnoose" in McLeod's journal, had just returned from a council with the Kelawatsets, from whom he had gleaned a number of salient details. According to "Starnoose," while Smith's men were "fixing Canoes," an axe was mislaid, prompting the Americans to seize a suspect who was "tyed and otherwise ill treated." (A day later, Smith denied "having used blows or any manner of violence" against the captive.) Upon recovery of the axe, the hostage was released. He happened to be a highly respected man and was "much irritated" at his treatment. He talked of reprisal but was overruled by a more influential leader.

A little while later the chief who advised caution decided he wanted to "ride a horse for amusement about the Camp" and "took the liberty of mounting one." Unfortunately, it was this man that Arthur Black, with gun in hand, brusquely ordered off the horse. (Like Smith, Arthur Black denied using force, asserting that he "ordered him to desist but not in an angry tone[,] neither did he present his gun.") Angered and humiliated, the chief then "gave his concurrence to the Plan in agitation." Moreover, the Indians claimed, the Americans had declared themselves "a different people" from the HBC men and threatened they would soon "monopolize the trade" and drive out the HBC.

Surprised at the HBC men's willingness to tolerate strangers who "evinced evil intentions" toward Indians, "Starnoose" also wondered why McLeod assisted men who boasted "they would soon possess themselves of the Country." When McLeod queried Jedediah Smith on this point, he retorted that "he did not doubt of it, but it was without his knowledge and must have been intimated to the Indians through the Medium of a Slave boy attached to his party," that is, the deceased Marion.

After collecting about thirty horses, Smith and McLeod's party proceeded toward another large Umpqua village. Enduring several gloomy days of rainfall, on October 21 they camped near the village, where they noticed two fresh graves. Upon questioning, the Umpquas told them the graves held men who were killed by Smith's trappers during the fight. McLeod requested the chief "Starnoose" to tell his people that they must hand over to him anything they had that belonged to Smith.

On October 22 the Umpquas produced a rifle and a musket, two pistols, 163 beaver skins, 42 otter skins, two shirts, half a dozen pencils, two vials of medicine, "some Books and other Paper" (unfortunately the books' titles were unrecorded), and two "Charts." Quite likely, the last items were two of Smith's preliminary field maps. The next day the Umpquas returned "421 Large Beavers" and four small ones, and five otter skins. On October 27 they delivered ten pounds of beads, a beaver trap, two muskets, and a cooking kettle. A day later McLeod's brigade reached "the entrance to the North Branch, where Mr. Smith's Party were destroyed."

There, wrote McLeod, "a Sad Spectacle of Indian barbarity presented itself to our View, the Skeletons of eleven of those Miserable Sufferers lying bleaching in the Sun." Where the remainder of the dead men were no one knew. After conducting a brief funeral ceremony, the white men turned back toward the seacoast and other Umpqua villages. At one village near Tahken-itch Creek they recovered a rifle, a pistol, two horses, and fifteen beaver skins. On November 1 they arrived at another village and received four beaver skins, a musket barrel, a blanket, a woolen shirt, some beads, and a few horses. On November 4 they took in two kettles and three saddles, and on the 10th they recovered three horses, two mules, seven beaver traps, a copper kettle and its cover, a rifle and a rifle barrel, some beads, and another parcel of "Books, journals & other papers," doubtless including Rogers's and Smith's tattered daybooks. Clearly, Smith's goods and livestock were indeed distributed among several Umpqua villages, but no evidence suggested the assault was the concerted act of a multi-village coalition.

By November 23 the campaign to recover Smith's possessions was drawing to a close. Continuously foul weather made for bad hunting and miserable camping, and it seemed unlikely that more property would be restored. Jedediah Smith told McLeod that he planned to press on to Fort Vancouver, where he hoped to sell his livestock to the HBC men and pay off "such of his Men as [were] pleased to accept their dismissal." McLeod replied that he was not empowered to make such an agreement but suggested that Smith might "settle that and other Matters with my Senior Officer." Five days later the rain let up and Smith departed for Fort Vancouver, accompanied by Michel Laframboise and two other HBC engagés as a "precautionary Measure."

By December 2 McLeod caught up with Smith's party, and under mixed rain and snow they proceeded together toward the post. Around December 9 Smith received twenty-three "Large Beavers and 1 Large land Otter," the last furs to be returned. When they reached the Willamette they found the surrounding lowlands inundated, so McLeod's men crafted two canoes and the party set out for the fort. Smith's arrival a few days later prompted a round of negotiations with Chief Factor McLoughlin and the imperious Sir George Simpson, who happened to show up just in time to supervise negotiations with Smith. In the course of their discussions, additional information surfaced to shed light on possible causes of the massacre.

McLeod had diligently aided Smith, expending valuable HBC time and energy. All told, Jedediah recovered eight rifles and muskets, eight traps, more than six hundred beaver skins, almost fifty otter skins, roughly forty horses and mules, and sundry camp gear and other items, including the fragmentary journals. Despite an official policy intended to eliminate competition with Americans, the HBC men viewed Jedediah Smith's sad plight with genuine concern. They took action in what McLoughlin would have denoted the spirit of Christian charity, but they did not entirely ignore the interests of either the Indians or the HBC.

McLeod's ability to retrieve as much of Smith's gear as he did illustrates the benefits of maintaining amicable relationships with Indians upon whose goodwill HBC profits depended. McLeod succeeded admirably at pressuring the Umpquas to restore substantial amounts of Smith's goods while maintaining the HBC policy of avoiding violence. It is hard to imagine that anyone could have done better. Perhaps Smith came to appreciate the wisdom of McLeod's diplomatic maneuvering, but his first impulse had been to shed rivers of Umpqua blood. Whatever may have been their faults, some HBC men brought to the wilderness an honorable sense of civility that a man like Jedediah Smith would have admired.

Sir George Simpson was not an easy man to deal with. A diminutive, bald-headed fellow with piercing eyes, Simpson was famously acerbic, brutally frank, and dictatorial, and he never lost sight of the HBC's interests and annual dividends. The image of Simpson, dapperly attired in a suit and sporting a silk neck-cloth and top hat while he perched stiffly at attention in an HBC canoe all the way from York Factory on Hudson's Bay to Fort Vancouver, seems weirdly out of place, even amusing. But Simpson was evidently a stranger to humor, and few men, even among HBC officers, spared him much affection. He displayed a singular devotion to his superiors, he drove himself hard, and he demanded the same from his many underlings.

On his previous visit to the Columbia in 1824–25, Simpson had announced that the Snake River country must be made a "fur desert" to keep out men such as Jedediah Smith. As of 1829 the HBC's "Governor and Committee" still considered the "impoverishment of the Country situated to the Southward of the Columbia" to be "the most effectual protection against opposition from the Americans." But even as the Fort Vancouver men dutifully applied Simpson's program, they offered invaluable assistance to Smith after the Umpqua River disaster.

Simpson was waiting at Fort Vancouver when Jedediah Smith and Alexander McLeod returned on December 14. McLoughlin upbraided McLeod for his failure to take his men south to trap the Sacramento as he was supposed to do. McLeod replied that he came back because he needed more horses, but McLoughlin suspected the real reason was that McLeod wished to spend some time with his family. McLoughlin and Simpson were irked that McLeod had devoted so much time to helping Smith that he neglected to keep his men trapping. The result, complained Simpson, was the "loss to us of the Services of this Expedition for the whole Season," which tallied to more than £1,000, "independent of the loss of Profits" the HBC stood to gain.

On Christmas Eve, 1828, Smith discussed his affairs with Simpson. Two days later Simpson penned a letter to Jedediah summarizing the substance of their meeting. McLeod was about to leave for "12 to 16 months" on another trapping expedition to California, and Simpson wanted to "come to a final understanding or Settlement" with Smith before McLeod departed. Simpson's letter would "guard against any misapprehension" as to details of the agreement. Smith's misfortune, wrote Simpson, had aroused "the most lively feelings of Sympathy and commiseration" among the HBC's "Gentlemen." Accordingly, McLeod had been sent to the Umpqua country to "ascertain the cause of their atrocious conduct," punish the perpetrators if necessary, and restore Smith's property. Simpson also took the opportunity to record, and thus preserve for future reference, details about the causes of the attack. The disturbing evidence he mustered casts an unflattering light on Smith and his men.

According to Simpson, McLeod learned at the site of the "Melancholy catastrophe" that "some harsh treatment" of the Umpquas by Smith's men had triggered the assault. Some Indians had been "beaten and one of them bound hands and feet for some very slight offense," presumably the theft of the axe. The trappers' mistreatment of the Indians "corroborated in their Minds a report that had preceded" Smith's arrival, doubtless a reference to smoke signals and runners that communicated news of the Americans' movements from tribe to tribe. Indians had constantly monitored the progress of Smith's brigade and its conflicts with Indians ever since they were on the way north from the Sacramento River, and perhaps the Umpquas knew that the trappers had killed many California Indians. Admitting that Smith might have had "some grounds" for his actions in

California, Simpson still believed that the Umpquas' attack stemmed from the Americans' "injudicious conduct and [their] unguarded situation" at camp.

A few months later, in a March 1829 update on Smith to the HBC's board of directors, Simpson mentioned other evidence that he likely acquired from McLeod. He recited again the Indians' overblown claim that Smith's party had been "destroying all the Natives that came within their reach," but then Simpson introduced some details that appear particularly damning. Simpson informed his superiors that the Umpquas viewed Smith's brigade with grave suspicion but formed no "plan of destruction" until Smith's "clerk" (Harrison Rogers) "attempted to force a Woman into his Tent." When her brother intervened, Simpson went on, Rogers knocked him to the ground and in that instant sealed the trappers' doom. According to the Indians' version, "seeing the opportunity favorable, as some of the people were asleep, others Eating and none on their guard, [the Umpquas] rose in a body and dispatched the whole party except the man who fled," meaning Arthur Black. The deed was done, said the Indians, "as a measure of Self Preservation."

Smith denied "some parts" of the Indian version but, Simpson remarked, "the whole story is well told, and carries the probability of truth." The absolute "truth" of these assertions might be questionable, but they doubtless reflect genuine Indian perceptions of the event. If indeed the allegations were true, the assault on Smith's party is readily explained and responsibility for it rests mainly with Smith and his trappers. Rogers's journal suggests that he was a forthright and decent man, and perhaps the attack was the sad result of a terrible misunderstanding. But it remains at least possible that for some reason he or another man made a fatally unwise decision to rape a Kelawatset woman at the Umpqua River camp. On the other hand, Simpson may have been inclined to accept the Indians' stories uncritically since they cast his trade rivals in the worst possible light.

An early-twentieth-century Coos Indian informant named George B. Wasson offered other details. Wasson said that when "an old Indian" plunged a knife into an elk carcass hanging from a tree at Smith's camp to "see what condition the meat was. . . . Mr. Turner the cook . . . kicked the old man out of the camp." A while later, reported Wasson, "some Indian boys came into camp with their legs bleeding from where the cook had whipt them with a horse whip." Thereupon, the Umpquas "all got their bows and arrows and massacred all the Smith party, except Turner[,] who dove in the river and got away." Still another Indian informant noted that the trouble erupted when a young lad mounted a mule and the white men assumed he was going to steal it. Sparse and somewhat indefinite though it may be, Indian testimony about the fight adds materially to the slim documentation of this important event and is worth considering.

Simpson wrote that McLeod's relief expedition recovered "nearly the whole" of Smith's goods, but this was well short of the truth. Smith had no means to reimburse the HBC's expenses, so Simpson had decided to "place the property which we have recovered at [Smith's] disposal without any charge or demand whatsoever." As for Smith's horses, Simpson was willing to take them off his hands for forty shillings apiece, "a higher price than we ever pay for Horses." Simpson judged Smith's poorly dressed and water-damaged beaver furs to be "of very bad quality[,] the worst indeed I ever saw." Considering what those furs had been through, Simpson was probably not exaggerating. He offered to purchase the lot of beavers at three dollars per skin and made a final bid of two pounds for each horse. Smith could either accept his offer or try to find another buyer for his furs and horses, which would be virtually impossible.

Jedediah Smith broached the idea of taking his men up the Columbia to the HBC post at Walla Walla, but Simpson thought this would be "the height of imprudence." Citing the "desperate hazards" of a lengthy trip through potentially hostile country where only large and well-armed HBC brigades dared to go, Simpson warned that such a decision would be "sporting with Life or courting danger to [the point of] madness." Instead, Simpson invited Smith to winter at Fort Vancouver and in springtime travel with him east to the Red River Settlement in Minnesota, courtesy of the HBC. From Red River, Smith could easily make his way south to Saint Louis. Alternately, he might remain at Fort Vancouver until the next autumn and travel with the Snake Country Expedition to the environs of the Great Salt Lake.

On December 29 Simpson handed Smith another letter that clarified several fine points of their discussions. He assured Smith that "the satisfaction we derive from these good offices, will repay the Hon[ble] Hudsons Bay Comp[y] amply for any loss or inconvenience sustained in rendering them." Simpson was relieved that Smith had decided to "pursue the safer yet more circuitous route by Red River" that would return him to Saint Louis by the following July. Accordingly, Smith sold his furs and livestock to the HBC for $2,500 to $3,000 and agreed to spend the winter at Fort Vancouver.

During many cold, gray days in the following two months, Jedediah found ample opportunities to examine the fort and learn about its operations. The HBC men were equally eager to acquire information from Smith. When Jedediah regaled the HBC men with tales of his California adventures, Simpson found it amusing that the Mexicans ignored the wealth in beaver fur that abounded so close to their settlements. Within five years the HBC had opened the 850-mile Siskiyou Trail from Fort Vancouver to San Francisco Bay. Operating secretly at first and later under agreements with Mexican officials, the HBC men harvested many furs in Mexican land. The company also operated a store at the small community of Yerba Buena (later San Francisco) from 1841 to 1848. Like Spaniards and Mexicans before them, the HBC trappers failed to discover North America's richest placer gold deposits in the gravelly, cobble-strewn streams where they hunted beavers. After 1848 most of that gold wound up in the hands of Americans.

Simpson optimistically suggested to his HBC superiors that when Smith's information about western geography became known in the states, American interest in the Oregon Country would dwindle. Thanks to effusive reports from Ashley and others, wrote Simpson, Americans naively believed that a trip across the continent posed few impediments. After bringing their

"Horses, Cattle, Agricultural instruments &c … to the height of Land in about Lat. 38," they imagined that they would simply "embark on large Rafts & Batteaux and glide down current" on the Multnomah several hundred miles to the "Land of Promise." Instead of drifting placidly down yet another version of the "river of the west," according to Smith's recital travelers would confront "Mountains which even Hunters cannot attempt to pass," and sandy wastes hundreds of miles in extent where starvation was all too common. In spite of Simpson's estimate that American trappers had taken £2,000 worth of beaver pelts from the Far West each year since 1824, he concluded that "we have little to apprehend from Settlers in this quarter, and from Indian Traders nothing." Sir George Simpson was no fool, but he could not foresee the future.

Jedediah Smith's letters to William Clark in December 1829 and Secretary of War John Eaton in October 1830 tell a different story. Both were written after he departed Fort Vancouver. Informing Clark of his difficulties with Indians and Mexicans in 1827 and 1828, Smith summarized the Umpqua River fight and its aftermath and acknowledged the HBC's hospitality during his stay at Fort Vancouver. But then Smith's patriotism took flight. "Until British interlopers are dismissed from off our territory," he asserted, "Americans will never be respected or acknowledged as patrons by Indians on the west side of the Rocky Mountains." "British influence is gaining ground every day," warned Jedediah, while Americans were "tormented and annoyed" by every Indian nation in the Far West.

When he returned to Saint Louis in October 1830 Smith hammered on the same theme in his letter to Secretary of War Eaton. After noting Ashley's success and the emergence of Smith, Jackson & Sublette, Jedediah explained that the traders' route from Saint Louis to the Rockies via South Pass easily accommodated wagons, and that grass for cattle was almost always available on the main route. Repeating his earlier assertion to Clark that "sickness and natural deaths are almost unknown," Smith provided a detailed description of Fort Vancouver, noting that a major expansion project was under way when he left in 1829.

The Hudson's Bay Company's post Fort Walla Walla, on the Walla
Walla River near the confluence of the Snake and Columbia rivers in
modern Washington State. Jedediah Smith passed by it in 1829.
"Old Fort Walla Walla," chromolithograph from Pacific Rail Road
Surveys, vol. 12, book 1. Author's collection.

More importantly, the Willamette River valley offered splendid
opportunities for farming and for raising cattle, hogs, sheep, and
horses.

Fort Vancouver's farmers annually harvested seven hundred
bushels of "full and plump" wheat as well as fields of oats and
barley. The farm boasted fourteen acres each of corn and peas
and abundant grape vines and apple trees. Smith estimated that
the HBC collected at least $250,000 worth of beaver furs each
year, and he claimed that many were taken inside U.S. territory.
Denouncing the "glaring and apparent" injustices of the joint-
occupancy treaty, Smith declared it operated to the "injury of
the United States" and should be "terminated, and each nation
confined to its territories." In closing he urged Eaton to lay all
these complaints "before President Jackson."

Jedediah Smith well understood that the fur trade played a
much larger role in national and international affairs than its relatively minor economic significance would suggest. Newspaper
accounts of Smith and his fellows' activities in the Far West con-

Clark's Fork of the Columbia River, in the vicinity of Flat Head
Lake north of modern Missoula, Montana, which Jedediah Smith
passed by in 1829. "View of the Clark's Fork and the Ridge of
Mountains, South of Flathead Lake, Looking Eastward,"
chromolithograph from Pacific Rail Road Surveys, vol. 12, book 1.
Author's collection.

tributed to the growing public and political sentiment in favor
of national expansionism that marked the Age of Jackson. Perhaps the discouraging assessment he offered Simpson at the fort
was meant to quiet HBC fears about the Americans' capacity to
interfere in their bailiwick. While men such as Smith and Ashley
called upon their government to take decisive action in Oregon,
British parliamentarians and HBC executives likewise worked
in concert to secure the region.

Arguments over territory such as the one that took place
between Johnson Gardner and Peter Skene Ogden in 1825 did
not happen simply because the mountain men were buck-
skinned thugs liable to pick a fight for no particular reason. The
Rocky Mountain men came from widely divergent geographic,
economic, and social sections of U.S. society and thus defy easy
characterization, but many embraced the expansive patriotic
spirit of the times. Conscious "manifest destinarians" or not,

Jedediah Smith passed the Kettle Falls, a famed landmark in
northeastern Washington, near the Hudson's Bay Company's post
Fort Colvile, on his eastward route from Fort Vancouver in 1829.
"Kettle Falls, Columbia River," chromolithograph from Pacific Rail
Road Surveys, vol. 12, book 1. Author's collection.

some acted as though they carried the flag with them wherever
they went—and some really did. Between 1800 and 1840 fur
traders played a crucial role in the contest between Britain and
the United States for sovereignty over the Columbia River and
the Pacific Northwest. Prominent among them was Jedediah
Smith, and in 1829 no American was better informed about the
Oregon Country and the HBC's operations there. Smith must
have felt some urgency to get back to the states so he could share
his knowledge with men who were in positions to reshape U.S.
policy on Oregon.

By early March 1829 Jedediah had learned that two American
trapping parties had spent part of the winter near the HBC's
Flathead Post, and he suddenly revised his exit strategy. One of
the outfits was Joshua Pilcher's Missouri Fur Company brigade.
In a final, desperate gesture to prevent his company from slid-

ing into bankruptcy, Pilcher would attempt to strike a deal with Simpson to combine their operations, only to be brusquely rebuffed. The other outfit was a Smith, Jackson & Sublette brigade led by David Jackson. Smith left Fort Vancouver to rejoin his partner on March 12, two weeks before George Simpson's anticipated departure. Arthur Black was the only survivor of the Umpqua fight to accompany Smith. Richard Leland remained at Fort Vancouver but got into some difficulty with the HBC and was shipped off to Canada with another trouble-maker in July. John Turner also stayed behind but soon returned to California. In 1846 Turner was among the men who rescued the forlorn survivors of the ill-fated Donner Party.

Of his journey away from Fort Vancouver, Smith wrote only that he ascended the Columbia, turned north at Fort Walla Walla, and followed "Clark's Fork" of the Columbia to the HBC post called Fort Colvile at Kettle Falls. Traveling in company with Jackson northward along a well-worn trail beside the Colvile River, he passed briefly into what is now British Columbia. After crossing the Selkirk Mountains, they turned south toward the Pend Oreille River in northeastern Washington and Lake Pend Oreille in the Idaho panhandle. Smith and his companions followed "Clark's Fork" of the Columbia, now the Flathead River, into Montana and turned north along Thompson River to the Thompson Lakes, about thirty miles southwest of present-day Kalispell. In the Kootenai River country they entered today's Glacier National Park and followed the North Fork of Clark's Fork of the Columbia to Flathead Lake. Then they headed south along the Big Hole River and the Beaverhead River and reentered Idaho through Monida Pass.

On August 5, 1829, Smith and Jackson met William Sublette on Henry's Fork of the Snake River near the "Three Tetons." The three men had not been together since the 1827 rendezvous and doubtless exchanged warm greetings. Jackson and Sublette updated Smith on their business affairs, and he must have been heartened to hear that the company was beginning to show a profit. In October 1827, while Smith trekked across the Nevada desert, William Sublette had traveled to Saint Louis, assembled another outfit, and paid off Smith, Jackson & Sublette's $7,821 promissory note to Ashley dating from July 1826. Sublette returned again to Saint Louis in October 1828 to deliver Ashley 7,107 pounds of beaver fur, 24 pounds of "castorum," 49 otter skins, and 73 muskrat skins. Sublette and Jackson planned for the "general rendezvous" of 1829 to take place in August at Pierre's Hole, in Idaho's Teton Basin.

While Sublette purchased trade goods, Ashley brokered the harvest of skins. Prices were very favorable, with beaver fur selling at five dollars per pound and castorum at four dollars. The otter skins sold for three dollars each, and the muskrats fetched twenty-five cents apiece. After deducting his fees, Ashley tallied the proceeds. As of October 26, 1828, Smith, Jackson & Sublette had cleared about sixteen thousand dollars. William Sublette spent the winter at Saint Louis and in early March 1829 departed for the rendezvous with fifty-five men and enough mules and horses to carry $9,500 worth of goods. One of Sublette's new recruits was Joseph L. Meek, a Virginian whose exciting western experiences were chronicled in a book published in 1870.

From the mouth of the Kansas River, Sublette's brigade headed through spring snow and rain to the Arkansas River, then north to follow the North Platte to the Sweetwater. A few miles east of South Pass they set a northwest course for the headwaters of the Wind River and the Popo Agie. Early in July 1829 Sublette's brigade encountered Robert Campbell and his trappers near modern Lander, Wyoming. Campbell and his men had trapped in Crow country that spring and made a good hunt. When Thomas Fitzpatrick arrived with David Jackson's fall and spring fur collections, Campbell held nearly the whole of Smith, Jackson & Sublette's furs. Before leaving for the rendezvous, Sublette dispatched his brother Milton and some trappers to the Big Horn–Yellowstone to make ready for the coming trapping season. After resupplying his own trappers and dispatching them in good order to new trapping grounds, William Sublette proceeded to the rendezvous.

After the 1829 rendezvous, Robert Campbell set off for Saint Louis to deliver to Ashley forty-five packs of beaver. Ashley sold

Smith, Jackson & Sublette's 4,076 pounds of beaver furs (at $5.25 a pound) for $21,476, and received $77 for seven otter skins and 14 pounds of castorum. Ashley deducted his 2.5 percent broker-age commission, amounting to $531.80, then added the proceeds to Smith, Jackson & Sublette's preexisting January 1829 credit of $6,684, yielding a total credit of $28,160. At the moment, their debt stood at $29,177. In April 1830 Campbell or someone else would sign a promissory note for the outstanding balance of $1,017. Campbell thereafter left the country for three years to attend to family affairs in Scotland.

Despite three tough years in the mountains, substantial prof-its still eluded Smith, Jackson & Sublette. Of course, Smith's misfortunes resulted in heavy losses of horses, furs, goods, and men, and he had been obliged to sell his furs at bargain prices in California and again at Fort Vancouver. Thanks to Jackson, Sub-lette, and Campbell, the losses were not greater. If it was to suc-ceed, Smith, Jackson & Sublette must generate profits before competition eliminated its advantages. One good year with no major catastrophes could pull the outfit out of red ink and put it well into black. Ashley skimmed some of their profits as a fur broker and supplier of goods and risked almost nothing, but his take was relatively small. Entrepreneurial field men might make a lot more money, but life in the West was extremely demand-ing, and they faced great risks on a daily basis. For the next year Smith, Jackson & Sublette had to keep its trappers busy, avoid another disaster, prevent costly losses, and above all, maintain high profit margins on the goods they sold at the rendezvous. By early 1830 they would hear news that inspired them to redouble their efforts: Bernard Pratte & Company, with John Astor's backing, was preparing to send caravans west to capture the mountain trade.

When the beaver hunters began arriving at the 1829 ren-dezvous there was no sign of Smith, Sublette, or Jackson. The trappers' meeting with their "long-absent Booshway [bour-geois]" took place on August 20 and, reported Joseph Meek, was marked by "excitement and elation." Gathered there were some 175 mountain men, most of them hirelings of Smith,

Jackson & Sublette, along with a number of free trappers and former HBC freemen operating on their own hook.

Remaining at Pierre's Hole for almost a month, wrote Meek, the trappers "indulged in their noisy sports and rejoicing." While Smith, Jackson & Sublette's hired men wallowed in revelry and high jinks, the three partners formulated strategy for the impending fall hunt. Remembering the kindness of his hosts at Fort Vancouver, and perhaps an unrecorded agreement, Jedediah insisted they refrain from trapping west of the mountains and avoid competing directly with the HBC "for the present." Jackson and Sublette agreed, perhaps reluctantly, that no Smith, Jackson & Sublette trappers would go further west than the forks of "the great Snake River" in eastern Idaho.

By early October Smith and Sublette's brigade ascended Henry's Fork and crossed Lewis and Clark's Northern Pass, then trapped their way to Henry's Lake, at the outer limits of Smith's territorial prescription, where they spent a few weeks. In early November they retreated to the Three Forks of the Missouri. Arriving at the Madison River via either Targhee Pass or Raynolds Pass, the party continued eastward past the Gallatin River toward the Yellowstone River. The brigade experienced several run-ins with Blackfeet raiders, resulting in a few deaths and more bad blood between Blackfeet and Americans.

At about this time, Joseph Meek recorded an account of a joke that Moses "Black" Harris played on Jedediah Smith. During a frigid trek over snow-packed mountains that winter, about one hundred horses and mules perished in deep snowdrifts. Smith sent Harris to climb a nearby mountaintop and ascertain how far it was to the prairies, where the livestock might find better forage and milder weather. When Moses Harris ambled back into camp, Smith asked him what he saw. According to Meek, Harris responded: "'I saw the city of St. Louis, and one fellow taking a drink!' . . . prefacing the assertion with a shocking oath. Smith asked no more questions. He understood by the man's answer that he had made no pleasing discoveries; and knew that they had still a weary way before them to reach the plains below. Besides, Smith was a religious man, and the coarse profanity of the mountaineers was very distasteful to him." Meek's story has the ring of authenticity and suggests that some of the mountain men enjoyed trying to rattle Jedediah Smith once in a while.

In early December 1829 Smith and Sublette's men descended to the freezing plains along the Bighorn River and came to the Shoshone River, which they named the "Stinking Fork" because of its sulphurous smell. It flowed through the geothermal springs region called "Colter's Hell" after the Lewis and Clark expedition veteran John Colter discovered it in 1807–08. Meek remarked of the Stinking Fork and its brimstone fumes, "[I]f it war hell, it war a more agreeable climate than I had been in for some time." The Shoshone River's headwaters lie in the mountains a few miles east of Yellowstone Lake, near what is now Cody, Wyoming. This was probably the closest Jedediah Smith ever came to viewing Yellowstone Lake or the hot springs, geyser basins, and other natural wonders of today's Yellowstone National Park.

Smith and William Sublette learned that Milton Sublette and forty trappers had spent the previous season hunting in the vicinity and were not far off. After scouts ascertained their whereabouts, Smith and Sublette cached their furs near the Shoshone River and joined Milton's brigade. Together they crossed the Absaroka Mountains from the Yellowstone to the Bighorn Basin and headed for the confluence of the Bighorn and the Wind rivers. In late December they established winter quarters at "Wind River, East side of the Rocky Mountains." By then David Jackson's brigade had probably also arrived. Joseph Meek recalled that "the men celebrated Christmas as best they might under the circumstances." Soon after settling in, Jedediah Smith, in consultation with his partners, wrote the important letters to William Clark and Secretary of War John Eaton mentioned earlier in this chapter. The partners also took advantage of the slack time to form plans for the coming year.

A few days later William Sublette and "Black" Harris departed "on snowshoes, with a train of pack dogs" from the winter camp on Wind River for Saint Louis. By mid-February 1830, after eight weeks on the icy trail, the hardy voyagers delivered Ashley another order for trade goods. Sublette spent the next several weeks assembling a stock of merchandise, and he dispatched a caravan from Saint Louis on April 10.

He delayed his own departure by four days while he secured a new license from William Clark that permitted the company to trade at "Camp Defiance, Horse Prairie, mouth of Lewis' Fork of the Columbia, junction of the Little Horn and the Big Horn, and at the Quamash flats of Lewis' Fork of the Columbia," with a capital investment of $8,205. "Camp Defiance" is the same belligerent-sounding name for the rendezvous site that Smith had used two and a half years earlier in his October 1827 letter to Governor Echeandía. "Quamash flats" refers to the Camas Prairie region in southeast Idaho's Snake River Plains. Their license empowered them to trade with Indians in an area encompassing Wyoming, Idaho, and Montana. Beaver trapping and hunting in Indian Country remained illegal, but if British competitors in the Oregon Country were to be defeated, then U.S. laws must be ignored.

Sublette hastened along the trail to catch up with his men, many of whom were greenhorn recruits. His westbound caravan boasted two important "firsts." Ten five-mule freight wagons and two small single-mule Dearborn wagons hauled blankets, beads, knives, guns, and other trade goods. Other wheeled vehicles had made part of the journey, but if Sublette's wagons were capable of rolling from Saint Louis to South Pass, then what would prevent wagons from going the rest of the way to Oregon? Sublette also proved that livestock could manage the trip. Several beef cattle and a lone milk cow trekked to the rendezvous with the trappers. Some beeves wound up in stew pots or roasted over fires, but others survived and returned to Saint Louis with the hardy cow. On July 16 Sublette's entourage reached the rendezvous site in the Wind River Valley, near the confluence of the Wind River and its southern tributary the Popo Agie.

After Sublette and Harris left the winter camp early in January 1830, Smith and Jackson's trappers set out on a 150-mile journey down to the Powder River to a new camp, where they waited out a particularly malevolent winter season. Until early April they huddled in their encampment, trading stories of their varied adventures, hunting bison, and killing time. When warm weather unlocked the ice-bound creeks, the trappers shook off their winter lethargy and set about the business of hunting beavers. David Jackson conducted one party into the Snake River country. Jedediah Smith and the remainder headed northwest from Powder River, passing the Tongue River, the Little Horn, and Clark's Fork, and then crossed Pryor's Gap into the Yellowstone country.

In the ensuing weeks Smith's men evidently worked up Clark's Fork of the Yellowstone in a southerly direction, then struck southeast along the western flank of Heart Mountain, about twenty miles north of present-day Cody, Wyoming. From there they headed south to the Shoshone River and continued southward, crossing the Greybull River on the western margin of Wyoming's Big Horn Basin. After crossing the Owl Creek Mountains, the brigade set a course for the 1830 rendezvous site near the confluence of the Wind and the Popo Agie rivers.

Jedediah Smith reached the Popo Agie and his final Rocky Mountain rendezvous early in July. The economic outlook appeared promising. Thanks to excellent hunts in 1829–30, the partners collected well above one hundred packs of beaver fur from their trappers. If all went well, those furs would yield a substantial profit, but Smith, Jackson & Sublette still owed William Ashley about $1,000 and had accumulated an additional debt of $23,000 for trade goods and other supplies.

It may have been William Sublette who broached the idea of dissolving the company. He learned at Saint Louis that the Astor-Chouteau company was preparing to send goods to the Rockies. The 1830 AFC brigade failed to reach the rendezvous, but future AFC caravans would succeed. At any rate, after some discussion the three partners decided to get out while the getting was good. As of August 1, 1830, Smith, Jackson & Sublette was no more. Late in July, the partners struck a bargain with five trappers—Thomas Fitzpatrick, James Bridger, Milton Sublette,

Jean Baptiste Gervais, and Henry Fraeb—who organized the famous Rocky Mountain Fur Company. The Rocky Mountain Fur Company's founders were experienced, almost legendary, mountain men, but not one of them possessed a genuine talent for making money. William Sublette became the new outfit's main wire-puller, and the five partners never escaped the web of indebtedness he wove around them.

On August 4 Smith, Sublette, and Jackson departed the 1830 rendezvous with seventy riders to safeguard the rich cargo of 170 packs of beaver fur loaded into ten wagons. After a relatively uneventful trip, they pulled into Saint Louis on October 10. Jedediah Smith had not seen Saint Louis for five long years. The city was larger and richer, and business was good. An entirely new town, Independence, was growing about 250 miles to the west on the banks of the Kansas River where it entered the Missouri. Large caravans of loaded wagons assembled at Independence each spring, making it for a few years a lively jumping off place for New Mexico–bound merchants on the Santa Fe Trail. Cantonment Leavenworth, forty miles up the Kansas River from Independence, was now the leading frontier army post. Old Fort Atkinson had been abandoned and lay in moldering ruins.

Newspapers trumpeted word that Smith, Jackson & Sublette brought in as much as $150,000 worth of beaver fur, but that was an exaggeration. One paper, the *Missouri Intelligencer*, enthused that "These hardy and sun-burnt *Mountaineers* . . . exhibited great demonstrations of satisfaction, at their near approach to their families and friends." Another paper, the *St. Louis Beacon*, patriotically opined that Smith, Jackson & Sublette's wagons had made such an easy trip that they "could have gone on to the mouth of the Columbia, [which] shows the folly and nonsense of those '*scientific*' characters who talk of the Rocky Mountains as the barrier which is to stop the westward march of the American people."

Soon after his arrival at Saint Louis, Jedediah Smith penned a letter to Robert Campbell's brother Hugh at Richmond, Virginia, to ask if he might handle the sale of Smith, Jackson & Sub-

lette's furs. Around November 18 Campbell's return letter with
some price information reached Smith, but by then the partners
had signed another contract authorizing Ashley to "take our
Furs forward to Philadelphia and N. York and dispose of the
Same." "Ashley beaver" still commanded a premium in the markets, and it may have seemed best to capitalize on that association. Ashley marketed nearly all of the furs to John Astor, and the
sale netted a whopping $84,500. The accounts were not finally
balanced until 1831, when each partner received at least $17,500.
But by then Jedediah Smith was dead.

About two weeks after reaching Saint Louis, Smith, Jackson,
and Sublette collaborated on another letter summarizing their
adventures and explaining their enmity for the British-American
joint occupancy of Oregon and sent it off to the secretary of war.
Like their earlier letter to Secretary Eaton, this one asserted that
wagons could make the long prairie crossing carrying as much
as 1,800 pounds each, and it stressed that "the ease and safety
with which it was done prove the facility of communicating over
land with the Pacific ocean." The partners declared that their
hired men remained healthy and robust throughout the trip, and
that plentiful grazing for livestock could be found "along the
whole route coming and going." A description of Fort Vancouver followed, and the closing paragraphs focused on why the
treaty of joint occupation ought to be terminated. The main reasons were unfair British commercial advantages, their "decisive"
influence over Indians in the region, and a somewhat overblown
fear that the British might use the Pacific coast as a staging area
to launch "privateers and vessels of war."

With these affairs settled, Smith turned to other long-deferred
interests. He was now, after all, a man of considerable means. If
financial independence had been his ambition then he had certainly achieved it. It would not do to ignore his family or his
own aspirations any longer. For one thing, he was eager to purchase a farm tract in Green Township, Ohio, adjacent to land
that his brother Ralph owned. For this purpose he forwarded to
Ralph a note for $1,500 to buy the land from a certain "Major
Tiller." He then bought a commodious house in Saint Louis on

Federal Avenue, soon to be renamed Broadway. Smith would live there briefly, and so would three of his brothers. Peter came to Saint Louis late in 1829, Ira arrived in December 1830, and Austin followed in January 1831.

While still on the inbound trail along the Kansas River on September 10, Jedediah had responded to brother Ralph's letter of April 3, informing him of their mother's death. Ralph indicated that he planned to travel to Saint Louis, and Jedediah urged him to do so, adding, "I am not under the necessity of visiting the Mountains again." At about this time Smith purchased two slaves, a thirty-eight-year-old man named William for $400, and a twenty-one-year-old woman named Elizabeth for $325.

In his published memoir, Joseph Meek recounted a tale concerning Smith's ownership of slaves that is corroborated nowhere else. As a sample of the mountaineers' roughhouse humor, Meek related an incident that took place when starvation stalked his camp during the winter of 1829–30. A "negro boy, belonging to Jedediah Smith," placed a porcupine on a fire to roast and when he momentarily turned his back, Meek and a trapper named Reece made off with it and devoured it. Other men witnessed the theft, but it seems that bigotry dissuaded them from handing white thieves over to a black man; besides, they found the hungry victim's mortification at his loss amusing. During "the following summer," according to Meek, "when Smith was in St. Louis, he gave the boy his freedom and two hundred dollars ... so that it became a saying in the mountains, that 'the nigger got his freedom for a porcupine.'"

Meek's narrative is a generally reliable source, and this anecdote may be based on fact. But the story is mysterious. Smith never recorded his opinion on slavery, and if he did own a slave in 1829, there is no evidence that he left Fort Vancouver with one. Perhaps he requested Sublette to bring the slave out with his 1829 brigade. Further, no surviving document records Jedediah's acquisition of any slaves prior to his return to Saint Louis. He was certainly in Saint Louis by mid-October 1830 and remained there for several months, so the manumission of a slave is a possibility. But there is no evidence to corroborate

Meek's story. Neither do we know who owned the slave named "John Ransa," who died at the Umpqua River.

In late January 1831 Jedediah mentioned more recent events in another letter to Ralph Smith: Ira had arrived on December 23 seeking employment as a typesetter, but "the vicinity had been previously supplied" and he found no work. Taking Ira under his wing, Jedediah enrolled him at a seminary college in Jacksonville, Illinois. Though he was not "altogether pleased" with it, he thought it might be a respectable institution and was willing "to give it a fair trial." Austin also made it safely to Saint Louis but seemed uncertain of his future, so Jedediah wrote to two other seminaries that might offer appropriate courses of study. He gently admonished Ralph for encouraging their youngest brothers, eighteen-year-old Benjamin and seventeen-year-old Nelson, to move to Saint Louis. Jedediah Smith knew the city too well to approve of such an idea, noting, "This is the last place to which youngsters should be sent." At the ripe old age of thirty-two years, he expressed a markedly paternal sense of responsibility for siblings who were not much younger than he had been upon arriving at Saint Louis nine years earlier. Perhaps inspired by his mother's death and his father's declining health, Jedediah also wrote to Ralph in February that the time had come to "make Some alterations." With one parent dead, "our Brothers are now in a different situation; but . . . this does not relieve me from my duty to my Father.... [I]t should be our desire and wish, to use an aged Father with careful and filial affection."

While he caught up with long-ignored family affairs, Jedediah considered two money-making opportunities for the immediate future. He first thought of investing as much as ten thousand dollars in a partnership with Robert Campbell. But sometime in January he decided to undertake a joint venture on the Santa Fe Trail with William Sublette and David Jackson. The three friends would conduct a wagon train carrying about twenty thousand dollars' worth of merchandise to New Mexico.

Late in January Smith's friend William Ashley contacted Missouri's Senator Thomas Hart Benton to request that the State

Department issue Jedediah the necessary passport for his planned "trading Expedition to the Mexican Provinces." The passport was issued on March 3, 1831. Sometimes such documents included physical descriptions of their bearers. Smith's passport survived, but unfortunately it contains no description of him. No one, it seems, ever took the time to write down what Jedediah Smith looked like. This was not so for William Sublette. A passport bearing the signature of Secretary of State Martin Van Buren, issued to Sublette on April 9, 1831, indicates that he stood six feet, two inches in height and had a "straight and open" forehead, light blue eyes, a "Roman" nose, "Light, or Sandy" hair, and a "fair" complexion and that his face was "Long & expressive with a scar on the left chin."

The commercial venture to New Mexico promised to be profitable, but it might have seemed unavoidable. For one thing, Thomas Fitzpatrick had delivered the Rocky Mountain Fur Company's order for goods to Saint Louis only in early May 1831, two months after the deadline stipulated in the company's agreement with Smith, Jackson & Sublette. If Smith, Jackson, and Sublette conveyed their goods to New Mexico, they might be sold either in the Mexican market or to the Rocky Mountain Fur Company or to other trappers in Taos and elsewhere.

Smith's Santa Fe Trail excursion also demonstrates that economic security had not eclipsed his love for exploration. For several years he nursed aspirations to recast his journals into a proper literary style and then publish a book recounting his adventures and discoveries. Smith had read plenty of expeditionary literature himself, and he knew that such publications sometimes found eager purchasers. Moreover, he could use the book as a platform to broadcast his views on the Far West, the joint occupation treaty, British competition, and the need for Americans to gain the upper hand in the Oregon Country.

Jedediah had seen much of the West, but he knew relatively little about New Mexico and its rivers, or the Santa Fe Trail's connections with interior Mexico. A voyage to Santa Fe would enable him to complete his book. Other American trappers, such as Charles Bent, Ewing Young, William Wolfskill, James

Ohio Pattie, and Kit Carson, had already moved to New Mexico and helped establish a usable trail west to California, as well as trails northward from the Arkansas and Platte rivers to the Rocky Mountains. Jedediah Smith undoubtedly wanted his maps to include reliable information about the region he knew least.

Smith had found just the fellow to help him bring his publishing project to fruition. Accompanying him on his final Rocky Mountain venture was Samuel Parkman, a well-educated young man who first went to the mountains with William Sublette's 1829 caravan. Jedediah recognized Parkman's talents and set him to work during the winter of 1830–31 "arranging the notes, and making maps of the route through which they had traveled." Parkman also commenced studying the Spanish language, the better to aid Smith and Sublette when they visited New Mexico. With Samuel Parkman to assist and translate in New Mexico and then polish Smith's manuscript, the publication of a book seemed eminently feasible. If that book had appeared, Jedediah Smith would have achieved perhaps his loftiest ambition. Gaining national honor and public acclaim, he would share the fame of other great Western explorers such as William Clark, Meriwether Lewis, Alexander McKenzie, and David Thompson. (For his part, Parkman found ample opportunities in New Mexico; he eventually became director of operations at a silver mine in Guanajuato, Mexico, where he died in 1873.)

Jedediah Smith pondered another intriguing possibility that spring. On March 2 he wrote a third letter to Secretary of War John Eaton. Only discovered in 2000, this remarkable letter is the most significant Smith item to be brought to light in decades. Unlike the letters to Eaton jointly prepared by Smith, Jackson, and Sublette, this one was the work of Jedediah Smith alone. He had recently learned that the government was considering plans to send "an exploring party to the Rocky Mountains under the direction of Lieut Holmes of the United States Army." Indeed, Smith and Holmes were acquainted, and Holmes had told Smith he wanted to hire him as a guide.

The "Holmes" in this case is 1st Lt. Reuben Holmes, a West Point graduate (1823) who was posted at Fort Atkinson during much of the 1820s, traveled with a military expedition up the Missouri River in 1825, and then served on commissary duty at Saint Louis from 1827 to 1832. Born in Connecticut in 1798, he was almost the same age as Jedediah Smith. Holmes was a fellow Yankee who developed a promising career in the frontier West, and like Smith, he died at a young age, perishing from cholera in November 1833. Doubtless the two men's trails had crossed from time to time over the years, and one can assume they were friends.

To Secretary Eaton, Smith noted, "I cannot consent to take a subordinate part in a business that several years experience had qualified me to control." He was nevertheless eager to participate in a government-funded expedition reminiscent of Lewis and Clark's epic journey. His experiences, he thought, vested him with sufficient knowledge and authority to qualify as a coleader with Holmes. He reminded Eaton that his "knowledge of our Western Territory [was] equal if not superior to that of any man in the country."

Smith assured Eaton that he was not merely seeking "public employment," for he had no need of money. Instead, he believed he "could do much to promote the objects of the expedition." With a hint of pride he wrote, "Having for several years hazarded all that a man can hazard and acquired more than the Government would be disposed to give any man for his services[,] I would look on the most liberal pay as no inducement to again encounter the hardships and dangers incident to the life of an explorer." Listing his various journeys, he pointed out that he had traveled in "many directions" and was familiar with "nearly all the passes between the waters of the Missouri and the Columbia and the Colorado of the West."

Smith mentioned he had just completed a manuscript map incorporating "all the information I have personally collected with all that was before known of our Western Territory," adding that he had logged "more than 10,000 miles" of western travel. Alluding to his vast store of "dearly purchased" information, he asserted that "the most enterprising and industrious explorer could not acquire the knowledge of the country which I already have in less than three years[,] and in all probability a much longer time would be required." In sum, he could not accept a secondary position, but he had no "wish to lock up the information;" rather, he wanted to "aid in the laudable design of bringing to light the resources of the country." In fact, a few months earlier, in December 1830, Smith had sent to one John Cremer a package of botanical specimen seeds that included gooseberries, service berries, choke cherries, buffalo berries, yellow and black currents, what may have been sweet grass (Smith called it "Scented Grass seed"), and some "Leaves of the Scented wood" from the "western coast south of the mouth of the Columbia river." He hoped they would "find a place in the gardens of the curious from the fact that they are natives of the most distant and wild territories of our republic," adding that perhaps he might "in some future time see them blooming in the gardens of the atlantic." Like the Indian artifacts he sent to William Clark, Smith's parcels of seeds evince his continuing interest in collecting and sharing items of potential interest to eastern scholars and the scientific community.

Smith urged Eaton to contact William Clark, William Ashley, or Senator Benton to verify his qualifications for the position. But, wrote Jedediah, "the business requires dispatch," and he assured Eaton that he could be ready to take the trail with just three days' notice. Undoubtedly, Smith's call for "dispatch" related to his impending departure for New Mexico. What a story this would have made, if only the secretary of war had responded favorably to Jedediah Smith's proposal. But no answer ever came, and nothing happened to postpone Smith's scheduled departure for Santa Fe. There would be no "Smith and Holmes Expedition." Among all of Smith's writings, this letter best captures his abiding passion for exploration and his personal ambition to emulate the likes of Lewis and Clark.

On April 10, 1831, Smith's caravan departed Saint Louis. Mustering seventy-four men and twenty-two mule-drawn wagons, the brigade included former partners William Sublette and David

Jackson, Jedediah's brothers Peter and Austin, and his two clerks, Samuel Parkman and Jonathon T. Warner. Smith owned eleven of the wagons, ten belonged to Jackson and Sublette, and one had been modified to mount a six-pounder cannon on its rear axle in case of trouble with Indians. By the time the caravan passed the last settlements, two more wagons and nine men had joined it for safety's sake. On April 31, while the wagon train paused briefly at Lexington, Jedediah Smith had Parkman draw up a new will. In an 1826 will, Smith had named his friend Robert Campbell as executor, but by 1831 it seemed likely that Campbell's chronic ailments might have the better of him. The new will named Smith's "particular and confidential friend," William Ashley, as executor of his estate in the event of Jedediah's death. Witnessed by Parkman and Warner, it guaranteed Jedediah's father a lifetime annuity of two hundred dollars annually and divided the remainder of the estate among Smith's siblings.

Unfortunately, Smith's 1831 trip is so poorly documented that few specifics are known. Resting and making last-minute preparations occupied a couple of days at Independence, the last town between Missouri and New Mexico. Just as the wagon train was about to leave Independence, Thomas Fitzpatrick caught up with it. Smith, Sublette, and Jackson agreed to furnish him with goods, one-third coming from Jedediah's assortment and two-thirds from Sublette and Jackson's. Fitzpatrick would accompany the caravan to New Mexico, purchase livestock at Santa Fe or Taos, and pack the trade goods north to his Rocky Mountain Fur Company partners at Cache Valley. By May 4 the wagon train was ten miles southwest of Independence at the confluence of the Big Blue and Kansas rivers.

Traffic had grown enormously since 1821. The road was well worn, numerous campsites and water holes had been identified, and maps and guides were practically unnecessary. By 1831 hundreds of Mexican, New Mexican, and American traders and fur hunters annually made the 1,700-mile round-trip between Saint Louis and Santa Fe. New Mexico markets became saturated by the middle 1820s, and most of the goods now went deeper into Mexico. Still, the trail was not without its perils. Pawnees, Arapahos, Comanches, and Cheyennes—buffalo hunters and warriors who lived in the southern prairies—were growing angry over the ceaseless parade of aliens who prowled through their land. Even when white men placated Indians with goods as a "toll" for crossing their land, the tribesmen sometimes raided horse herds and fights occasionally broke out. But relatively few men were killed on the trail.

Nature also posed diverse threats to Santa Fe Trail travelers. Stifling summer temperatures and vicious winter blizzards, clouds of insects, choking dust storms, heavy winds, drenching rains, and flooded streams could make the trek a misery. Sometimes game was exceedingly scarce. In addition, there was a one-hundred-mile stretch of trail in central Kansas, called the "water scrape" or the "Cimarron Cutoff," that deviated from the main route. Taking this alternate trail could shave several days off the trip, but the cutoff offered almost no water for humans or livestock. Though traders resorted to it with some frequency over the years, it was always a risky proposition, and sometimes disasters befell travelers on the cutoff.

In the first few years of the trail's use, traders usually loaded their packs of goods on horses and mules. After about 1825, the vast majority of traffic on the trail consisted of large wagons drawn by mules or oxen. In 1826–28 the U.S. Congress funded a survey of the trail, and 1829 saw the first U.S. Army escort, under Major Bennett Riley, accompany the traders' caravan to the Arkansas River, which marked the boundary between the United States and the Republic of Mexico. Major Riley's tour of the trail was prompted by traders' complaints that Indian "depredations" had become more frequent over the past few years. Still, by 1830 the trip had been reduced to a standardized routine, and losses of men, goods, and livestock were rare. In 1831 Jedediah Smith had good reasons to suppose that the trek would be a pleasure cruise compared to what he had endured for the past nine years.

Wending its way unmolested across the plains to the Arkansas River, Smith's caravan followed the river westward. Tragedy struck on May 19, however, when Pawnee warriors murdered a clerk of Sublette and Jackson's named Minter near the Pawnee Fork of the Arkansas. By May 24 the weather was hot and dry and the wagons were perched at the threshold of the bleak Cimarron Cutoff. The caravan plunged southwestward into the desert. Not a drop of water was found for three days, and by the fourth morning the dehydrated livestock were on the verge of collapse. Parched men mounted equally parched horses and fanned out in different directions to search the scorched flatlands for water.

Jedediah Smith and Thomas Fitzpatrick rode south of the caravan, hoping to find a spring along the route they meant to travel. Spotting a depression that ordinarily might have contained water, they headed for it, but the prevailing drought had drained it. Smith suggested that Fitzpatrick should remain there and try digging for water while he went closer to the Cimarron to investigate another likely spot two or three miles ahead. Perhaps Fitzpatrick watched Smith slowly ride out of sight before he started scratching into the damp earth. "He was last seen," reported a contemporary, "by a spy-glass, about three miles from Fitzpatrick."

None of his companions ever saw Jedediah Smith again, alive or dead. He stumbled onto a band of Comanche warriors, who surrounded him at the next waterhole and murdered him. According to Josiah Gregg's classic Santa Fe Trail chronicle, *Commerce of the Prairies* (1844), in 1831 more than three hundred traders and hired hands freighted a quarter of a million dollars in goods to New and Old Mexico and only two men—Smith and Minter—died on the trail. The spring near which Smith died has been tentatively identified as Fargo Spring, sometimes called Wagon Body Spring, located on the north bank of the Cimarron in western Grant or Stevens County, Kansas.

Smith's final fifteen minutes of life, it was said, passed while the Comanches debated in Spanish the best means of dispatching him. What had gone wrong? Was it just plain bad luck, or had Smith made a final, fatal error in judgment? Did the thirst that turned his throat into parchment dull the razor-sharp instincts that had kept him alive all those years in the wilderness? Did he momentarily cease his constant scanning and processing of the environment—the key to self-preservation in Indian Country—and thus fail to detect the presence of probable enemies before it was too late to escape? How could he have forgotten the admonition of poor Minter's death just a week earlier? What had been the substance of his halting conversations with the comancheros with whom he spoke just minutes before the Comanches killed him? These questions cannot be answered, but one thing is certain: Smith wound up in the wrong place at the wrong time, and in an utterly random instant the Comanches snuffed out a most promising life. Smith might just as well have been struck dead by a bolt of lightning. In truth, this was no hero's death.

Jedediah Smith led a remarkable life, to say the least. The force of his austere personality must have been impressive, and his native intellect and keen observational powers served him well. His character had been forged and tempered in danger, privation, and suffering with his fellow trappers in the Far West. Many of his experiences seem all but incredible. He had yielded completely to his romantic fascination with the Great West, and he had achieved great things. He left an enormous legacy in the history of western American exploration. Admired and respected for his wisdom by highly placed and powerful men whose opinions he helped shape, Jedediah S. Smith was also an inspired and esteemed leader of some of American history's most rambunctious hyperindividualists—the mountain men.

"The Things of Time"
An Assessment of Jedediah Smith

JEDEDIAH Strong Smith was a man of many parts, to be sure. A true Jacksonian-era man, Jedediah compulsively sought to better his economic circumstances, no matter what the risks. Smith was one of those "perpetual motion" characters who sometimes blaze across the stage of history. Indeed, he seems to have been almost incapable of indulging in relaxation. At the time he died, Jedediah Smith was quite possibly on the threshold of genuine fame, and if his adventures had been published, he would be far better known than he is today.

Central to the mythology of Jedediah Smith is the persistent assertion that he played a role as a missionary to Indians by "preaching" to some far western Indian tribes, specifically to Flathead Indians during the winter of 1824–25. The result, some Smith enthusiasts believe, was that a Flathead delegation went to Saint Louis in 1830 to request further religious instruction. The story attracted Dale Morgan's attention in 1967, and he devoted several pages in an article to sorting out the evidence. Morgan noted that Edwin L. Sabin's *Kit Carson Days* (1914) was the first source to suggest that Smith served as a "missionary" to the Flatheads and that his story would make a good hagiography. Thereafter, a "religious legend" became embedded in the mythic version of "Bible totin'" Jedediah Smith. Morgan himself sheepishly confessed that even in the absence of conclusive evidence, he had "tacitly admitted in print that Jedediah Smith carried a Bible with him into the West."

Smith spent only four weeks among the Flatheads, in November–December 1824. He did not speak Salish, and sign language—had he mastered it by this early date—would have been totally inadequate to convey abstract theological messages. No Smith journal entry mentions a Bible, and he cites "chapter-and-verse" scripture nowhere in any surviving journal or letter. Indeed, only Harrison Rogers penned a complete "prayer" in any surviving journal related to Smith's expeditions. In March 1828, while among the Maidus in California, Smith wrote, "If missionaries could be useful in Civilizing and Christianizing any Indians in the World their efforts should be turned toward this valley." His usage of the conditional voice indicates that he himself had not done so. In the same passage he characterized the Maidus as "the lowest intermediate link between man and the Brute creation," and within a few days Jedediah and his men would kill several of them.

Out of twelve books listed in Smith's estate, only three dealt with religious topics: a Bible, a collection of "Wesleyan hymns," and a tome entitled *Evidences of Christianity*. We may assume that Smith possessed all these books, but none appear in the documentary record of his travels. His eulogist described Jedediah as a true Christian "[w]ithout being connected with any church.... He made religion an active, practical principle, from the duties of which, nothing could seduce him." Jedediah was a pious Protestant Christian, certainly, but not so devout that he refused to travel on the Sabbath, as would numerous western migrants in the overland trail years.

Dale Morgan correctly concluded that the assertion that Jedediah Smith acted as a missionary "simply vanishes under close inspection." Declaring that "we must resist any tendency to convert Jedediah into an essentially religious hero," Morgan dismissed the "Sunday school stereotype" of Smith as a feeble invention and expressed his hope that future research would be aimed instead at an accurate depiction of the "whole man." Smith was unquestionably a man of deep faith, but his western career was economically, not ecclesiastically, motivated. Examples abound of men and women who attempted to missionize Western Indians, but Jedediah Smith did not.

Texts on several monuments, however, maintain that he did. One in Walworth County, South Dakota, claims that Smith was "truly a missionary by example," that he "carried a Bible with him where ever he went," and that his "worth as an explorer, his resourcefulness as a leader, and his skill as a mountain man were only surpassed by his integrity and faith." Three monuments in Sacramento County, California, including one erected in 1981, refer to him as the "Bible Toter" or "Bible Totin' Jed Smith" and boldly proclaim him as the "First Great Protestant Missionary To Mountain Men."

Perhaps such references contribute to Jedediah's reputation as a dour fellow who never cracked a joke. Dale Morgan suspected that Jedediah "may have been entirely humorless," finding only two remarks in his surviving journals and letters that offered even "the ghost of a smile in them, and these contain as much of wryness as of humor." But, as we have seen, Smith's journals do offer a fair number of passages displaying a dry sense of humor. Nonetheless, Jedediah's customary language was doubtless tamer than that of his fellow trappers. A missionary named Samuel Parker penned a wonderful comment about the trappers' jargon during the 1835 rendezvous. While grousing about the uncivil mountain men who seemed perfectly oblivious to his religious instruction, he fumed they were "proficients in one study, the study of profuseness of language in their oaths and blasphemy. They disdain common-place phrases which prevail among the impious vulgar in civilized countries, and have many set phrases, which they appear to have manufactured among themselves, which they have committed to memory, and which, in their imprecations, they bring into almost every sentence and on all occasions. By varying the tones of their voices, they make them expressive of joy, hope, grief, and anger."

If Jedediah Smith ever resorted to the irreverent, colorful, and amusing jargon associated with characters such as "Black" Harris or Joseph Meek, whom Smith knew well, no hint of it emerges in his prose. Indeed, his eulogist averred, though the "gentle and affable" Jedediah lived for nine years in a "lawless country" where "his ears [were] constantly filled with the language of the profane and dissolute, no evil communication proceeded out of his mouth."

One minor item that merits brief notice is the occasional use by writers of a diminutive form of Smith's first name, "'Diah," which turns up now and again in biographies. This familial nickname appears twice in a single letter from Dr. Titus Simons's son Solomon to Peter Smith dated November 22, 1829, and nowhere else. Both Maurice Sullivan and Dale Morgan used it on occasion, which encouraged other writers to do likewise. Perhaps sisters and brothers fondly referred to him as "'Diah," but Jedediah signed all of his extant letters much more formally, either as "J. S. Smith" or "Jedediah S. Smith." No evidence suggests that the nickname was ever used by anyone else.

A clear sense of what sort of man Jedediah was remains elusive, posing a strange problem for biographers, who would like nothing better than to feel that they have come to "know" their subject. Despite a deficiency of hard evidence, a few comments may be hazarded to trace the main contours of Jedediah Smith's personality. No one who interacted with Smith, except Mexican officials in California and a few HBC men, ever wrote a negative critique of him. Many Indians' testimony would undoubtedly be highly unfavorable, but not all. He was certainly a personable man; otherwise he could not have risen so high and so fast in the trappers' fraternity.

Sound business sense, which Smith certainly did possess, did not necessarily make a good brigade leader. (Ironically, as we have seen, disasters and plain bad luck more than once thoroughly trumped Smith's aptitude for making money, and in some years he lost a great deal more than he gained for his company.) The trappers who risked their necks to travel with Smith to California and elsewhere must have observed in Jedediah other, perhaps more useful, characteristics that might make the razor's edge of difference between life and death in a perilous situation.

Jedediah Smith rarely lost his temper. He kept cool under desperate circumstances and usually made wise decisions. Like the best militia officers of his era, Smith could lead his men into deadly situations only because he merited their goodwill and trust. A strutting martinet, or a dour psalmster for that matter, would be unlikely to elicit much allegiance from the "reckless breed of men." But Smith did win his men's affection, respect, and admiration. It is a tribute to his steadiness, wisdom, and intelligence that his partners, most of his hired hands, and many Saint Louis businessmen and politicians held him in such high regard. And of course, informed contemporaries acknowledged that practically no one understood Western American geography better than Jedediah Smith did.

Jedediah's eulogist claimed that, "in all his dealings with the Indians, he was strictly honorable.... [H]e made it a rule, never to molest them, except in defense of his own life and property, and those of his party." But Smith's behavior was by no means universally saintly. In many instances Jedediah's "affable and gentle" nature did not restrain him from murdering Indians when he thought that circumstances justified it. In fact, it was Smith's broad conception of the requirement to defend his "life and property" that prompted his preemptive killings and ultimately triggered the disaster on the Umpqua River. Similarly, his agreements with Mexican officials were conditional at best, and he often resorted to duplicity and deception when dealing with authorities he did not respect. His interactions with HBC men sometimes reveal similar discontinuities.

David J. Weber noted that most historians, "supposing that the pious Smith could not have been deceitful, have given Smith the benefit of the doubt" regarding his troubles in California. For many years Jedediah's version of these events has been accepted without much criticism. Recently discovered evidence, however, casts doubt on Smith's account and suggests that he was at best disingenuous and at worst a determined liar, truly the sly Yankee that Mexican authorities feared. Smith himself wrote only a few lines that imply a broadly imperialistic view of his expeditions. But in his diary he once alluded to the "restless enterprise that ... is leading our country-men to all parts of the world," adding, "it can now be said there is not a breeze of heaven but spreads an american flag." Uniting his economic self-interest with a growing conviction that he was destined to achieve great things, Jedediah Smith was a walking symbol of

Jacksonian America, and his behavior in California in 1826–28 was not entirely beyond reproach. A strain of ethnocentrism, if not outright bigotry, emerges from Smith's own interpretation of his dealings with Governor Echeandía and other Mexican officials, especially during his second detention in California. Recognition of Smith's self-serving and devious explanation of this experience is by no means a novel idea. In 1936 Maurice Sullivan cast some doubt on Smith's biased version of the story, noting that he "felt that he had been oppressed in California [so] he presents in his journal a none too favorable picture of the people" there. Sullivan also thought Smith's suspicion that Mexicans instigated the "Mohave massacre" was "putting the matter rather strongly." Finally, Sullivan observed that Smith "was stubbornly determined to do as he pleased," despite Mexican officials' orders.

Jedediah Smith is now assured a permanent and prominent place in the annals of North American exploration. He will ever stand in the first rank of great explorers. And yet, it would not do to forget that Smith was surely a man of his time. Embracing the exuberant promise of a great American future, he was sometimes an ardent expansionist and always an economic go-getter. Reflecting the crosscurrents of inconsistent ideology in Jacksonian America, Jedediah was simultaneously pious, humanistic, and bigoted. His journals preserve exciting and illuminating details about his journeys of exploration, the daily lives of mountain men, and his varied dealings with Indians, Mexicans, and the HBC men. His journals also present a handful of little windows through which readers may peer into the deeper regions of his unusual mind and gain glimpses of his personality. Caught up as he was in the "things of time," Jedediah often contrasted his own life experiences against the unlimited endurance of eternal salvation. In spite of his achievements, tragedies, and wealth, he evidently never questioned his abiding faith, but he often agonized over his perceived spiritual lapses and berated himself as a prodigal son who failed to provide for his family.

Jedediah Smith's life can be characterized as comet-like or meteoric, burning briefly but ever so brightly. Truly, few men in

Western American history achieved so much in so few years. Perhaps, though, if one cares to indulge in analogies, it would be equally appropriate to envision his life as a classic case of what can happen when a promising, talented, capable, and energetic man simply cannot avoid burning the candle at both ends.

Accounts of Smith's Death

WILLIAM Sublette and Austin Smith recorded brief summaries of Jedediah Smith's final hour, based on second- and thirdhand accounts that they heard at Santa Fe. Austin Smith also prepared an obituary that was published in two Illinois weekly newspapers. While obviously similar, their accounts differ slightly and are worth considering individually. Their information came from a few daring comanchero traders who almost certainly had been the last non-Indians to see Smith alive. It is quite likely that they witnessed his murder from a distance.

By late August, William Sublette had concluded his business in New Mexico and his wagons were on the trail back to Saint Louis. On September 24, 1831, the caravan paused at Walnut Creek, a popular camping spot on the Arkansas River about three hundred miles west of the settlements. While there, William Sublette scribbled a note to William Ashley to tell him Smith was dead. He wrote simply, "On our Way out to Santafee we lost Mr. Minter[,] killed on the pawnee fork we suppose by the pawnees[.] [I]t happened on the 19th of June[.] Mr. J. S. Smith was killed on the Cimeron June 27th by the Comanches. We met with no other losses by Indians & arrive in Santafee July 4th." (Sublette mistakenly wrote a dateline of "June;" both Minter and Smith died in May.) At the end of August, Austin and Peter Smith and a small party of men left Santa Fe for California to purchase mules, an ironic reprise of Jedediah's ventures.

At the same time that Sublette wrote to Ashley, Austin Smith posted the sad news to his father. "Your son Jedediah," he wrote:

was killed on the Semerone the 27th of May on his way to Santa fé by the Curmanch Indians, his party was in distress for water, and he had gone alone in search of the above river which he found, when he was attacked by fifteen or twenty of them—they succeeded in alarming his animal[,] not daring to fire on him so long as they kept face to face, so soon as his horse turned they fired, and wounded him in the shoulder[.] [H]e then fired his gun, and killed their head chief[.] [I]t is supposed they then <u>rushed</u> upon him, and despatched him— such my farther is the fate of him who you loved.

On May 24, 1831, three days before Jedediah was killed, Ira Smith had written a letter to Ashley requesting one hundred dollars on Jedediah's account. He plaintively added, "[P]leas give me information if you have anything from him since he left Saint Louis[,] or should you hear any thing pleas let me know if convenient." Ashley had no news to report, but Austin Smith supplied Ira a few details in a letter posted on the same day as the one he sent to their father. Jedediah, he wrote,

> took a due South course from the one we were travelling.... The Spanish traders who trade with those Indians informed me, that he saw the Indians before they attacked him, but supposed there could be no chance of escape, he therefore went boldly up, with the hope of making peace with them, but found that his only chance was defense, he killed the head Chief.... I have his gun and pistols, got from the Indians by the traders.... [T]he Spanish traders say the Indians succeeded in alarming the horse he was riding so as to get his back to them,... they then ... wounded him in the shoulder; he faced them and killed the Chief.

In turn, Ira Smith provided information from Austin about Jedediah's death to a newspaper at Jacksonville, Illinois. First printed in Jacksonville's *Illinois Patriot,* on October 29, 1831, an identical obituary appeared in Vandalia's *Illinois Intelligencer.* Saint Louis papers completely overlooked Smith's death, and no other newspaper obituaries have surfaced. Austin Smith's obituary letter contains a long-known but misinterpreted bit of significant evidence that sheds light on Jedediah Smith's final minutes. In the *Illinois Patriot* there appears the following sentence: "The Spanish traders trafficking with these Indians told us *that they saw brother a short time before the Indians attacked him, and told him there was no hope for escape,* so he went boldly up to them in hopes that he could effect a conciliation" [italics added for emphasis]. The import of this sentence seems clear: Smith had evidently encountered and apparently spoken or otherwise communicated with the comancheros while he searched for water, but they were unable or unwilling to assist him. He then rode "boldly" to his death.

There is another gem among Jedediah Smith's postmortem notices. In June 1832 an anonymous admirer's detailed and illuminating eulogy "of our distinguished countryman" appeared in the *Illinois Monthly Magazine* published at Alton. Tentatively identified as the *Illinois Monthly Magazine*'s editor James Hall (or less likely, Charles Keemle, a former mountain man and editor of the weekly Saint Louis *Beacon*), the eulogist was certainly acquainted with Smith. He noted with surprise that Jedediah's death and accomplishments had "been entirely unnoticed" at Saint Louis. But the eulogist refused to "cast into oblivion the memory of one so richly deserving an imperishable monument," declaring that Smith's story "ought to be cherished by every American."

During a conversation at Saint Louis in March 1831, Jedediah had proudly informed the writer, "I started into the mountains, with the determination of becoming a first rate hunter, of making myself thoroughly acquainted with the character and habits of the Indians, of tracing the sources of the Columbia river, and following it to its mouth; and of making the whole profitable to me, and I have perfectly succeeded."

The eulogist affirmed that Smith "took notes of all his travels and adventures," and more importantly, "these notes have been copied, preparatory for the press." He also learned that Smith, Jackson, Sublette, and Parkman had collaborated on drafting "a new, large, and beautiful map" that would supplant all contemporary maps of the West, and that plans were afoot to publish it, too. The sad truth is that Smith's map, or more likely several maps, vanished within a few years at most. None were ever published, and even today not a single original map has surfaced. (Researcher George R. Brooks discovered a promotional advertisement dating to 1840 in a Saint Louis newspaper for "The Journal and Travels of JEDEDIAH S. SMITH," but evidently nothing came of it. Still, as Brooks pointed out, the publishing solicitation indicated that Smith's material was still substantially intact at the time.) Imploring the nation never to forget Smith, the "greatest American traveller," his eulogist predicted that publication of his journals would secure "all the honor that is justly due him." As it turned out, an entire century passed before Jedediah Smith received the recognition he richly deserved.

APPENDIX B

Smith's Probate Records

SHORTLY after receiving word of Jedediah Smith's death, William Ashley commenced the onerous process of administering his estate. On November 9, 1831, he posted a bond for $30,000 and was granted a power of attorney over the estate. A preliminary accounting showed Smith's assets to be worth about $15,700. In combination with an estimated $20,000 worth of goods that "Mr. Parkman and one of Mr. Smith's brothers" disposed of at Santa Fe in the autumn of 1831 and a few additional items, Smith's estate totaled roughly $40,000. Some tangible assets were sold, and some of Jedediah's personal belongings went to friends and family members.

From Smith's estate William Sublette bought thirty-two mules and four horses, as well as "9 Rifle Guns" and "5 Shot Guns" (most of them damaged), sixteen "Spanish Blankets," a box of tinware, fifteen pounds of gunpowder, and ten "Spanish Saddles." Austin purchased his brother's "catalogue of books" for fifty dollars. Jedediah's library is known to have included such titles as "Clapperstone's *Second Expedition into Africa,* Rollin's *Ancient History, History of Ancient Greece,* Morris's *Gazetter, The Seaman's Daily Assistant, Natural Theology, Evidences of Christianity, Theological Dictionary,* Henry's *Exposition* in six volumes, and *Josephus* in four."

Perhaps as souvenirs or perhaps for future sale, Jedediah Smith had acquired a bow and arrows and the sixteen "Spanish Blankets" that Sublette bought. They were enclosed in a large trunk along with several beaver skins, "a lot of Grey Bear skins" (one of them was supposed to be the bear that mauled Jedediah in 1823), "one skin shirt," "sundry small skins," "horns of various kinds," and "other Indian curiosities." Most of these items were turned over to Ira Smith, who perhaps distributed them to his sisters and brothers. In 1832 Jedediah's slaves, William and Elizabeth, were hired out to someone at $135 for the year, and then they disappear from the record. Numerous outstanding bills were paid or collected, as the case warranted. There would be money enough to assure Smith's family comfortable lives.

In November 1832, Ira Smith informed William Ashley that he meant to take over the administration of Jedediah's estate. There is no evidence that the transfer was marked by rancor, but Ira petitioned to have Ashley's power of attorney revoked. In February 1833 the County Court of Saint Louis heard a case, *Ashley v. Smith,* in which Ashley's lawyer challenged Ira Smith to justify the revocation of Ashley's appointment. Ira won the case and became executor of Jedediah's estate in March. A few months later Ashley turned over roughly $9,000 in assets. Thereafter, in accordance with Jedediah's 1831 will, Ira issued lifetime annuities to his father, his brothers and sisters, and dear friends such as Dr. Titus Simons. In 1834, for example, Smith's father and siblings received $4,500 from Jedediah's estate.

From a historical point of view, by far the most important item among Jedediah Smith's belongings was the manuscript that he and Parkman had worked up. It carried the rather cumbersome title "A manuscript Journal of the Travels of Jedediah S. Smith through the Rocky Mountains and west of the Same, together with a description of the Country and the Customs and Manners of the different Tribes of Indians through which he traveled," for so it is recorded twice in the probate records. Perhaps the manuscript had reposed in the "box containing papers, books, &c" that Smith left with Ashley before leaving for New Mexico. An appraisal of the manuscript set its value at an impressive sum, two thousand dollars. One of three men who examined and evaluated it was William Clark, the explorer whom Jedediah greatly admired. Unfortunately, only portions of the manuscript have so far been recovered. If a complete copy were to appear today, it would likely fetch a king's ransom.

Bibliographic Essay

ANY Jedediah Smith biographer must begin by acknowledging a deep debt to the meticulous work of the scholars who rescued Smith from oblivion in the early to mid-twentieth century. No fur trade historian can do without Hiram Martin Chittenden's pathbreaking *A History of the American Fur Trade of the Far West,* 2 vols. (New York: Harper & Brothers, 1902, and various reprints). The first scholarly treatment of the western fur trade, it includes several chapters on the Ashley-Smith era. Harrison C. Dale's *The Ashley-Smith Explorations and the Discovery of a Central Route to the Pacific 1822–1829* (Glendale, Calif.: The Arthur H. Clark Company, 1918; rev. ed., 1941) was the first book to focus on Smith and Ashley, and the first to bring substantial portions of Harrison Rogers's journals into print. John G. Neihardt penned the first Smith biography to gain pubic attention, *The Splendid Wayfaring* (New York: Macmillan Company, 1920), but the book was hampered by a lack of sources.

Serious Smith scholarship began in the 1930s, when Maurice S. Sullivan, a California writer and assiduous Smith enthusiast, found a descendent in Texas who possessed most of Samuel Parkman's circa-1830 transcription of Jedediah's journals covering 1821 to 1828. From this material Sullivan produced two important books. *The Travels of Jedediah Smith: A Documentary Outline* (Santa Ana, Calif.: Fine Arts Press, 1934) presented Smith's recently discovered journal along with several of Sir George Simpson's letters and Alexander Roderic McLeod's journal, detailing his effort to help Smith recover his possessions after the 1829 Umpqua fight. Useful but less important is Sullivan's *Jedediah Smith: Trader and Trailbreaker* (New York: Press of the

Pioneers, 1936). Dale L. Morgan's authoritative biography, *Jedediah Smith and the Opening of the West* (New York: Bobbs-Merrill, 1953), portrayed Smith as a "genuine American hero" and framed his career within the national and international contexts of the Missouri River and Rocky Mountain fur trade.

Several publications appeared after Morgan's 1953 biography that permitted a substantial refinement in scholars' assessments of Smith. Ironically, perhaps the most important one came to light just a year later, and Dale L. Morgan coauthored the work. In 1953 the historical cartographer Carl I. Wheat discovered, "almost by accident," among the collections of the American Geographical Society a copy of John C. Frémont's 1845 map of the West bearing annotations lifted from Smith's maps. In collaboration, Morgan and Wheat published *Jedediah S. Smith and His Maps of the American West* (San Francisco: California Historical Society, 1954). A rare book, it thoroughly evaluates the significance of Smith's lost manuscript maps and reproduces several Smith-influenced contemporary maps. Two excellent articles by Robert West Howard, "Back East Background of Jedediah Strong Smith," *Pacific Historian*, 12: 2 and 12: 3 (Spring and Summer 1968), shed light on Smith's youth and family connections. D. W. Garber likewise amplified Morgan's research on Jedediah's youth and family history with additional material in *Jedediah Strong Smith: Fur Trader from Ohio* (Stockton, Calif.: University of the Pacific, 1972).

Offering a wide range of source material for the Ashley-Henry and Ashley-Smith outfits are Richard M. Clokey's biography, *William H. Ashley: Enterprise and Politics in the Trans-Mississippi West* (Norman: University of Oklahoma Press, 1980), and Dale L. Morgan's massive documentary compilation, *The West of William H. Ashley* (Denver: Old West Publishing Company, 1964). Two items shed light on the 1823 Arikara battle and its aftermath: Donald McKay Frost's *Notes on General Ashley: The Overland Trail and South Pass* (Barre, Mass.: Barre Gazette, 1960) reprints numerous relevant documents. Also useful is Doane Robinson, ed., "Official Correspondence of the Leavenworth Expedition into South Dakota in 1823," *South Dakota His-*

torical Collections, vol. 1 (Aberdeen, S.Dak.: News Printing Company, 1902, reprinted 1972, South Dakota State Historical Society), which presents letters detailing military action surrounding the "Arikara Campaign."

George R. Brooks's excellent *The Southwest Expedition of Jedediah S. Smith: His Personal Account of the Journey to California, 1826–1827* (Glendale, Calif.: The Arthur H. Clark Company, 1977) resulted from the recovery of Samuel Parkman's transcription of a lost Smith journal covering his travels to California in 1826 and 1827. Brooks also prepared a superior reediting of Harrison Rogers' "Daybook I," covering November 26, 1826, to January 27, 1827. Charles L. Camp's *James Clyman: Frontiersman* (Portland, Oreg.: Champeog Press, 1960) includes Clyman's brief narrative of his adventures in 1823–25 with Smith and the Ashley men. In the middle 1980s Spanish borderlands expert David J. Weber discovered significant additional Smith materials in the Mexican archives. A dossier of letters long suspected to exist, they clarify Smith's dealings with the californios. Among other things, they offer persuasive evidence that he deliberately disobeyed Echeandía's orders to leave California by a specified route. Presented in *The Californios vs. Jedediah Smith, 1826–1827: A New Cache of Documents* (Spokane, Wash.: The Arthur H. Clark Company, 1990), these documents shed much new light on Smith's detentions in California.

Sources useful for investigating Smith's dealings with the Hudson's Bay Company include Richard G. Montgomery's *The White-Headed Eagle: John McLoughlin, Builder of an Empire* (New York: The Macmillan Company, 1934); Frederick Merk's *Fur Trade and Empire: George Simpson's Journal, 1824–1825* (revised ed., Cambridge, Mass.: The Belknap Press of Harvard University Press, 1968); and Gloria Griffen Cline's *Peter Skene Ogden and the Hudson's Bay Company* (Norman: University of Oklahoma Press, 1974). John Phillip Reid's *Contested Empire: Peter Skene Ogden and the Snake River Expeditions* (Norman: University of Oklahoma Press, 2002) includes a detailed and innovative analysis of the Johnson Gardner–Peter Skene Ogden affair and Smith's relations with Ogden.

The mythology surrounding Jedediah Smith's pop-culture image has generated several articles and pamphlets. Rev. Don M. Chase's *He Opened the West and Led the First White Explorers through Northwest California May–June 1829* (Crescent City, Calif.: Del Norte Triplicate Press, 1958) presents Chase's argument that Smith was a missionary to western Indians. The main issues in dispute are covered in Don Chase, "Was It Jedediah Smith?" *Pacific Historian* 15: 3 (Fall 1971); and Clifford M. Drury, "Another Myth Answered" and Don Chase, "Don Chase's Rejoinder," both in *Pacific Historian* 17: 1 (Spring 1973). Dale L. Morgan's careful dissection of the evidence behind the missionary claim appears in "Jedediah Smith Today," *Pacific Historian* 11: 2 (Spring 1967). Raymund F. Wood's *Jedediah Smith and His Monuments* (Stockton, Calif.: The Jedediah Smith Society, 1999) offers photographs and transcriptions of sixty-six monuments commemorating Smith. Wood also penned an article describing the religious "fundamentalism" shared alike by Smith, Rogers, and the Catholic fathers José Bernardo Sánchez and Narciso Durán in "Jedediah Smith: A Protestant in Catholic California," *Pacific Historian* 21: 3 (Fall 1977). Barton H. Barbour's "Mountain Men and Missionaries in the Far West: Jedediah S. Smith and Marcus and Narcissa Whitman," in Richard Etulain, ed., *Western Lives: A Biographical History of the American West* (Albuquerque: University of New Mexico Press, 2004) summarizes the missionary mythology and compares Smith's western experiences with those of the Whitmans.

Reliable general surveys of the Rocky Mountain fur trade era include Don Berry's *A Majority of Scoundrels: An Informal History of the Rocky Mountain Fur Company* (New York: Harper & Brothers, 1961), and Robert M. Utley's *A Life Wild and Perilous: Mountain Men and the Paths to the Pacific* (New York: Henry Holt and Company, 1997). Robert Glass Cleland's *This Reckless Breed of Men: The Trappers and Fur Traders of the Southwest* (New York: Alfred K. Knopf, 1950) features some Smith material in a narrative of the southwestern fur trade. Fred R. Gowans's *Rocky Mountain Rendezvous* (Provo, Utah: Brigham Young University Press, 1975) assembles much useful source material for the rendezvous era, some of it bearing on Smith. Barton H. Barbour's *Fort Union and the Upper Missouri Fur Trade* (Norman: University of Oklahoma Press, 2001) examines numerous aspects of the western fur trade and provides background on commerce and competition in Saint Louis in Jedediah Smith's era.

Several biographies of Rocky Mountain fur traders and military men whose careers intersected with Smith's have proven useful in this study of Smith. John E. Sunder's *Joshua Pilcher: Fur Trader and Indian Agent* (Norman: University of Oklahoma Press, 1968) treats one of Smith's competitors. Sunder's *Bill Sublette: Mountain Man* (Norman: University of Oklahoma Press, 1959) covers Smith's partner and friend. Francis Fuller Victor's *The River of the West* (Hartford, Conn.: R. W. Bliss & Co., 1870) is a respectable ghost-written biography of the colorful mountain man, Joseph L. Meek. If not entirely credible, it presents a wealth of details and anecdotes found nowhere else. A more scholarly treatment is Harvey L. Tobie's *No Man Like Joe: The Life and Times of Joseph L. Meek* (Portland, Oreg.: Binsford & Mort, 1949). T. D. Bonner's *The Life and Adventures of James P. Beckwourth, Mountaineer, Scout, Pioneer, and Chief of the Crow Nation of Indians* (reprint of 1892 edition, Williamstown, Mass.: Corner House Publishers, 1977) and Roger L. Nichols' *General Henry Atkinson: A Western Military Career* (Norman: University of Oklahoma Press, 1965) provided useful detail and background. LeRoy R. Hafen, ed., *The Mountain Men and the Fur Trade of the Far West,* 10 vols. (Glendale, Calif.: The Arthur H. Clark Company, 1965–72) presents more than three hundred brief biographies of the Rocky Mountain men, a number of whom were Smith's companions or business associates.

Most of the extant archival materials bearing on Smith are housed in the Missouri Historical Society's fur trade history collections at Saint Louis. Of special importance are the Jedediah Strong Smith Papers, the William H. Ashley Papers, and the William L. Sublette Papers. Additional important Smith letters and some Ashley materials are in the Western History Collections of the University of Missouri at Columbia. The Manuscripts

Department of the Kansas State Historical Society, at Topeka, holds a handful of important Smith letters. Smith's estate records, containing financial details and information about his possessions, are found in Probate File #960, Clerk of the Probate Court, Saint Louis, administered by the Missouri State Archives. Copies of Smith's obituaries are found in the Illinois Newspaper Project files at the University Library at the University of Illinois, Urbana-Champaign. The anonymous eulogy "Jedediah Strong Smith" published in the *Illinois Monthly Magazine* at Alton in June 1832 offers a great deal of information derived from Smith himself about his career and future plans on the eve of his death.

A few government documents include references to Smith. By far the most significant is Smith's 1830 letter to Secretary of War John Eaton. Lost in the National Archives files for 175 years, it was brought to light in 2000 by James S. Hutchins of Vienna, Virginia, and reprinted in *Museum of the Fur Trade Quarterly*, 37:1 (2001). The original letter is in the National Archives and Records Administration, Records of the Office of the Secretary of War (Record Group 107), entry 258, "Applications, 1820–46." In addition, two items in the Congressional serial set, U.S. Congress, Senate, 20: 2, Senate Executive Document No. 67 (1828), and U.S. Congress, Senate, 22: 1, Senate Executive Document No. 90 (1832), contain much information on western fur trade conditions and the government's efforts to monitor it, including details supplied by Smith or someone close to him, such as William Ashley.

Index

References to illustrations appear in italics.